# My Musical Notes

# My Musical Notes

## A Journey in Classical Piano between the World Wars and Beyond

Gaby Casadesus

*Translated by Lawrence Lockwood*

*In collaboration with
Thérèse Casadesus Rawson*

HAMILTON BOOKS
AN IMPRINT OF
ROWMAN & LITTLEFIELD
*Lanham • Boulder • New York • London*

Published by Hamilton Books
An imprint of The Rowman & Littlefield Publishing Group, Inc.
4501 Forbes Boulevard, Suite 200, Lanham, Maryland 20706
www.rowman.com

86-90 Paul Street, London EC2A 4NE, United Kingdom

British Library Cataloguing in Publication Information Available

**Library of Congress Cataloging-in-Publication Data**

Names: Casadesus, Gaby, author. | Lockwood, Lawrence, translator. | Rawson, Thérèse
Casadesus, 1942– writer of foreword.
Title: My musical notes : a journey in classical piano between the world wars and
beyond / Gaby Casadesus ; translated by Lawrence Lockwood ; with Thérèse
Casadesus Rawson.
Other titles: Mes noces musicales. English
Description: Lanham : Hamilton Books, 2024. | Includes index. | Summary: "An inside
view of the life of internationally famous twentieth-century French concert pianists,
Robert and Gaby Casadesus who left Paris in 1940 and emigrated to the United States
on the eve of the German invasion. The husband and wife team went on to become
some of the most revered cultural figures in French musical repertory"— Provided by
publisher.
Identifiers: LCCN 2024022181 (print) | LCCN 2024022182 (ebook) | ISBN
9780761874584 (paperback) | ISBN 9780761874591 (epub)
Subjects: LCSH: Casadesus, Robert, 1899–1972. | Casadesus, Gaby. | Pianists—
France—Biography. | LCGFT: Biographies.
Classification: LCC ML417.C417 C413 2024  (print) | LCC ML417.C417  (ebook) |
DDC 786.2092/2 [B]—dc23/eng/202405014
LC record available at https://lccn.loc.gov/2024022181
LC ebook record available at https://lccn.loc.gov/2024022182

♾️ The paper used in this publication meets the minimum requirements of American
National Standard for Information Sciences—Permanence of Paper for Printed Library
Materials, ANSI/NISO Z39.48-1992.

*In memory of Gaby Casadesus, who was the source of inspiration to so many musicians devoted to the French piano repertoire.*

# Contents

# Foreword

## by
## Thérèse Casadesus Rawson

Gaby Casadesus (1901–1999), French classical pianist and pedagogue, is still renowned today as a one of the significant women soloists of the twentieth century, as well as a revered teacher of the French piano repertoire, having known Claude Debussy and Gabriel Fauré and, more importantly, Maurice Ravel, a personal friend who imparted many of his stylistic ideas to her.

Born Gabrielle L'Hôte in Marseille, she entered the Paris Conservatory at ten years old, where she became a favorite pupil of Marguerite Long and Louis Diémer. She was also awarded the First Prize in piano at sixteen years old, then the coveted Prix Pagès, the most prestigious award available to women at the time.

Her memoirs begin with these Conservatory years where she met her future husband Robert (1899–1972), himself a star pupil at that institution. As a young student, she counted Felix Mendelssohn and the French baroque keyboard composers among her favorites.

These memoirs relate the history of her joint career with her husband as a piano duo—recording iconic interpretations of four-hand and two piano repertoire—then as a piano trio with their son Jean (1927–1972). She also relates countless encounters with famous conductors (Toscanini, Stokowski, Szell, Bernstein, and many more) and their world-wide tours as husband and wife, as well as their family life spanning two World Wars. These recollections provide contemporary audiences a fascinating account of the mid-twentieth-century lifestyle of classical musicians: they are told in a conversational rather than academic style. They portray a woman who managed to balance her own career as a pianist and teacher with that of her husband's, all the while raising three children. In her later years, she founded the Robert

Casadesus International Piano Competition in Cleveland in tribute to her late husband. Gaby Casadesus also taught masterclasses for decades at the American Conservatory in Fontainebleau (where Nadia Boulanger had also taught for decades) as well as for several years at the Académie Ravel in Saint-Jean-de-Luz and the Salzburg Mozarteum. She was much sought after as a jury member for international piano competitions and many of her former students continue to impart her legacy.

# Acknowledgments

The Gaby Casadesus story was originally captured in a series of interviews in 1988 with French music journalist, Jacqueline Muller, who formerly worked in artist relations at *CBS France*.

The extended Casadesus family is grateful to Madame Muller for documenting this first person account of Gaby's tireless contributions to the field of classical music. Their interviews became *Mes Noces Musicales*, published in France in 1989, which today provides the only official recounting one of the most extraordinary husband and wife teams in twentieth-century classical music, Robert and Gaby Casadesus. Translated and republished in English for the first time as *My Musical Notes*, this 2024 edition brings their legendary story to a larger audience. For the first time in decades, classical music afficionados are treated to an inside view of Robert and Gaby's creative partnership, the ups and downs of international touring between the wars, and their stewardship of that remarkable institution known as the American Conservatory at Fontainebleau, France. Robert and Gaby's seemingly star-crossed journey, which abruptly ended in 1972, produced thousands of small stars which even today continue to come into view thanks to their dedication to piano pedagogy. It is almost impossible to list the number of students who entered the duo's orbit either through masterclasses, indirectly through their voluminous CBS recordings, or from the concert hall. Thus, only a fraction of them can be acknowledged here. Many of the luminaries who are documented in this book hardly need an introduction, but those creative collaborators who helped sustain Fontainebleau deserve special mention. At the top of the list are undoubtedly composer Maurice Ravel and their late son Jean.

On the twenty-fifth anniversary of Gaby Casadesus'passing, her grandsons Carter Casadesus Rawson and Ramsay Casadesus Rawson and I honor her legacy with this French to English translation of her 1988 memoirs, *Mes noces musicales: Conversations avec Jacqueline Muller* (Paris: Buchet-Chastel 1989), a collection of interviews with a celebrated French classical music journalist, Jacqueline Muller, and having them published in the United States.

Thérèse Casadesus Rawson and her sons wish to acknowledge those who moved or continue to move that legacy forward between Robert's passing in 1972 and Gaby's in 1999—in alphabetical order (*–deceased):

Philippe Bianconi
Guy Casadesus*
Gréco Casadesus
Philippe Entremont
Guy and Gildas Gourlay
Jay Gottlieb
Grant Johannesen*
Bond Johnson
Joseph Kerr
Philip Lasser
Robert Levin
Lawrence Lockwood
Jacqueline Muller
Robert Russ / Sony Music
Gabriele Slizyte
Debra Takakjian
The Rawson family
The Lagardère family

# A Note on Translations

This book was originally published as *Mes noces musicales: Conversations avec Jacqueline Muller* (Paris: Buchet-Chastel, 1989), by Gaby Casadesus.

In the English translation, the choice to use ellipses and contractions in English was intended to better render the French conversational style of these interviews which were never intended as an academic publication.

## Chapter 1

# First Meeting and Our Beginnings

How did I meet Robert? It's quite a story, as is the case with every love story. Both of us attended the Paris Conservatory on the Rue de Madrid, but fate didn't immediately treat us favorably.

When I think about it now, after so many years, it still amuses me to point out that things weren't so obvious. Quite frequently, I'd heard people mentioning him, and, quite often, when I arrived for classes, someone would say: "You know? . . . Casadesus came in a moment ago!" Yet who was this Casadesus that everyone was talking about? He had a sound reputation as a talented pianist, but, apart from that, I didn't know anything about him. Furthermore, I didn't have any idea of how old he was. This anecdote goes back to 1916.

To my enormous disappointment, I'd just started in Louis Diémer's class. I'd hoped to join Alfred Cortot's class, but, just before the acceptance competition, I'd had a severe bout of the flu, and Cortot, who thought that I wouldn't be able to take part, didn't include me on the list. Despite my absence on the previous days, I successfully completed the competition with Schumann's *Toccata*. I'd played it extremely well, and I was accepted. But none of the faculty members requested me as a student. Thus, Diémer, who taught male students, had ended up with a shortage of students. In that era, mixing of genders in classes was inconceivable. Male students on one side, female students on the other. The war had reached a zenith, and most of the male students were away for military service. Indeed, these circumstances meant that another girl and I were the only female students admitted to Diémer's class. Something that was even more unbelievable was that he didn't have any right to accept female students. The reason is rather amusing: Diémer had married one of his female students, and his father-in-law insisted upon a clause in the marriage contract—where it was stipulated that he'd never give lessons to female students. . . . And here you have a gentleman more than seventy years old who, on account of the war, gained the legal right to tear up his marriage

1

contract—whereupon he received a notarized authorization allowing him to teach female students.

With great dejection, I started attending his class and nevertheless earned my first prize in 1918. I'd wished so much to study under Cortot, who was the most popular faculty member at that time. Furthermore, I'd been an unregistered student for his classes, and he was interested in the way that I played. Therefore, I logically should have been admitted to his class if I hadn't been stricken with an ill-timed case of the flu.

In 1913, I'd performed for Gustave Lyon, the Director of the Maison Pleyel, and he advised my mother to introduce me to Cortot. Therefore, I went to Cortot's home. I was greeted rather unenthusiastically. With considerable haste, he said to me, "I can't listen to you. I don't have any time!" Then he nevertheless inquired: "How old are you?" "I'm eleven, Maestro," I replied, "and this is what I'm going to play," and then I sat down at the piano, whereupon I played Mendelssohn's *Rondo Capriccioso*, which was quite familiar to me, because I'd played it at a concert for the opening of the Hôtel Lutétia two years earlier. Cortot immediately advised me to seek an introduction to Mme. Long. "You couldn't receive better instruction in technique!" That's how I became a student of Marguerite Long, with whom I earned my first medal in 1915. When I was leaving after having won my medal, she said to me, with that tone that she could so readily adopt: "Even though I'm angry with him (I don't know why they were at odds), you must go to Cortot now. He sent you to me, and now I must send you back!" The wretched flu led to a quite different outcome.

Like every student, I also took courses in the History of Music department, and that's where other people mentioned to me quite frequently that Casadesus had just left. He inspired numerous comments: "You know, Casadesus is fantastic; he's a wonderful pianist!" "He came here to see his teacher—Diémer, who adores him." From all of the evidence, his presence didn't go unnoticed. Everyone was talking about him, and I was indisputably the only person who hadn't even seen him.

At last, I happened to meet him one day. I recall that I was accompanied by my mother. At that time, young ladies never went out alone, and it was out of the question for me to go to the Conservatory without being accompanied. I was fifteen years old, and I'd just been admitted to the advanced section. "There's Casadesus!" whispered one of my classmates whom we'd just met on the sidewalk. "Casadesus? But it's impossible for that person to be him. He's too young," I replied, with complete surprise at my discovery.

I just couldn't believe that this was truly the one, the Casadesus that everyone was talking about. In fact, the name was familiar to me because it was often heard in the musical world. It was only later that I understood that people were referring to his uncles instead of him. I immediately found

Casadesus to be charming, and I wondered about what impression I may have made upon him because I was wearing socks that day! What could he have thought about a young girl who was wearing socks?

Later on, we met several times in the Ensemble section, without anything further. Then, one day in June 1917, shortly before my end of year examination, he offered to hear me. I was going to play Chopin's *Barcarolle*, and I can recall that my mother responded: "I'd be very pleased if you could hear my daughter." My mother was an exceptionally talented pianist, and she taught piano. She's the one who got me started at the piano and followed my progress until I entered the Conservatory. She was a passionate admirer of Schumann, and I always played Schumann using my mother's scores, which I carefully preserved. Therefore, I accepted Robert's invitation. At that time, he was living on the Rue Rochechouart with the entire Casadesus family. The apartment included a studio that was used as a rehearsal room. I played the *Barcarolle* for him, and he gave me some advice that I found to be most helpful. He seemed friendly, and, moreover, I believed that he must be an extremely generous person, because he'd taken the time to hear me perform.

During the month of October in that same year, my mother and I went to listen to him at the Salle des Agriculteurs, where he was giving his first public recital. I think that he'd offered us invitations. I don't remember this detail that well! I don't have a very precise recollection of the program either. It certainly did include Schumann's *Fantaisie* in any case. Perhaps Beethoven's *Appassionata*, too. When the concert ended, he introduced us to his grandfather and his Aunt Rosette, who'd been seated on the stage in order to hear him play. After this recital, I understood that he was a far from ordinary pianist. I was astonished by the perfection of his performance. My mother was also deeply impressed. He was undeniably extremely talented. Then, not long after, a horrible event overwhelmed my life. My mother died from a sudden stroke in the month of December. She'd been affected by bronchitis somewhat earlier, but, in 1917, medical diagnostic investigations were still extremely incomplete, and a patient's blood pressure wasn't routinely tested . . . so that no one was aware of the status of her blood pressure. My mother needed to follow a salt-free diet because she developed an elevated albumin level when I was born. Like many people, she didn't feel like pursuing treatment, and she believed that it would be useless. Hence, she'd suspended her diet. Moreover, she was very worried about my elder sister who'd just left her husband and was returning to live with us. My mother was extremely sensitive. She'd always made sacrifices for us, and she'd given piano lessons in order to add to the income earned by my father, who was a civil servant in the Finance Ministry.

One morning, my sister and I needed to go out. Our mother stayed alone with a lady who came to do sewing, and then she had that stroke. When we returned, I immediately went out looking for a doctor—because we didn't have a telephone. When he examined her, the doctor said, "Your mother's still young,—she was forty-eight—but her arteries must be twenty years older." There was no way of saving her life, and she died during the night.

When I told Robert about my mother's death, he was shaken. He comforted me by saying that he'd greatly admired her and that he'd discovered in her genuine artistic qualities. Robert showed intense sensitivity, and my mother's death brought us closer together. He began writing to me regularly. He also visited me . . . and he encouraged me to work as hard as possible in order to earn my prize under highly favorable conditions, because he told me, "That would have pleased her so much."

The war was raging, and Paris was being bombarded. Big Bertha was firing its shells almost every hour. At night, we often hid in the cellar.

In January 1918, Robert informed me that he was going to be called for military service. He belonged to the 1919 levy, and he'd just completed his review board examination. He subsequently became more affectionate and closer, but he hadn't mentioned marriage yet.

One day, my father invited him to have lunch with us. He arrived in uniform. His appearance was beyond belief. Pants that were too short or too long—I can't recall which—combined with a type of short jacket that was too tight. Because we were surprised by his appearance, he said to us with a smile, but with great seriousness, that how he looked was wholly unimportant, because, in any instance, he was going to be killed. . . . In making apocalyptic utterances Robert manifested a certain flair for exaggeration, which he enjoyed displaying at certain times.

He left in the Spring. Initially, he went to Dun-sur-Auron, in the Berry region for his induction and was assigned to an artillery unit even though he'd completed his military training with the cavalry!

The year 1918 was undoubtedly the most difficult period in the war. Because of the bombardment that was becoming more intense; my father wanted me to move to the country. It must be recognized that, at that point, Parisians were fleeing the city. I refused to leave because I absolutely wanted to complete my competitive examination. I won the prize on my first try, and I was pleased.

After my prize, I accompanied my sister, who'd reconciled with her husband, to Cabourg in order to spend the summer. I gave small recitals for vacationers, and this activity was extremely pleasurable. It was during this period that Robert began courting me by mail.

Then, when it was least expected, the Armistice was announced. Robert was sent to Versailles, and he was assigned to military music. He was delighted with his garrison. He was playing the snare drum! Instead of the military drum because he claimed that he hadn't managed to make his hands move properly for performing drum rolls. . . . He was distressed about it. . . . His superiors allowed him to continue studying Harmony at the Conservatory, and, for that entire year, he came to the Rue de Madrid to take his courses. His garrison was quartered in a marvelous building opposite the Château de Versailles. During his free time, he took strolls in the park, and that's where he composed his first piano compositions, which he dedicated to me. The whole history of the Château is recounted in these compositions that are still unpublished. . . . The staircases and the two Trianons profoundly inspired him.

After the prize in Harmony that he'd received in the class given by Xavier Leroux and Jean Gallon, he returned to Paris, where he was appointed as a cyclist-orderly at the École Militaire. He was responsible for transporting money, and he took on this role very seriously. His prize was unfortunately overshadowed by an extremely painful event in his family.

On the day that he received his prize, Robert lost his beloved grandfather. Upon returning to the Rue Rochechouart, he went to announce the good news to his grandfather before ascending to the studio in order to show his examination results to his uncles. When he came downstairs again, he found his grandfather dead with a newspaper on his knees. Robert's grandfather had been somewhat listless because he'd experienced a bronchial infection earlier, but there weren't any signs that would have let anyone expect a sudden death. Did he die from joy because of the announcement of his grandson's prize?

Robert was deeply troubled by this sudden death. He'd greatly admired his grandfather, and, throughout his life, he recalled having heard his grandfather playing the guitar or the mandolin in the evening before bedtime.

Robert continued his military service until 1920. He took advantage of his lengthy free time at the École Militaire by composing. Unfortunately, he didn't keep any of his scores because he considered them unworthy of being saved for posterity.

He was released from his military obligations just when he won the Diémer Prize, which he obtained with unanimous approval. The examination program included: a sonata by Beethoven, Schumann's *Études symphoniques*, and Liszt's *Campanella*. The prize no longer exists, but it was actually equivalent to today's international prizes. It was accompanied by a sum of 4,000 francs, which wasn't an enormous amount . . . and the winner was also hired for two orchestra performances in Paris. This was an important prize, because it conveyed a distinction that surpassed the Conservatory's degree and was highly coveted by young pianists.

From that time on, Robert was courting me persistently, and then everything became quite simple. One day, without any hesitation in his voice, he said to me: "You must become my wife." In those days, it was out of the question to become someone's lover without marrying him . . . there wasn't an option of becoming lovers either. I told him that we were too young, that it was crazy. . . . I'd been acquainted with another young man, but that didn't matter. The way that Robert behaved toward me when my mother died, displaying sincere affection, and the way that he encouraged me so that I could win my prize—all this had touched me deeply. . . . I found him to be quite attractive and I looked up to him both as a man and as an artist. . . . From then on, we began spending a lot of time together.

From 1921 onward, Robert began giving concerts on a regular basis. In spite of the wartime interruption when he could devote much less attention to the piano, he retained a magnificent naturalness. His captain at the Arvor camp had become fond of him, and, because he knew that Robert was an excellent pianist, the captain designated him as the supervisor of the Foyer du Soldat. This position, with its quaint charm, conveyed responsibility for organizing all of the musical events that were intended to entertain the troops. The situation offered Robert an opportunity to play excerpts from *Carmen* or *l'Arlésienne*, as well as Dranem's songs. He also provided accompaniments for all the young men who were capable of singing popular tunes. Robert adored the entire repertoire, and I recall that he was delighted to play for us whenever he visited our home, which my father and sister enjoyed tremendously. He could spend hours playing and singing all of these songs. He was fully capable of recreating the *Boeuf sur le Toit*'s ambiance.

The *Boeuf sur le Toit* was the cabaret where all of the young musicians gathered. An extraordinary spirit prevailed there. Robert adored going there to listen to Darius Milhaud, Erik Satie, or Jean Wiener and Clément Doucet.

After his demobilization, Robert began traveling to Le Havre regularly in order to give piano lessons. His uncle, Marius Casadesus, gave violin lessons there several times per month and he'd obtained this position for Robert. Even today, I still know people who remember the courses given by these two members of the Casadesus family.

For Robert, this was also the beginning of his concerts throughout France.

During this period, we often visited the Lemaigre family, who were friends who lived in a mansion in the Passy neighborhood, on the Rue Raynouard. This neighborhood bore no resemblance to what it has become today. I can recall that I'd arrive at the Passy metro station, which was the end of the line in those times. The Rue Raynouard was bordered by houses surrounded by gardens, such as Balzac's house, which is the only one of these houses to have been preserved today. Moreover, that was the last house, because, afterward, there weren't any more residences of this kind. The site of the Maison de la Radio was occupied by a gas plant, which was hardly compatible with urban development . . . the view of the Seine was superb, and the Lemaigres' garden was teeming with flowers. They even had a splendid Judas tree. Mr. Lemaigre was an alumnus of the École Normale Supérieure, and he'd served as the

Director of the Lycée Louis-le-Grand in Arcueil. He knew people who were utterly fascinating and who belonged to all sorts of milieux. Sacha Guitry had been one of his students, and I found that to be quite amusing. Mme. Lemaigre often accompanied me to concerts. We'd listened to Robert together when he performed Ernest Chausson's *Concert* during the war. The Lemaigres often invited us to dinner. Robert gladly sat down at the piano, and, in order to entertain our friends, who were enthusiastic Wagnerians, he played *Tristan, the Meistersingers,* or *Tannhäuser.* These evenings thrilled us. One evening, the session continued until 5:00 a.m., and I had to spend the night at their home. My father was furious about it, and he claimed that I was misusing the freedom that he'd allowed.

We were thinking of marriage at this point, but my father had firmly warned us that he'd oppose it, so long as Robert lacked a financially stable position. In those days, there was no notion of helping a young couple in any way whatsoever. We were expected to shoulder our responsibilities by ourselves. Robert had just been appointed as an instructor for the three-month summer session at the Fontainebleau Conservatory, where his uncle Francis was one of the founders, and this outcome produced a strong impression upon my father. Moreover, he was thinking of resuming a family life because, fairly recently, he'd met a lady with whom he wished to share the rest of his life. I was opposed to his remarriage, and my father knew that I'd never agree to live in his house with anyone other than my mother. I exhibited the inflexibility of youth and a lack of experience with life. These circumstances worked in our favor, and my father finally consented to our engagement.

For my part, I began giving lessons to my mother's students who asked me to continue their instruction after her death. In spite of these positive aspects, my father feared that our marriage would end up failing. Sometimes he said to me with an extremely worried tone: "Remember that you're both pianists. One of you will necessarily be better than the other. If it's him, that will be very good, but then it will be the end of your career. If it's you, things will be even worse." Actually, he didn't have any idea of a musician's life, and, because my sister, a harpist, was unhappy with her husband, who was a violist, he believed that we were going to face the same problems or the same obstacles.

Our friends interceded in our favor. The Lemaigres, who were our greatest supporters, valued Robert's knowledge in non-musical realms. Mr. Lemaigre had even given him a few courses in Greek and Latin culture! Finally, my father recognized that Robert wasn't such a terrible choice.

As a Catholic, I wanted to have a church wedding, but Robert hadn't been baptized, even though the Casadesus family was Catholic. His grandfather, who'd been educated by narrow-minded priests, detested religion and he'd decreed that his descendants should never set foot inside a church. Robert didn't hesitate to be baptized, so that we could be married in a church according to my intentions. He underwent religious training from the priest who officiated for my first communion. This priest was an intelligent and cultivated person. He immediately persuaded Robert to study the Gospels, which fascinated him to such an extent that, one day, he told me that he never would have believed that catechism could be so interesting.

We were married on July 16, 1921, at the church of Saint-François Xavier, which is just a stone's throw from here. The weather was splendid, precisely in the way that is uniquely Parisian when summer begins. The entire Casadesus family was present: Robert's father, his beloved Aunt Rosette, his other aunts, his uncles, and his cousins.

We asked the composer Henri Rabaud, Gustave Lyon, and my uncle Raynaud, who was my mother's brother and a conductor, to be our witnesses. Thus, our wedding took place under musical auspices.

The reception took place on the Rue Vaneau, right here, in this room where we're speaking to each other today.

Before my wedding, my father, my sister, and I were living on the Rue de Petrograd, but we wanted to leave an apartment that was haunted by sad memories. One day, my father visited this apartment, and he was fascinated by the fifth floor, which offered a superb view of Paris' rooftops. Without hesitation, he paid a deposit of fifty francs to the concierge, so that she'd keep the apartment for him. When I showed Robert the apartment, he fell in love with it, too! Furthermore, he never wanted to leave Rue Vaneau, even when a building that blocked our view was erected across from us. No other apartment could be deemed acceptable in his opinion.

On the evening of our wedding, we went to Fontainebleau, not because it was fashionable to spend a wedding night there but because Robert would be starting to give his classes on the following Monday. We only had Sunday for any kind of honeymoon trip. . . . Robert told me that we couldn't afford a real trip, but that we'd catch up later. He was right, because, during fifty years of living together, we found plenty of opportunities to travel.

We'd rented a small room with a bathroom, and we ate our meals with the students in the Conservatory's refectory, which was located in the Henri II Gallery. Francis Casadesus had obtained permission to lodge American students in the Château and also to establish a restaurant there. A few years later, however, the restaurant was shut down because fire hazards were feared.

During the first two summers, we lived in that same room overlooking the market. During the third year, when we'd acquired somewhat more money, we were able to treat ourselves to a small apartment with two rooms and a kitchen, across from one of the town's military barracks. This was the pinnacle of luxury! Robert had been dazzled by the vast expanse of the sky that was visible through our windows. Finally, we'd be spared from the market's odors, which weren't always agreeable at the height of the summer! After returning from Fontainebleau, we were unable to live on the Rue Vaneau because my father, who'd been assigned to Boulogne-sur-Mer, had leased the apartment. Furthermore, I'd been involved in a few altercations with the physician who lived on the floor beneath us and couldn't tolerate my five hours of piano playing every day! At that time, I feared that two pianists may have driven him insane.

Therefore, we set up our household in the apartment where Robert was living, at 54 rue du Four, exactly across from the Théâtre du Vieux-Colombier. When he was a bachelor, he'd lived there with his Aunt Rosette, and he wanted her to continue living with us. Aunt Rosette was unmarried, and he feared that she'd die if she were abandoned. . . . She took care of him like a son. He brought her his fees, and she gave him his pocket money, as he told me. I found this situation to be touching and astonishing. In order to please my husband, I ultimately gave in to his wishes, and Aunt Rosette shared our life for ten years. Initially on Rue du Four, and then on Rue Vaneau, which became our residence in 1924.

During this time, we often received visits from Ravel, Caplet, and Szymanowski, with whom we spent long evenings chatting or playing music, purely for our own entertainment. Actually, we were working a lot. I was planning to compete for the Pagès Prize, and long hours at my piano were required, so that we went out rather infrequently. When we went out, it was to the theatre or to hear cabaret singers, which is something that Robert adored. We were extremely dedicated!

The lessons that we were giving allowed us to live suitably, but we nevertheless needed to watch our budget quite closely. I can recall that, when Robert left for a tour in Belgium, I didn't go with him so as to avoid incurring extra expenses.

Every month, I went to give lessons in Rouen. While Robert was giving courses in Le Havre. We took the same train. I got off first . . . in Rouen, I had the pleasure of spending time with my father, who'd just been appointed as the Chief Customs Administrator there.

Robert had decided to give a yearly recital in Paris, and he prepared his programs with considerable diligence. We were entirely responsible for the costs, including rental of the hall. These recitals were given at the Salle des Agriculteurs, which no longer exists today. I recall that Albert Roussel attended one of them.

Aunt Rosette helped me to prepare the envelopes that were used to send announcements to our friends and acquaintances, along with information encouraging them to buy tickets . . . Our hope was to cover the costs . . . because we didn't anticipate earning profits from a transaction of this kind. The two of us took responsibility for everything, while the impresario didn't

bother with much at all. He only began to play an active role at the point
when Robert received superb reviews in the press, and these reviews began
appearing without delay.

During this period, Robert played Stravinsky's *Petrushka* at the Paris
Opera with Ernest Ansermet as the conductor. Ansermet, who'd appreciated
Robert's interpretation and characterized it as "brilliant," immediately invited
Robert to begin performing with him in Geneva. This was as worthwhile as
any lengthy speeches, especially when the source was a conductor whose
reputation was already extremely well established.

Then there was a completely unexpected event of a type that often functions like a "starting block" for a runner . . . Robert was asked to replace a
pianist who suddenly became ill.

Serge Koussevitzky had hired Edouard Rissler to interpret Beethoven's *4th
Concerto* at the Paris Opera. Rissler experienced a slight stroke a few days
before the scheduled date. He had to be replaced immediately. Koussevitzky
contacted Robert, who, because fate sometimes works in one's favor, had
been practicing this very concerto. Robert agreed. He greatly admired Rissler.
In one week, we'd perfected the concerto together, with two pianos, and
Robert was able to fulfill his role as the substitute. Koussevitzky had been
reigning supreme in Paris since the day of his arrival from Russia. His wife
was very influential in Paris. She belonged to a wealthy family, and they
hadn't left their native country without resources.

Initially, Koussevitzky was a bass player, and he'd never studied conducting. Indeed, he wasn't the only person for whom this situation arose. This
was also what happened with Arturo Toscanini, who'd been a cellist. As was
true for many conductors, it was a matter of blind luck that he'd stepped up
to the podium at a moment's notice so as to replace a conductor who was
unavailable. Because Toscanini knew the program by heart on account of
having played it so many times in the role of a solo cellist, he was asked to
conduct. He displayed such authority and was so capable of imparting what
he felt to his colleagues that he decided to exchange his cello for a conductor's baton. For Serge Koussevitzky, it was a different story. In Russia, at the
beginning of the century, bassists faced the public when they performed. One
evening, a young girl who was in a theatre box caught his eye. The attraction
was mutual. The young couple ultimately met, and they fell in love. This girl
was the daughter of a member of the Duma, who imposed a requirement for
their marriage: that his future son-in-law should abandon the bass, which the
father considered unworthy of being associated with his social position. In
exchange, he offered Koussevitzky an orchestra where he could become the
conductor. The father's command was executed. The orchestra was established by hiring Moscow's best musicians, so that a lot of problems for its
conductor were avoided. . . . . The story is true. It was recounted to us when

we visited the USSR. In spite of the musicians who were capable of all sorts of miracles, Koussevitzky turned out to be a marvelous conductor who was extremely talented, and, right away, he achieved overwhelming success. Like anyone for whom conducting isn't his first position, he was an extremely demanding conductor who behaved toward his musicians as if he were a czar, to such an extent that, when he left Russia, the orchestra decided not to replace him and to perform without a conductor.

Koussevitzky therefore arrived in Paris accompanied by his wife and a sizeable fortune. He immediately organized concerts at the Opera. He also returned to the bass. I can recall that he gave a concert with Henri Casadesus at the former Salle Pleyel and that the concert consisted of viol and bass compositions. Koussevitzky possessed a perfect mastery of the bass, which is rarely regarded as a soloist's instrument.

The concert with Robert took place in an overflowing hall and it was enormously successful. In response to enthusiastic applause and numerous curtain calls, Robert sat down at the piano and performed a short composition as a solo encore. Koussevitzky clearly didn't appreciate this initiative because he believed that Robert should have asked for permission. . . . He mentioned it to Robert and held a slight grudge thereafter. . . . It is indisputable that the laudatory articles that appeared on the day after the concert were a tangible influence for the continuation of his career. In spite of this troublesome incident with the encore, Koussevitzky hired Robert again for the following year. Robert used to say, "The best proof of success is being hired again. The first time, you can offer something new, a different style, and a different approach to a given work. That's relatively easy. What's necessary is for people to want to hear you a second time . . . a third time . . . etc."

From then on, the appearances continued one after another. Mr. Lyon, the manager of the Salle Pleyel, who'd known Robert when he was quite young, offered him a recital in Geneva. The Pleyel organization assumed responsibility for all of the expenses. Robert was phenomenally successful, and there were favorable articles. When favorable articles come out, progress unfolds much more quickly.

Robert also began participating in concerts at the Théâtre du Vieux-Colombier, and these concerts were especially oriented toward premieres of contemporary works. That is where Robert performed the earliest works by Caplet and Ravel. Ravel frequently attended these evenings, and he responded enthusiastically to Robert's interpretation of *Gaspard de la nuit*. He came to congratulate Robert during the intermission, and he said: "Finally, you've played *Le Gibet* with the sound and especially with the tempo that I've wanted, whereas everyone else insists on playing it faster. It's a thrilling work with this same haunting note that's repeated like a tolling bell," and he'd added: "You must be a composer because you understand other people's music so well." This praise gave my husband immense pleasure. Then, Ravel asked him:

> Would you agree to recording certain compositions that are too difficult for me, if you could replace me? I signed a contract with Eolian in London to produce recordings of some of my piano compositions, but I don't think that I'm capable of performing everything myself. Certainly, your name won't appear, but I'll compensate you for your work.

Indeed, he turned out to be very generous. I should reveal that my husband agreed to this "deal" for the fee, because, although it was a pleasure to play Ravel, releasing a recording of his interpretation on piano rolls was hardly of interest to him. Recordings were in their infancy, and no one could imagine the importance that this invention would acquire for musicians' careers as time went on.

Therefore, we sailed from Calais toward Dover with Maurice Ravel. Personally speaking, I'd already been aboard a boat in my childhood when I was living in Algeria, and it was very enjoyable to undertake a crossing again. For Robert, however, this was his first time. Moreover, the English Channel's reputation was unfavorable, and, as soon as we'd boarded, he led us to the deck so that we'd be in the open air. . . . Ravel, whom I'd feared to be an old man turned out to be a very pleasant traveling companion and very cheerful. In Dover, we rushed aboard the train that would be taking us to London, and we enjoyed a good cup of tea accompanied by cookies that were offered to us. Our crossing had been somewhat choppy.

Upon arriving at Charing Cross, we proceeded to our hotel, where an invitation from the singer Mme. Alvar was waiting for us, because she'd arranged a dinner in honor of Ravel.

The dinner was followed by a private concert. Ravel played his *Sonatine*. He seemed to be tense, or somewhat stiff. It was obvious that he was experiencing stage fright. . . . There's nothing more difficult than sitting down at an unfamiliar piano and attempting to play the *Sonatine* . . . The fact that the composition is called a sonatina doesn't mean that it's easy to play! Then Mme. Alvar sang some of Ravel's art songs with Ravel himself accompanying her. For his part, Robert performed *Forlane* and the *Toccata*.

This was the same evening we heard the first performance of the *Duo pour violon et violoncelle*, which overwhelmed us with its beauty. The violinist Jelly d'Aranyi, who was only eighteen years old, was the performer, along with a wonderful cellist, who was a very handsome young man and whose name was Kindler. Later, we met him again in the United States, in Washington, where he'd become a conductor. D'Aranyi was attired with a simple shawl draped around her "in the Spanish way." She had a striking appearance. They played this sonata with such youthfulness and so much spirit! It's an extraordinary work and is one of the most beautiful that Ravel wrote, although it's largely unknown, perhaps because it's difficult for both performers and listeners. . . . We heard it performed on other occasions by extremely well-known musicians, although they unfortunately played it rather poorly. Ravel was enchanted by this performance. Later in the evening, he brought us into the library with the performers, and he asked d'Aranyi to play gypsy folklore music for him.

D'Aranyi, who was Hungarian, was hardly reluctant, and she played enthusiastically for at least two hours, without any interruptions. She was dazzling, and Ravel was overjoyed.

When we came back to our hotel extremely late that night, Ravel excitedly confided to us that, as soon as he returned, he'd be rushing to Montfort-l'Amaury in order to work in quiet surroundings. Shortly thereafter, he completed *Tzigane*, which he dedicated to Jelly d'Aranyi. Thus, this evening in London was the source of the extraordinary creation that *Tzigane* embodies.

Insofar as the recordings on piano rolls are concerned, it isn't really clear, even today, to tell who is playing what. Is it Ravel? Is it Robert? I'm personally convinced that Robert is the person performing the *Toccata*. It is undeniable that Ravel was somewhat apprehensive when he approached a piano. Although he was a quite talented pianist, he wasn't a virtuoso. There was a sense that he wasn't truly at ease. His wrists lacked the flexibility that's absolutely necessary for playing the piano. Furthermore, he knew it. It was obvious that he was trying too hard.

A few years later, in 1932, I was sitting beside him at an evening event, and he confided to me: "I'm working on composing a concerto for both hands"—he'd just completed his *Concerto pour la main gauche*—"an easy one because the Americans have asked me to be the performer." "I'm going to have to work on my piano playing, because, even if the score doesn't involve serious difficulties, I never succeed at properly playing what I've written. I'm going to ask Marguerite (Long) to help me make all of my fingers nimble." Indeed, he'd actually written this concerto for himself, even though Marguerite Long, who was always highly capable of making events turn out favorably for herself, had persuaded Ravel that she should be performing it in the United States. The project didn't come to fruition, however, because the Americans wanted Ravel and no one else as the pianist. Ultimately, Ravel became ill, and this trip was no longer possible. And it's actually Marguerite Long who created the *Concerto en sol*, in Paris, with Ravel conducting.

# Chapter 2

# The Casadesus Tribe

I haven't spoken yet about the Casadesus family, or let's say the Casadesus tribe, whose fame is owed to their grandfather, Luis, a Catalan from Figueras who emigrated to Paris.

He adored music and he'd begun playing the violin, although his grandmother threw his violin out with the trash because she didn't want him to become a musician. Subsequently, he took up a new direction with the guitar and mandolin. His mother, who was an actress, traveled frequently, and he was brought up by his grandmother. Luis was born in 1850.

In 1870, he went to France, joined the army, and obtained citizenship. He met a young French girl, Mathilde Sénéchal, who'd also been born in 1850, and they were married. They had thirteen children, among whom eight became musicians. Although he couldn't become a musician himself, he insisted that his children should be musicians. He'd suffered greatly from not becoming a violinist, because, in his opinion, it was necessary to be a violinist to join an orchestra. The concept of being a soloist was alien to him. It was necessary to gain stable employment, and only an orchestra could offer it.

Grandfather Luis was a cashier for a cookie-producing company, and, on weekends, he led orchestras for small dances in Montmartre. That allowed him to earn a bit more money for bringing up his numerous children.

Francis, the oldest, immediately began playing in his father's small Saturday night orchestras. He became the founder of the American Conservatory of Fontainebleau. He was an opera composer and was a contemporary of Gustave Charpentier. Like Charpentier, he was a member of the group known as the "Montmartre School." He was also a conductor. Francis Casadesus died in 1954, just after celebrating his eighty-fourth birthday.

All the Casadesus children began earning a living when they were approximately fourteen years old.

Robert's father was an actor and a singer at the "Boîte à Fursy." He was born in 1878.

He was a member of Sacha Guitry's troupe. In the 1920's, Charles Dullin appointed him to be the Director of the Théâtre Français in New York. This was the era when Americans held the French in high esteem for having resisted the invaders! Robert Casadesus had truncated his name, and he let himself be known as Robert Casa. He'd completed training in *solfège*. Later, he was the person who oversaw our son Jean's practice when he was preparing for his first medal in *solfège*. Robert played the piano extremely well, and he could truly play anything, although he preferred singing.

There was also Henri, the founder of the Société des Instruments Anciens, which was a well-renowned ensemble. Henri was born in 1879. As a violist, he belonged to the acclaimed Quatuor Capet before the First World War. His second wife, Marie-Louise, who was a harpist, was the mother of Gisèle and Christian Casadesus, who are well-known in the realm of theatre.

Aunt Rosette, who was born in 1873 and who was highly significant in Robert's life, as well as in our family's life, was an extremely talented pianist. She'd also started working at the age of fourteen in her father's orchestras. She didn't pursue a career as a musician, but she was an excellent teacher. She was perfect with children.

Marcel, who was born in 1882, studied the cello. Unfortunately, he was killed during the First World War.

All of the Casadesus children were students at the Paris Conservatory, except for Régina, who became a harpsichordist. She was born in 1886 and would have been delighted to receive training at the Conservatory as her brothers did. Luis didn't want her to attend this den of perdition for girls, however! This circumstance didn't prevent her from obtaining piano training with Isidore Philipp, outside the Conservatory. Later, she decided upon the harpsichord, to join her brother Henri's Societé des Instruments Anciens.

Cécile, who was born in 1884, didn't pursue a musical career either, although she gave piano lessons. As for Marius, the youngest, who was born in 1892, he was brought up by his sister Rosette, because their mother had a stroke at the time of his birth, which left her partially handicapped. Indeed, she died in 1907. Marius, who was a brilliant violinist, also played the *violino piccolo* in the Société des Instruments Anciens. Later, he formed the Quatuor Casadesus, and Robert often performed with him in concerts. Marius' son, Gréco, who was born in 1950, is an extraordinarily gifted composer who composes for the cinema.

Robert was the oldest member of the next generation. Furthermore, there was only an age difference of eight years in relation to his Uncle Marius. They were practically brought up together.

At the age of twenty, Robert Casa (Robert's father) had an affair with another student at the Conservatory, where he was studying diction. Her family name was Varnet, and we never knew her first name. . . . At that time, it was unthinkable to have a child without being married.

This simply wasn't done! When Robert was born, his mother didn't want to keep him. She even considered placing him with Public Assistance so that she could avoid disclosing to her parents that she'd become a mother. Without hesitation, Robert Casa took his son in his arms and brought him home. It was said in the family that Miss Varnet, who was of Swedish origin, had come to Paris to study there. The entire Casadesus family was firmly arrayed against her because they were furious at her for wishing to abandon her child. Robert Casa therefore brought this newborn to his mother. When she saw the infant, she said: "He's a real Casadesus! He has the Casadesus forehead! I'll take care of him. That will simply only mean one more child in this house!"

Initially, Aunt Cécile, who was fifteen years old, cared for him. She was full of tenderness and kindness for Robert, and that explains the affection that he always maintained for her.

Robert Casa had acknowledged his son when he was born on April 7, 1899, but Robert never knew his mother. It appears that she did attempt to see him when he won his prize. The boy was fourteen years old at that time, but the family expressed its opposition. It was inconceivable for a woman who had abandoned her child to be admitted into the family. She was a nonperson to them, and the entire tribe turned its back on her.

Shortly after his birth, Robert was sent to a wet nurse in Caen. One day when his father visited this woman, he was thunderstruck by the squalor surrounding the baby. Robert Casa brought his son back to Paris immediately, and the entire family was delighted to rescue this little fellow.

One day when Grandfather Luis took Robert on his knees, as he liked to do, when Robert must have been eighteen or twenty months old, Luis was astonished to hear the child singing with the bells: "Ding, ding, dong, ding, ding, dong." Then Luis made Robert sing the entire sequence. The little boy repeated it perfectly! Thus, it was perhaps the bells of a church in Caen that were the source of Robert's musical calling! It has always been said that a person's early childhood years can determine his or her life. That idea proved to be true for Robert.

Robert's grandfather wanted him to learn the violin, always according to the perspective of secure employment. His uncles had succeeded by means of this path. One of them had even joined the Orchestre Colonne. Therefore, Robert would learn the violin, too.

Robert wouldn't hear of it, however. He laid down his violin and took a seat in front of the piano.

At that time, the family was living in the Faubourg Poissonnière. When Aunt Cécile married, Aunt Rosette took the reins and continued Robert's upbringing. He was three or four years old, and Robert quite naturally regarded Aunt Rosette as his mother until her death. I told you that she never married. It seems that she always said, "I don't want to leave my little Robert." She is also the one who took care of her mother and another young nephew for many years. This woman truly sacrificed herself for everyone. She took responsibility for bringing up her youngest brother, Marius. She kept the household operating. She was really the captain of the Casadesus ship! Without her, I don't know what would have become of the tribe, but that was also the tragedy of her life.

She's the person who got Robert started at the piano. When he was seven years old, she took him once a month to Mlle Simon, who was Antoine-François Marmontel's assistant teacher. Aunt Régina had been one of her students. Miss Simon emphasized practicing phrasing, sound, and precision. For her, clarity was fundamental. Also, sound. She was fantastic! She adored Schumann. I don't believe that she'd have been very interested in Mozart. As for Chopin, he was all right, but he wasn't comparable to Schumann.

She was that type of woman who never marries although she nonetheless remains impassioned and even ardent. . . . It's odd, but I've always found this intensity among female musicians. Aunt Rosette was completely this type of person. She was ardent, somewhat excessive. . . . As for Miss Simon, she always dressed in male attire. It must have been George Sand who inspired her.

Aunt Régina had introduced Robert to Isidore Philipp, who was that era's eminent piano teacher. "This child is extremely gifted," Philipp observed, "but he needs to practice. He should be working with Pierret." Pierret was Philipp's teaching assistant. His life ended tragically. He committed suicide at the age of thirty. Robert told me that he was fantastic. He only had one idea: strengthening the hands. During this period, Robert could barely extend his hand for an octave. He was probably about nine years old. Pierret immediately made him practice one of Chopin's chords that Philipp always used for this type of exercise: Do, E flat, F sharp, La, Do. Pierret went so far as to twist Robert's fingers to demonstrate the exercises. He almost injured Robert because he emphasized development of flexibility so much. Robert always told me that Pierret had certainly contributed to acquisition of flexibility and technique, because Miss Simon never would have developed a technique of this kind. She was far more interested in musicality than technique. Pierret was terrifying. He almost went so far as to break students' fingers. . . . He insisted upon flexibility of the joints. He made students practice extension. Indeed, Robert possessed wonderful hands! I don't know whether that's because of Pierret. . . . In those days, students put up with everything from their instructors. No one bore grudges, and, foremost, no one dared argue.

Robert quickly began taking part in minor competitions. He won a prize for his interpretation of *L'harmonieux forgeron*, although he hadn't been able to play it using the pedal, because he was too small to reach it! A young girl who'd been able to use the pedal won the *Femina* prize. This young girl was Yvonne Lefébure. I have a photo of this event, where Robert can be seen next to her. There was even an article about them in *Comoedia*.

Robert was eight years old. In 1911, Robert won a *solfège* prize offered by Albert Lavignac. In 1912, he auditioned for Louis Diémer and was admitted to his class, where he won a first prize at the end of the first year, when he was fourteen years old. For this competition, Robert played Gabriel Fauré's *Variations* in the presence of Fauré himself, who was then serving as an administrator of the Paris Conservatory and as a jury member. After Robert's performance, Fauré patted him on the cheek and said, "You'll be a good little pianist!" He'd been dazzled by Robert. That day, Robert Casa understood that his son shouldn't enter the profession immediately, as the family tradition would have required. He said with profound seriousness: "Now, you'll really be able to get to work!" As if Robert hadn't worked hard already to achieve such a result!

Every summer, Robert spent his vacations in places where his father had been hired for the season. Therefore, he went to Cancale, Cabourg, and Houlgate. Robert Casa brought part of his family with him: his mother, his sister—Aunt Rosette, and Robert. That must have been a formidable entourage! Robert often told me that they'd eaten oysters in Cancale. Everyone except for Robert had drunk a small glass of alcohol to avoid catching typhoid. Robert unfortunately contracted this terrible disease. . . . It happened just after his prize, and wagging tongues in the family said that his illness occurred because he'd worked excessively and because his weary body couldn't defend itself. His illness occurred simply because he'd eaten oysters during the month of August! To restore his health, it was considered advisable to feed him sheep's or lambs' brains. The next day when he'd been feeling better, he had a 104-degree fever again! After this bout of typhoid, it seems that he remained unwell for an entire year. In addition, he was still growing, and this absorbed his energy, as it does for all children. The result was that Robert grew a lot . . . and gained weight.

For the rest of his life, Robert possessed an iron constitution. I never saw him ill, except for an occasional episode of the flu.

After his convalescence, he joined Lucien Capet's class. This is one of the things that made the greatest impression during his life, because Capet was exceptionally influential. I was in Capet's class, too, and I've retained an inextinguishable recollection of it. Capet received public recognition on account of his quartet: the Quatuor Capet, which was renowned worldwide.

Robert possessed the good fortune of being born into a family of musicians. His uncles, Henri and Marcel, were members of the Quatuor Capet, and, when rehearsals weren't taking place at Capet's home, they occurred in the Casadesus studio. In this way, when Robert was a young child, he heard every quartet as he quietly sat on a chair during rehearsals. He knew Beethoven's *Quartets* by heart. It can be said that this was the milk that nourished him. . . . This was extraordinary training for him. Like all quartets, the Quatuor rehearsed at least two hours per day, and Beethoven was the foundation of its repertoire. Occasionally, they played Haydn or César Franck, but Beethoven predominated. Furthermore, Beethoven was the family deity.

Robert subsequently transcribed Beethoven's *Quartets* so that we could play them in a version for four hands. That's why I know them by heart, too. . . . We often played them in the evening, after dinner. This was excellent discipline.

After his typhoid episode, Robert therefore became a pupil of Capet, who taught the Chamber Music section. He was also taking courses in Harmony.

During his first year with Capet, his explanations and descriptions were literally overwhelming. When he was having us practice Franck's *Sonata*, I can recall that he said: "You're going to see a long dark pathway. . . . At the end of this pathway, everything will become clear. That's the direction that you need to go in." During the second year, he was somewhat less overwhelming, because he was repeating himself. Capet was a genuinely great man! Whenever he could do so, he allowed Robert to play, because Robert was a fantastic sight reader. "Young Robert," as he was known. Robert was always referred to as "young" Robert, so as not to confuse him with Robert the Elder, namely his father. Frequently, people said: "Robert the Elder is coming for lunch. No one mentioned it to Young Robert."

Very soon, Robert began playing in piano-violin duos with his uncle Marius. The small difference in terms of their ages had brought them together. They always played by heart. I don't know how they were able to learn so quickly! When we relocated to the United States, Marius was quite sad because he'd lost his partner. Marius had created a superb quartet in addition to his participation in his brother Henri's Société des Instruments anciens. The Société toured just about everywhere in the world—to America, to Russia. The family was very well-known at that time. Today, period instruments are fashionable, but, when the twentieth century began, no one even knew what a *viola da gamba* was! Henri contributed enormously to the rediscovery of period instruments. He wrote about methods, and he arranged compositions so that they could be played with period instruments, although this activity didn't prevent him from composing operettas, too. Robert's father also wrote operettas that were performed at the Gaîté lyrique. I heard them, of course, but the one who was most successful in this domain was indisputably Henri.

Moreover, he was a Director of the Gaîté lyrique, and he was also a conductor. As for me, I gave the first performance of my husband's *Sonate pour piano et alto* with Henri.

You'll see that, when I mention a "tribe of musicians" to you, I'm not far from the truth!

# Chapter 3

# Entering the Profession

When he was sixteen, Robert began accompanying students from classes given by Mme. Aiglon, who was the wife of Xavier Leroux, his harmony teacher. She was an excellent singer, and Leroux was a renowned singing teacher. Robert had been highly pleased to accept this position, and I believe that he received a modest stipend for his work as an accompanist.

With a friend's help, he also joined the Opéra Comique, where he was a substitute in the percussion section. Indeed, he played the triangle or the celesta. He was also being paid there, and it can be said that these experiences were his start as a professional musician. His experience as a percussionist was quite useful later in terms of his work with orchestration. Contrary to what people believe, percussion is extremely difficult. It's necessary to know everything about a score unless you're counting each bar. . . . Robert always acknowledged that performing as a substitute had aided him tremendously. Moreover, our son Jean followed his father's example, and, when we were living in the United States, he took percussion courses in New York and adored them.

Robert told me an anecdote about a personal experience when he was a substitute percussionist. This was something that had happened at the Théâtre des Arts, when *Ma mère l'Oye* was being performed as a ballet with orchestration by Maurice Ravel, who was conducting. At one point, Ravel stopped and said to the triangle player: "Play louder! Nobody can hear anything! We can't hear the triangle. It has to be louder and more resounding!" Robert was profoundly impressed that Ravel, who didn't know him then, would have said this to him. Later, Robert often said to conductors who were directing *Ma mère l'Oye:* "Be especially sure that the triangle can be heard. It's particularly important. That's what Ravel wanted."

Robert was in great demand because he could sight read music so well. All of his friends who were preparing for the Prix de Rome in composition asked him to play their cantatas.

Robert played for numerous premières. In 1925 or 1926, Olivier Messiaen, who was still very young, asked Robert to play one of his works for the Société nationale de musique. In those days, he often interpreted works by the Polish composer Karol Szymanowski, who was living in Paris then. There were several societies where premieres took place: the Triptyque, the SMI, and the Société nationale.

It could be said that Robert's career truly began in 1924. As I recall, he gave twenty-five concerts that year! There were tours of Switzerland and Belgium. In Basel, he'd even performed with Weingartner, who possessed a reputation as an eminent Beethoven conductor, and they gave a performance of Beethoven's works. Throughout his life, Robert kept making regular trips to Belgium and Switzerland.

During this period, he was also hired for concerts in Spain. The earliest concerts were devoted to Ravel's work. We went to Le Belvédère at Montfort l'Amaury, to prepare with Ravel for concerts that were given in the following way: Ravel and Robert playing four hands. Always. Then Ravel would accompany a female singer. Robert would perform a solo afterwards, either *Gaspard de la Nuit*, or *Le Tombeau de Couperin*. Then he played the *Trio* with his uncle Marius and the cellist Maurice Maréchal.

Ravel greatly enjoyed Spain. One day, in Barcelona, he encouraged Robert to listen to *sardanas*. In fact, it was customary after Sunday Mass for *sardanas* to be performed in church squares. These rhythms made a strong impression on Robert, and they later inspired him to compose three *sardanas*. Although Ravel was born in the Basque region, he deeply loved these dances that are Catalan, as you know.

Ravel also introduced Robert to *horchata*, a beverage made from sweetened almond milk with a rather distinctive flavor.

Ravel and Robert always engaged in long conversations between concerts. A genuine friendship existed between them. Of course, they had long conversations about music. Ravel completely agreed with Robert about the importance of Beethoven's *Quartets*. In Ravel's opinion, the *Symphonies* were less successful. He regarded them as rather erratic. I think that he didn't like them very much, and that was a bit surprising to me.

On the other hand, Ravel said that, for Mozart, everything was a success: his quartets, his symphonies, and his operas. These opinions only added to Robert's pleasure in playing Mozart. You know how much this composer was present in his programs throughout his career.

Ravel's letter to Robert, March 20, 1926 from *Mes Noces Musicales*, is translated below:

Le Belvédère, Montfort l'Amaury (S. et O.)

My dear friend,

My Sonata for violin and piano, half done, and that my publisher is waiting for, 2 *Chansons madécasses*, hardly begun, that I promised for the end of April. My operetta, the 1st note of which I haven't yet written, which is commissioned for next season.

And I must soon go to Milan for the last rehearsals of *l'Enfant et les Sortilèges*. I would like to seek refuge in St Jean de Luz. Upon further thought, I'm barricading myself in Montfort as I did last year.

Do convey my apologies to Miss Fity as I await a more favorable time, and receive the most cordial feelings of your MR.

A thousand thanks for the *Préludes* and the dedication. I received them as I got home the day before yesterday and haven't yet had time to look at them of course.[1]

I believe that Ravel influenced him greatly. Robert had told me how much Ravel admired Chopin. One day, Robert had stated that he didn't enjoy the *Tarantella* very much and that he considered it to be rather unremarkable. Ravel responded: "It's necessary to play the *Tarantella*, even if it's just for the last chord, which is superb!" Afterward, Robert played it as an encore quite frequently.

Ravel had also spoken to him about Mozart's *Clarinet Quintets*. Robert wasn't yet familiar with them during this period. Subsequently, he transcribed them, and we often played these quintets together. They were seldom heard in concerts during the 1920s. It should be said that, during this period, a substantial number of works that are familiar today were never played, Mozart, for example, was never fashionable in the way that he has been for the past forty years. Of course, people thought that Mozart's creations were satisfactory and that they were appealing, but they were not enraptured in response to his works as people are today. As for Ravel, he was already enraptured.

The 1920s . . . that was the heyday of Honegger's *Le Roi David.*

Arthur Honegger was a friend from the Conservatory. We saw him quite often. When we went to the United States for the first time, we played Robert's *Concerto pour deux pianos* for him just before our departure, and he enthusiastically wrote: "That's going to be incredible!" He'd just achieved enormous success with his *Le Roi David.* Ravel believed that Honegger was a musician with a German cultural identity. In Ravel's eyes, Honegger wasn't French at all. . . . It is a certainty that, among composers in the Groupe des Six,[2] Ravel attributed a German cultural background to Honegger.

It was very unusual for Ravel to speak unfavorably of another composer or another musician. For him, the heritage that a person bears within himself was primordial. Not the heritage that's attributable to a person's birthplace but

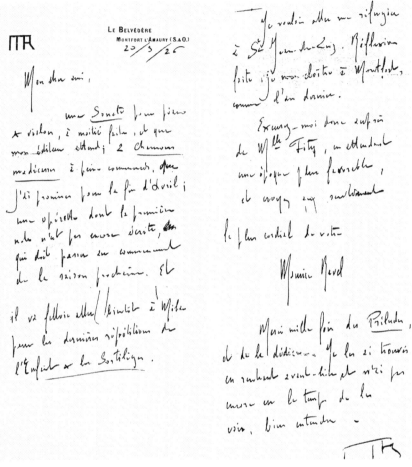

**Figure 3.1. A 1926 letter by Maurice Ravel to Robert Casadesus.** *Fond Casadesus, Bibliothèque Nationale, Paris, France.*

the heritage that we carry within our blood. . . . Everything that our parents have passed on to us while giving us life.

He adored Darius Milhaud. He said that Milhaud was the most interesting member of the Groupe des Six. It's true that all his works from the 1920s are excellent. Milhaud had carried out very original and fascinating research in the domain of harmonics. Ravel never mentioned Poulenc. He wouldn't say anything unfavorable about him. He didn't talk about him. . . . Ravel liked Satie, although not to the point of saying "It's necessary to play Satie," as the Groupe des Six was recommending at one time. Robert did play Satie. Compositions that he found interesting.

It's indisputable that the Groupe des Six influenced musical life during this period. I remember that Ravel once said in a conversation: "I need to renew myself. I can't go on constantly following the same path. *Daphnis et Chloé* or the *Rhapsodie espagnole* have been heard often enough. It was unbelievably successful, but now I must move on to something else." I wondered to myself: "But why does he want to change when he has created such beautiful things?" That's why Robert and I were so amazed in London by the performance of his *Duo pour violon et violoncelle*. It had seemed to us that this composition opened the door to a new facet of its composer. I'd like to emphasize that it's an extremely important work. Moreover, he himself was aware of it because, at that time, he only talked about this composition.

He'd also told us that hens could be heard clucking in his *Sonate pour violon et piano*, because, in France, when someone takes a walk in the countryside, background sounds always include: "Cluck, cluck, cluck, cluck, cluck, cock-a-doodle-doo." That's what inspired him to choose this theme for his sonata. For Ravel, it conveyed an aura of authenticity.

In this respect, it was said that he'd composed another finale for this sonata, although he'd changed it before leaving for America or after returning. I don't know anymore. Jazz was beginning to find a path in his head. It's true that it was arriving in France then because of the first recordings that were made in the United States. Mr. Lyon's son had brought us some records, and we were immediately interested in these new rhythms. It's obvious that, in the blues portion of his *Sonate pour violon et piano*, Ravel was strongly influenced by jazz.

In 1924, Robert was the first musician to devote an entire recital to Ravel. The program included *Jeux d'eau*, the *Sonatina*, the *Alborada del gracioso, Scarbo*, and the *Toccata* from the *Tombeau de Couperin*. He'd gone to Montfort l'Amaury to work with Ravel, and the concert was given in the original Salle Pleyel on the Rue Rochechouart. The recital was also broadcast, which was a milestone in that era. . . . Ravel attended the concert, and he subsequently sent Robert a charming letter where he said: "Did I tell you the other evening that *Jeux d'eau* (among other works) has never been played so well?"

Ravel frequently used express messages. Telephones in people's homes were a rarity during this period. "Get me a room! We'll take the train." It's necessary to point out that the train was always used for traveling. That took up a lot of time, and yet we were leading an extremely active life regardless! In addition to our courses in Le Havre for Robert and in Rouen for me, Robert was giving courses once a month in the home of one of Raoul Pugno's friends. He sometimes taught eight hours of courses in one day. During 1924–1925, he had an enormous number of students.

Bringing up Ravel again, I believe that he was extremely impressed by Robert's musical talents. He wasn't a person who gave lessons, but, when they were preparing a concert together, Ravel indicated a tempo for him. In this way, Robert was familiar with all of Ravel's wishes.

Ravel wasn't someone who offered exaggerated expressions of friendship, but I recall that, at the beginning of our relationship, when he was writing to Robert, he began his letters with "Dear Sir," and that, later, his greetings changed to "Dear friend."

Robert dedicated his *24 Préludes* to Ravel after composing them in 1924. For Robert, Ravel was indisputably one of the leading lights in the musical firmament.

He was an extremely simple man, a man who was genuine, sincere, and free from false pretenses. He spoke sparingly. When Ravel played *Ma mère l'Oye* for four hands with Robert (when we played it together with Robert, I'd play Ravel's part, namely the treble part, and Robert would play the bass part), he had the habit of adding a chord that isn't in the score at a certain point in *La Belle et la Bête.* One day, a musicologist who'd heard our recording asked why we'd been adding this chord that doesn't appear in the score. We responded that Ravel added it when he played this composition. Later, we spoke about it with Philippe Entremont, who confirmed that Ravel had inserted this chord in the orchestra version. When I revised the piano edition, I added the chord, and I explained why.

I never knew Debussy, but, one day, Robert had heard him accompanying the singer Ninon Vallin at the Salle Gaveau. He told me that he'd observed a precise, subtle, and consistently exact touch. I'd met Debussy's daughter, the one who died at an early age, because, after Debussy's death, I'd gone to play before Mme. Debussy, who'd relocated to the Hôtel Plaza-Athénée with her young daughter. Mme. Debussy had wanted to hear me play the *Préludes.* Her daughter was fourteen, and I was fifteen. She played the piano very well. For me, she played the *Gradus ad Parnassum* that her father had composed for her. We never met again because she died from croup when she was sixteen.

In fact, I could've had a chance to meet Debussy because he was a member of the jury when I took the entrance examination for the preparatory class. In the waiting room, someone told me: "Watch out! He'll plug his ears. He hates it when people play loudly." It seemed that he hated resounding chords and didn't tolerate anyone pounding the piano. I didn't even see his face among the jury members because I was concentrating on playing without mistakes. . . . This examination was difficult for a young girl. We had to wait our turns in a type of cubbyhole that was illuminated by a small light. This was a fearful moment! Applicants were tormented by stage fright. I've kept a dreadful memory of it. This competition period is a time that will never be forgotten. . . . When I completed my examination, everyone was waiting in a large hall.

There was always a rumor that the jury had fallen behind with its schedule. "You won't get to play the whole thing. They'll make you stop." Therefore, applicants knew that only a small portion of their performances would be heard and that it would be necessary for their allotted time to be the best. Alongside the hall where the competition took place, there was a glass door, and all the mothers were awaiting their candidate children behind it. It was rather ridiculous, because I don't really know whether they could have heard anything among the commotion created by students who were awaiting their turns and by those who'd already completed the examination. Indeed, the situation has hardly changed since then.

The examination hall was extremely large, and it was decorated with huge academic paintings. At one end, there was a small platform with a piano. It is always necessary to take time to adjust the chair to a proper height. This is a tricky moment because the height of the keyboard in relation to oneself is essential for playing.

The attendant instructed us to enter, and he shouted our names and ages, while helping us sometimes adjust the chair. The grand piano remained open. Its sound echoed in a fantastic way within this hall, and I can understand why Debussy would plug his ears, because, if a person played this piano loudly, it was frightful. When I was a member of the jury myself and when I returned to the hall, I became aware of this. Indeed, whenever anyone plays loudly, it feels like Russian percussive music is being played. . . . The first time that I sat on the jury side, I was quite emotional because it reminded me of the time when I'd competed. The stakes are so high! I also understood that a certain strictness was necessary because prizes can't be given to everyone. It's somewhat difficult to armor oneself in such a way, but people get used to it.

It's necessary to avoid being enthusiastic about a given candidate too soon, because the next candidate or candidates may be better. That's the problem with competitions. If random selection were to designate you as number one and if there are forty candidates, it still isn't known what the level of competition will be when you're being heard, because the jury may turn out to be too strict or not strict enough. Perhaps the level will only be determined with the tenth candidate. It may be said that it isn't possible to arrive at a judgment before Number 10. Hence, the first candidate will be at a disadvantage. As for the final candidates, they may also be competing at a point when everyone's falling asleep. . . . It's believed that it isn't favorable to compete around three o'clock in the afternoon. . . . That's the jury's naptime! I was a jury member at the Paris Conservatory in the era of Claude Delvincourt, Raymond Loucheur, and Raymond Gallois-Montbrun. In turn, Robert was frequently a jury member in international competitions, notably for the first Queen Elizabeth Competition in Brussels.

## NOTES

1. Maurice Ravel's letter to Robert Casadesus, March 20, 1926, translated from the letters in Gaby Casadesus's *Mes Noces Musicales* (Paris: Buchet Chastel, 1989), 31.

2. The Groupe des Six: six composers whose spiritual father was Erik Satie. They came together under Jean Cocteau's leadership in order to facilitate dissemination of a new type of music, while working in a close relationship with painters and poets. Their names were: Georges Auric, Francis Poulenc, Arthur Honegger, Darius Milhaud, Louis Durey, and Germaine Tailleferre.

# Chapter 4

# The American Conservatory at Fontainebleau

The beginnings of the Fontainebleau School were extremely brilliant, especially because there were first-rate faculty members: Charles-Marie Widor was a composition teacher there, and Nadia Boulanger was his assistant. Robert (Casadesus) was under the authority of Isidore Philipp.[1] The Conservatory had been opened by Walter Damrosch, the famous American orchestra conductor who'd paraded on Fontainebleau's streets holding the Stars and Stripes with his outstretched arm, followed by American soldiers and by Francis Casadesus, the School's founding director.

The story of the creation of the American Conservatory at Fontainebleau coincided with the end of the First World War. At the point when American military music arrived in France simultaneously with the American Army, it went on to take up residence in Chaumont.

Francis Casadesus, who was fifty years old at that time, was in a reserve unit at Chaumont, where he was administering the Military Music School. The School included several French musicians although its student body especially consisted of Americans.

They were so enthusiastic about the instruction that was offered to them, especially for woodwinds—flutes and clarinets—that Damrosch, who was conducting the New York Philharmonic at this time, considered it necessary to maintain contact and believed that musicians from his orchestra should travel to France in order to work with French instructors. Francis Casadesus came up with the idea of mentioning it to Mr. Fragneau, the Prefect of Seine-et-Marne, who immediately adopted every necessary measure for musicians to be housed in the Fontainebleau Château's Louis XV wing and for courses to be given there.

We'd invited Saint-Saëns, who was already a quite elderly gentleman, to one of the first concerts, so as to introduce him to Damrosch. Displaying the qualities that were distinctively his, Saint-Saëns took it upon himself to interrupt the singer who was interpreting one of his art songs, because he believed that she wasn't singing it in tune! Robert confided to me that he'd refused to play Saint-Saëns for this concert because, at that time, Robert was hardly enthusiastic about his music. Hence, it was Madeleine de Valmalète who played the *Danse macabre*, a brilliant work transcribed by Liszt for the piano. Later, Robert changed his opinion and frequently played Saint-Saëns' *Concerto Nº 4*.

During the School's early years of operation, there were as many as one hundred students per session. In agreement with Damrosch, Francis had created an actual conservatory where every type of instrument was taught, along with singing. The Americans responded enthusiastically to this approach. An American, Mrs. Tuttle, took responsibility for recruiting students in the United States. She reserved their ship passages for them, and she organized everything. On July 1, 1921, young Americans, male and female, were arriving at Fontainebleau. When it became known on the other side of the Atlantic that Isidore Philipp was one of the teachers, there was an actual flood of pianists. Composers came, too, including Aaron Copland, who continued to be loyal supporters. Organ instruction was especially important at the School for an extremely long period.

These young Americans brought a new way of life to the Château. The young ladies let their long hair dry outside the windows, and artillery trainees who were quartered at the Artillery School not far from the Château were therefore drawn to the grounds! At the time, this "incident" was problematic for Francis, who wasn't actually responsible for it . . . to such an extent that lodging in the Château had to be suspended. The classrooms and the instruction studios were retained. This arrangement created a terrible racket. . . . People who passed by the Château during the height of the summer could hear a veritable cacophony because we were practicing with open windows.

Initially, Robert was Isidore Philipp's assistant teacher from July 1921 to July 1924. At that time, he was giving two courses lasting half an hour apiece to each of his students every week. In 1924, because his career was developing successfully, he resigned. In addition, although he'd been enthusiastic about the technique taught by Philipp, he was also quite frustrated because Philipp only allowed composers such as Widor, Vidal, and Saint-Saëns to be performed. Works by Ravel or Debussy were hardly ever played. Robert found it unacceptable for these two composers to be so rarely performed.

In 1935, Robert was asked to replace Isidore Philipp as the director of piano instruction.

Therefore, we were linked to the Fontainebleau School for practically our entire lives because I'm still teaching there today. For my part, I started teaching in 1936. During those years and until the war, Robert only taught masterclasses every two weeks.

During our summers at Fontainebleau, we planned to meet after classes, at approximately 4:00 p.m., at the Château's main square. Then we'd take off for bicycle rides in the forest. We often went to Recloses, where a former schoolmate of my father-in-law owned a restaurant. Robert adored bicycling. From time to time, I "stalled" a bit, but then he'd push me to climb the hills! We were familiar with every nook and cranny in the forest: the Fairies' Pond, the Apremont boulders.

At the outbreak of World War II, it was out of the question to have American students traveling to Fontainebleau. That was considered far too dangerous. Many students wrote to us to ask whether it wouldn't be possible to offer courses during our stay in the United States, because we usually spent three months there from January to April. Then things turned out differently. We stayed in the United States. We sent a telegram to Paris in order to find out whether we could run the School in the United States during the summer. Robert, who was in his very early forties, was eligible for military service, but, for propaganda purposes, he received a special authorization from the Ministry of War to complete his tour. Hence, we were expecting to return to France in April. When events took an unfavorable turn and when Norway was invaded, we concluded that, because of the number of requests that had been received, we could possibly offer the summer courses in the United States. Very quickly, we received permission to stay three months more for the School. Therefore, we rented an apartment in Princeton, where we'd gone to give a concert. Fortunately, we'd brought the boys with us! Jean had earned a first place *solfège* medal, and, as a reward, we'd decided that he should accompany us. Perhaps if he'd only received a second-place medal, he'd have stayed in Paris. . . . You know how parents are!

In January 1940, we therefore took the southern Atlantic line, the Italian line. We embarked with our two sons and a trunk on the "Rex," and, during the crossing, we learned that Italy would be entering the war. We didn't have any doubts about it. In France, euphoria reigned. Everywhere, it was being proclaimed: "The Germans aren't strong at all!" The husband of one of my students, who was a pilot, told us, "You know, we fly over the borders. Nothing happens. Nothing moves. No one knows where they are." Naturally, they were in Poland! They were proceeding to overpower Poland! France was sound asleep. People were sure that the war wouldn't be fought in Paris. . . . It would unfold in Syria, but certainly not in France.

Because of Robert's having performed frequently in Germany, he was receiving many requests from German concert organizations, who were furious that we wouldn't be returning from the United States.

I always believed that we'd made a good decision by staying in the United States. We were doing valuable work that contributed to our country's reputation. If we'd returned to France, two options existed for us: we could continue playing and we'd have been accused of collaboration with the enemy, or we could hide in a corner and stop working for years. Neither option was favorable.

We were lucky enough to have a student who knew the headmaster of a school in Newport, Rhode Island. We ran the Fontainebleau School there for two summer months. We immediately had thirty piano students, including Grant Johannesen, who later played a key role in establishing the Robert Casadesus International Piano Competition in Cleveland, Ohio.

The School operated in Newport for two years. As you know, however, the American naval base in Newport was one of the most important bases in the United States. When the United States entered the war, we were literally kicked out, because the School overlooked the base, the shore, and the sea. All of this territory had been requisitioned, and the authorities possibly feared that we would send signals to German submarines.

Therefore, we relocated to Great Barrington, Massachusetts. This town was extremely close to the famous Berkshire Festival (Tanglewood) that Serge Koussevitzky had founded. This is where we celebrated the liberation of Paris and our forthcoming return to France in order to bring the School back to its point of origin.

At the end of 1945, Robert was approached by René Dommange, the Director of Éditions Durand, who was a member of the Committee for the Fontainebleau School, and by Jean-Paul Alaux, the President of the Fontainebleau Écoles d'Art, to become the Director of the American Conservatory. Robert enthusiastically agreed, because he was delighted to repatriate the School to France after five years of exile.

Hence, our return was planned for the summer of 1946. At that point, a real battle broke out because the American authorities deemed the return to be premature on account of the shortages that still existed in France after the occupation years. Only Walter Damrosch and a portion of the Committee supported us. On the French side, it was advisable to proceed quickly, because, after the Germans' departure, the Château had been reclaimed, and we were able to begin activities again in the Louis XV wing, although there was a project for possible establishment of a museum there, so that it was wise to occupy the premises without delay.

On July 4, 1946, which was Independence Day for the Americans, the School therefore opened its doors again with approximately twenty young Americans who'd followed us, in spite of the pessimistic advice they'd been given all around for attempting to dissuade them from embarking upon this adventure.

I became a real surrogate mother for a very large family. I took charge of food. We were still subject to rationing, and the Americans had unfailingly warned students that they were coming at their own risk. I performed wonders in order to ensure a supply of food, by arranging for crates filled with milk, soap, and all of the essentials to be sent from the United States, because we lacked everything, even toilet paper. . . . I imported corn meal that the baker didn't like, but it was better than nothing.

We were living in the Château. The bathrooms were sumptuous with their bulging bathtubs and their silver faucets with a swan's neck shape. Nonetheless, we only had a tiny stove for heating our breakfast. . . . We ate our meals with the students at the refectory on Rue Saint Honoré, and that spared me from any cooking chores.

At the end of this first summer, Robert had a commitment at the Lucerne Festival, where he was scheduled to perform Saint-Saëns' *Concerto N° 4*, with Paul Paray conducting. Then we thought that it would be a good idea to bring our young Americans with us. Words became a reality, and we left for our expedition to Switzerland, an expedition with a distinctive "very large family" image.

During this period, Nadia Boulanger hadn't yet returned to the School. As you know, she administered Fontainebleau later, until her death in 1979. During the war, she'd also resided in the United States, in California, not far from the Stravinskys, and she taught composition there.

Robert, therefore, took on the position of Director of the American Conservatory after our return, and he did so until 1948. Nadia succeeded him when our daughter Thérèse contracted poliomyelitis in the same year. This episode in our lives was truly a tragedy.

Our young daughter, who was barely six years old, was stricken with poliomyelitis after being exposed to an American student living at the Château.

This young man had been ill, and he was diagnosed with meningitis. Shortly thereafter, our son Guy, who was sixteen years old, also complained of headaches. I immediately took him to the hospital, where they performed a spinal tap that revealed that meningitis wasn't involved. The doctors told me that I could take him home and that there was no risk of any kind of infection. A therapy that I followed scrupulously had been prescribed. After three days, Guy was feeling much better, while Thérèse, in turn, was complaining of experiencing headaches . . . and a sore throat. Furthermore, she had a high fever. We immediately requested an appointment with a physician in Paris who observed that her reflexes on the left side of her body weren't as strong as on the right side. When he returned to examine her again on the following day, he announced that Thérèse had polio. . . . The poor child was tossing from one side to another in her bed. It was dreadful. . . . We transferred her as quickly as possible by ambulance to the American Hospital in Neuilly.

I only returned to Fontainebleau in 1971, when Robert gave a recital for the School's fiftieth anniversary. I didn't go into the apartment, and I only went there when Nadia was ill . . . much later . . . I couldn't bear revisiting places that reminded me of this terrible misfortune.

Indeed, the young flutist did have polio. He recovered relatively well, and we encountered him later in the United States, where he was a flutist in an orchestra.

Robert was severely stricken by this tragedy. The boys left for Switzerland with him, and I stayed with Thérèse at the American Hospital in Neuilly, where she was undergoing intensive treatment that unfortunately failed to offer positive results. Robert waited six months and then, when he saw that Thérèse could hardly remain standing on her legs, he was crushed. At that time, people were saying that he'd never played so well in his life, with so much sensitivity. . . . You know how people are.

This ordeal was heartbreaking for all of us. We'd been so happy . . . two handsome sons, along with an adorable and beautiful daughter who'd never been ill.

After three weeks of treatment in Neuilly, we joined Robert and the boys in Switzerland, although not without difficulty, because, according to the Swiss viewpoint, risks of infection continued for four weeks, and we quickly began to understand that we were undesirables, even in terms of our best friends. . . . We were obliged to go into hiding for a week. I was furious and I found this attitude to be shocking.

Robert returned to France with the boys, and I remained alone with Thérèse for a month so that she could undergo motor rehabilitation therapy that was said to be highly effective.

Nadia therefore became Robert's successor at Fontainebleau. Afterward, she never failed to send her wishes to Thérèse on her birthdays. . . . She kept a notebook where she recorded the birth dates of her acquaintances. She kept insisting that Robert *should* come to give courses. She wanted to maintain the level of the School. In turn, Jean was appointed as a teacher in 1952–1953. Nadia had hired him as a coaching instructor for Robert when he began playing for the New York Philharmonic. Jean taught at Fontainebleau each summer until he died.

Ultimately, Nadia and Jean no longer saw eye to eye. Nadia believed that he was seeking to change too many things. In fact, Jean hoped that the School would have stronger anchor points in American universities, notably at the State University of New York in Binghamton, where he was teaching, so that they could become catalysts for the Fontainebleau Conservatory. On the other hand, Nadia remained loyal to a form of tradition that was possibly valid. Indeed, she didn't like to argue with Jean. She considered him too young. Of course, Jean spoke English perfectly. He was quite familiar with the American mindset on account of having spent his teenage years in the United States. Jean often discussed his ideas with François Valéry who was for many years President of the Fontainebleau Schools. Even today, he says to me: "Oh, if we'd just listened to Jean.

After Jean's death, Nadia asked me to become his successor. At that time, I responded that I was indeed interested in masterclasses, although I didn't want to give regular courses for two months.

Therefore, I gave masterclasses, and that's how I met Émile Naoumoff, who was one of Nadia's last students and to whom she was deeply attached. She especially wanted to guide him toward composition. She said that it was necessary to let him compose what he wished, and that he could be corrected afterward. The attitude that she showed toward this young man was quite touching. She who'd wielded so much authority became much more flexible with age. He was also a very gifted pianist, and he was full of ideas. Because I thought it was a shame that he wasn't essentially being encouraged to pursue the piano, I recall having said to his mother, "You know, Chopin was a wonderful composer, but that didn't prevent him from being an excellent pianist, too. If your son possesses true talent as a composer, this shouldn't divert him from practicing the piano thoroughly." Even today, she still thanks me for having given her this advice. The Fontainebleau School always has a place in my life. I'm a member of the Board, I give classes there, and I'm interested in keeping up with its progress . . . Francis, Damrosch, Robert, Jean, Nadia, it's already so far away.

## NOTE

1. Isidore Philipp, who was born in Budapest in 1863, died in Paris in 1958.

## Chapter 5

# Two Pianos and Four Hands

I always wanted to pursue a career. At the beginning of my marriage, I was performing under the name Gabrielle L'Hôte-Casadesus. We often played four hands for our own enjoyment: Schubert, Mozart, and Robert's scores. Then we started playing two piano repertoires. The first time was in Nancy. We played a Mozart *Concerto* that we'd already been practicing for some time for our own pleasure. One day, when he observed that our two names—Gabrielle L'Hôte Casadesus and Robert Casadesus—as they appeared side by side on a poster—were occupying excessive space, Robert said to me: "I don't understand why you're performing under this name. Why couldn't we just perform under the name Robert and Gaby Casadesus? Clara Schumann didn't let herself be known as Clara Wieck Schumann, as far as I know."

In fact, I feared that this would create problems with all the Casadesus family members who were musicians! Marius, who was the leader of the Quatuor Casadesus, had been furious when Henri's second wife, who was a harpist, had chosen *Quatuor Casadesus* for the harpists' ensemble that she'd formed. She'd nevertheless included "harp" in the subtitle, but, because "*Quatuor*" appeared in large type, Marius said that people would only confuse the two quartets. He added "Women should keep their maiden names." No one ever reproached us for letting ourselves be known as Robert and Gaby Casadesus.

The situation became rather complicated when our young cousin, Jean-Claude, took the surname of his mother, Gisèle, who was married to Lucien Probst, and whose children quite obviously had their father's surname. Jean-Claude therefore had to seek permission to bear his mother's surname. Doing this could have created confusion with our son Jean, who, in turn, wasn't bothered at all by his cousin's using the surname Casadesus. On several occasions, confusion did occur, even though it only involved radio fees. Jean received Jean-Claude's fee payments and vice versa! When Jean's accident took place, some people believed that it was Jean-Claude because Jean had been given Claude as another of his first names. I'd given him this additional first name when he was born, saying to myself, "Jean is perhaps somewhat ordinary. If he wishes to let himself be known as Jean-Claude, he can." Double names were fashionable at that time. This situation meant that, when his death was announced and because both first names are always used in the United States, there were persons in France who believed that it was Jean-Claude who'd just been killed in an automobile crash . . . there was a brief interval of confusion.

We were working a lot, and our only entertainment was dinners in our friends' homes. During this period, dinners often ended with brief concerts. Robert easily sat down at the piano, and he did it more easily than I. We often visited our friends, the Cohendy family; the husband was a physician. We'd spend time with them later in Varengeville-sur-Mer. In their home, we always met extremely interesting people. That's where we got to know Mme. Costallat, who was the wife of Emmanuel Chabrier's publisher. We were introduced to composer Albert Roussel there, too.

In 1925, we went on a vacation to Varengeville for the first time, and, once again, we encountered Albert Roussel, who owned a house there. We were visiting with our friends the Cohendys, and we spent time practicing in the home of neighbors who generously lent us their piano.

On several occasions, we visited Roussel. Mme. Roussel was delighted to show me her clematis vines, and she wanted to give me a shoot from one of her vines for our house. The Roussels were growing extremely rare plants. In Paris, they were surrounded by particularly beautiful furniture and by strange or even exotic items. Both possessed refined taste and were exceptionally learned, indeed more so than many musicians in general.

Regarding these dinners with private concerts, we often met other musicians on those occasions. That's how we became acquainted with Hugues Cuénod. His very high-pitched voice was an oddity. Robert would play alone or piano four hands with me. During this period, we also attended the Orchestre Pasdeloup frequently and the Cirque d'Hiver, where concerts took place as well. Rhené-Bâton was the conductor at the Cirque d'Hiver then. I'd auditioned there, too, after my prize. Paul Paray conducted the Lamoureux Orchestra at the Salle Gaveau, and Gabriel Pierné was conducting the *Concerts Colonne* at the Théâtre du Châtelet.

Speaking of Pierné, I can say that, sometime after, I was to play Saint-Saëns' *Concerto N° 4* with him. He'd never heard me play before. He only knew that I'd just won the Pagès Prize and that I was a quite talented pianist.

He made me come to his home for rehearsals. He was living on the Rue de Tournon, on a ground floor with a garden, and he also occupied the first floor. His apartment was delightful. I went there one morning, and I recall that, when he saw me, he seemed slightly worried when he noticed that I was so thin and so young. "Be careful, be careful," he said. "You'll need to play like a virtuoso. You can't interpret this work without having a lot of power and a lot of emphasis for the strong chords and the rhythm!" He was undoubtedly wondering whether I'd be capable of mastering my material in the vast hall at the Théâtre du Châtelet.

The concert went extremely well, but, when I reconsider it today, I believe that he was right to speak to me in that way, because there's no question that the Conservatory prepares a person for competitions more than for performing with an orchestra that's intended to be heard in a concert hall.

Fortunately, I'd acquired the opportunity to play with what was then known as the "Ensemble des concerts," which was a type of reduced orchestra consisting of a violin, a viola, a cello, and a flute. I believe that this allowed me to rehearse the soloist's entrances within a concerto. Therefore, I already had a concept of the cues, which is something that a person absolutely cannot imagine when practicing accompanied by a second piano. It's so striking to hear an orchestra alongside oneself for the first time!

I recall having played a Mozart concerto with the Pasdeloup Orchestra when I was very young and how I was driven to tears when I heard a cello phrase whose beauty is impossible to envision before you hear it. Of course, we can always read the orchestral score, but that has nothing to do with the actual presence of a specific instrument. Today, recordings of orchestras performing alone are available for soloists, and this allows them to practice concertos seriously before gathering for first rehearsals. And, in addition, we can also listen to recordings of our colleagues, which can be good . . . or detrimental. . . . It should very much be kept in mind that, in those days, we didn't have anything of the sort.

I can also recall Robert's first concerts that were broadcast. I needed to go to the homes of friends who owned a radio to hear him. I must say instead that I tried to hear him! The radio transmission was dreadful. Only a sort of amalgamation of undefinable sounds could be heard. Furthermore, it was the same thing with the telephone. We didn't have a telephone until 1923 or 1924. At the beginning of our marriage, when we were living on Rue du Four, the concierge, who was the only one with a telephone, would call me from the courtyard: "Mme. Robert, there's a call for you!" and I'd come down from the first floor to receive the call. Moreover, people only made telephone calls in emergency situations.

During this period, Robert had an opportunity to perform before Anatole France one day. It was at the home of our friends the Lonchond family, who'd invited us to lunch. Dr. Lonchond was an archeologist. This was the time when the Affaire Caillaux trial was taking place. Anatole France was in a state of extreme excitement. He'd stated in a firm tone: "There's no way I'll defend him as I once defended Dreyfus." I can assure you that this occasion has remained engraved upon my memory. You can imagine—being in the presence of the famous Anatole France! Furthermore, that was the only time that we ever met him. He died a year later. After lunch, we chatted before sitting down at the piano. He was sitting in an armchair in a very dignified way with his long white beard that gave him the appearance of a patriarch. Our friends had insisted that he should hear Robert. Robert played Ravel, and I played Franck. It was obvious that Anatole France's tastes were more inclined toward Franck! He listened to Ravel quite attentively, and he seemed to enjoy Robert's performance. I recall that Robert had ended this mini-recital with the *Toccata*, which he played marvelously well, as he maintained the rhythm from beginning to end. As an expression of appreciation, Anatole France gave my husband an autographed photo that we've treasured.

In 1925, Robert was invited to play in Zurich. Zurich had an exceptional reputation for its cultural life at that time. Robert had given a recital, and he'd played with orchestra led by Volkmar Andreae. This excellent conductor was so kind as to welcome into his home the soloists whom he was conducting, and we were given a room there. He owned an extremely beautiful house, and, in particular, an extremely comprehensive musical library. Among other items, it was possible to find every edition of all of the most significant concertos. His house was near the home of Mathilde Wesendonck, who inspired Richard Wagner's *Wesendonck Lieder.* In addition, Wagner was often a guest in his muse's home. It was understandable that he'd enjoyed this superb location, which provided an impregnable view of the lake and multicolored gardens.

Volkmar was the Director of the Zurich Conservatory, and he'd been a friend of Ferruccio Busoni. He was a significant figure in the world of music. He was extremely kind to us, a touch paternalistic, because, in his eyes, we were young.

He told us how he'd once had the honor of turning pages for Brahms during a concert when Brahms was performing one of his piano concertos. I don't know any more whether this was the first or the second concerto, but Andreae told us that he'd remarked after the second concert—the concert was given twice—that he'd performed a passage more slowly than during the first concert. It seemed that Brahms had replied, "I'm an artist, not a machine!" I don't know whether this story is true, because Andreae loved to make up stories. He'd also told us that Ferruccio Busoni had given the entirety of Mozart's concerti under his baton. Ernest Ansermet, who was pre-eminent in Geneva at that time, was regarded as a formidable avant-gardist. It must be said that it was difficult to find two conductors who were more different than those two. There was a lot of debate about Ansermet, even when people thought that he conducted Debussy, Ravel, and Stravinsky perfectly well. People didn't like him when he was conducting Beethoven, however. It was said that he lacked the range of capabilities for conducting this repertoire. Later, however, what he'd done on behalf of music in general was acknowledged. He had a completely exceptional sense of how these new scores should be read. He was quite familiar with Stravinsky and Prokofiev. He adored Ravel, but I don't know whether they ever met.

Ansermet had completed studies in higher mathematics. He didn't hesitate to say that it was impermissible to create atonal music. In fact, he was intensely anti-Schönberg and intensely pro-Stravinsky. He had a superb sense of rhythm. He was a born musician with an extremely strong personality. He had an infallible ear and iron authority. He could ensure that new types of music would be played at a time when no one knew about them.

Today, every conductor knows *The Rite of Spring* by heart, but, in the beginning, it was extremely difficult, especially in terms of rhythm. The rhythm changes with each measure. There are beats at three, five, and seven. You need to be very alert! Once you've heard it, I'd say that fewer problems arise. At that time, however, everything still needed to be done. Orchestra musicians had to learn everything.

When there are many young musicians in an orchestra, they can sight read very quickly and are ready for all sorts of miracles, especially if they like the conductor . . . I believe that this is what happened with Ansermet. He opened the door for many new works, both in Geneva and during his travels.

To some extent, we followed the same routes that he did. We went to Russia after him and then to America. We often spoke with each other about his tours, his successes, and his critics. We formed genuine bonds of friendship apart from our professional relations. We visited his home, and we knew his wife very well. Later, during the war, we met in the United States, where he came to conduct regularly, because, as a Swiss citizen, he could travel freely. He also conducted Robert's works. He was one of the eminent figures in twentieth-century music.

In 1926, we bought a five horsepower Citroën. A big event! Neither Robert nor I were mechanically talented, but, like everyone in France, we'd dreamed of having a car. One of my students who was an extremely talented pianist—she became a famous singer under the name Renée Gili—had married a fellow who was well-off enough to own a large garage, near L'Étoile. As a specialist in the field, he'd assured us that he'd find a high-quality second-hand automobile for us. It was one of those small convertible cars with two seats in front and one seat in the rear. It was June, and we needed to obtain our drivers licenses quickly if we wished to enjoy our purchase during the summer. The garage owner had told us that it was incredibly easy and that, by taking ten lessons, we'd be able to receive our licenses. We took ten lessons together, thinking that at least one of us would indeed be successful. . . . So much stress! After the second lesson, we were taken to the Place de l'Étoile, and even though the traffic was nothing like it is now, it was already congested enough.

I can recall that, on the day of the test, the examiner "grilled" Robert intensively. From me, he only expected driving. He must have been thinking, "She's small and delicate, and I need to see whether she can handle the steering wheel," whereas Robert, who was a sturdy person, didn't seem to display any problems with driving.

To our great joy, we got our licenses on the first try! Robert immediately went to pick up the car from the garage, and he remembered his first trip for his entire life! He had to go to the Salle Pleyel, which was on the Rue Rochechouart then. He parked, but he forgot to use the parking brake—the Rue Rochechouart is on an incline—and he had to chase the car in order to stop it. That was a good start! On this very same day, he came by to pick me up on the Avenue de l'Opéra where I'd been shopping. He arrived late and was furious because other drivers had called him a "road hog:" he had trouble using the clutch and couldn't restart the car. Therefore, he was holding up traffic. We started together, and we proceeded onto the Rue du Faubourg St.-Honoré, while we stayed in first gear because we were following a bus. Suddenly, the bus stopped, and Robert pressed the accelerator instead of using the brakes! Quite obviously, we crashed into the rear of the bus, and we needed to leave our car at the Place Vendôme so that someone could come and get it started again. This was Robert's debut as a driver! I can tell you for sure that he became an excellent driver afterward.

That same year, we decided to drive down to Saint-Tropez with our car. We had a few adventures: cows and hens along the road that prolonged our traveling time . . . driving through villages, the condition of the roads . . . each trip was truly an adventure, or, indeed, an epic! I've kept a marvelous recollection of that visit. It was like a dream! Bathing in the sea was fantastic! I've always enjoyed swimming, and I didn't hesitate to swim far out because I've never been afraid.

We went to Sénéquier, which was already a fashionable location. Celebrities from the arts world came there to eat the delicious pastries, and we often ran into Colette, who was spending part of the year at her house in Saint-Tropez. The harbor had a distinctive charm. Of course, there weren't any of the large yachts that anchor there today, and the atmosphere wasn't snobbish at all. It was more of an informal atmosphere, with excellent small restaurants where people sampled regional specialties. I can remember eating eggplant for the first time. The cuisine was somewhat exotic for us as Parisians.

After this ideal vacation, we returned to Paris. Robert had concerts in Brussels and in Holland. Our friends, the Chauvel-Bize family (the garage owner and his wife, who was my former student), then suggested that they could take me to meet Robert in Holland. They owned a superb "Voisin" that could go one hundred kilometers per hour. For that era, this vehicle was a comet! It took us one day to reach Amsterdam. We had to cross rivers by ferries that took hours to wait for. It was a lot of fun, but also stressful. We arrived in time for Robert's concert, where he was playing with the Concertgebouw Orchestra. We needed to be back on the road the following morning. After a late-night supper following the concert, we all went to sleep late. So late that we didn't leave until ten o'clock in the morning. I needed to be in Paris by four o'clock in the afternoon, to give a lesson. Mr. Chauvel-Bize was ready to give it a try. It was November.

Our visibility wasn't perfect, because of fog. At Septeuil, we had an accident. It had rained, it was the season for harvesting beets, and the road was slippery. I wasn't aware of these conditions. I was sitting in the rear and was serving as the navigator, with my face buried in the map. On a hilltop, our friend came face to face with a truck. The truckdriver must have been frightened when he saw us and started braking quickly. He skidded, and Mr. Chauvel-Bize ended up in a ditch. The car didn't turn over, but Mr. Chauvel-Bize and I, who were on the left side, were injured. I lost consciousness, and Robert, who'd been sitting beside me in the rear, was scared to death. My eyes were open, but I wasn't conscious. Robert was doubly scared because I was six weeks pregnant, and he feared that I'd have a miscarriage. They carried me to a nearby farm, and I remained in a coma for several hours. Then I was taken to Paris in an ambulance. I spent two or three days completely unconscious. Dr. Vincent, who was Maurice Ravel's physician, was summoned, and he didn't hesitate to say to Robert: "You know, things with the head—either they're very serious, or they're nothing." Indeed, I recovered quickly enough but not entirely. In my bed, I could hear Robert giving lessons and, one day, I happened to remark that the piano was terribly out of tune. That wasn't true at all. In fact, my hearing wasn't the same for both ears. That drove me crazy. I didn't want to go to concerts anymore . . . and then I accompanied Robert when he was giving concerts in Switzerland. One day, we were walking at an altitude of five hundred meters, and, suddenly, I felt a clicking sound in my ear, and I could hear normally once again. I barely came within an inch of becoming like Gabriel Fauré, who suffered so much at the end of his life from this awful hearing problem that's even more horrible for musicians. . . . In my case, however, I was only twenty-five years old.

This reminds me of the few memories I have of Gabriel Fauré. He was the director of the Conservatory when Robert and I were there. He was already a quite elderly man. Robert and I attended the premiere for his quintet. This is indeed an especially difficult composition in the way that Beethoven's final piano sonatas are. In this regard, it was said that he was only able to hear with one ear when he composed it. It's true that his hearing was poor, and I recall that, during competitions, he'd ring a bell to be allowed to speak. "My child, I'm going to give you the tempo for the eighth note." Then the candidate began in that way, with the tempo indicated by Fauré for the public sight-reading examination His voice was barely audible.

Like every person who is deaf, they either speak very loudly, or they can barely be heard. . . . When I was competing, I didn't hear him say, so to speak, "for the eighth note." Sometimes, people encountered him in the hallways. He walked very uneasily and had all an elderly man's ways. He always gave the impression of losing his pants. On the other hand, he had a magnificent head that was covered with white fleecy hair.

For this premiere—it must have been during the 1920's—that took place in the hall at the former Conservatory, we were seated in the uppermost balcony. Students always had to climb to the uppermost floor. Cortot, Thibaud, and Casals were performing. We found it very moving.

Like Beethoven, who was also deaf, Fauré composed at his desk, instead of at the piano. Robert played his *Fantaisie* for Fauré. That was in Cannes. Afterward, Fauré wrote to Henri Casadesus to let him know how pleased he'd been to hear Robert's interpretation.

The year 1927 was an exceptional year for us, because it was the year when our first child, our son Jean, was born. Robert gave fifty-four concerts that year. In October, he took part in the opening ceremony for the new Salle Pleyel. The program was totally exceptional. Judge for yourself: Wagner's *Overture from the Meistersingers*, Franck's *Variations symphoniques*, Debussy's *Deux nocturnes*, Manuel de Falla's *Nuits dans les Jardins d'Espagne*, *l'Oiseau de Feu* under the baton of Stravinsky himself, *L'Apprenti Sorcier* by Paul Dukas, and, as a finale, Ravel's *Valse*, with the composer conducting. The Orchestra for the Conservatory's Société des Concerts was led by conductor Philippe Gaubert. I don't think that such a program could have been offered to us today.

Robert also agreed to do what were known as small tours. One of them was a tour of Burgundy. These series weren't well paid, and we were responsible for all the expenses: travel, hotels, and meals. The organizers frequently gave receptions after concerts, and perhaps this is what killed poor André Hekking, who was a marvelous cellist who played in duos with Robert. He loved the Burgundy of the after-concert events too much! The audiences were small: one hundred to one hundred and fifty. Yet Robert loved the audiences for these small tours as much as his audiences in London or Amsterdam.

At Easter, we took advantage of a stay with family members who lived in Vendôme to visit the Loire châteaux, which neither Robert nor I were familiar with yet! The roads were so poor and so full of potholes that I said to Robert: "I can't go on. Otherwise, I'm going to go into labor." I was seven months pregnant. . . . I got out of the car, and I preferred to walk. We were in Azay-le-Rideau, and I think that I walked as far as Langeais.

When I reached Langeais, I got a hotel room, and I lay down for the whole afternoon.

There was yet another adventure with our car at the time I was going to give birth. We owned a superb yellow B 14 Citroën with a red stripe. My father was very disappointed that we'd chosen this color, because, at that time, all the taxis in Paris were yellow. We absolutely loved this car. We'd bought it just before the baby's birth because we had ambitious vacation plans, and Robert wanted his child to be traveling under the best possible conditions. I recall that, at the end of June, we'd just obtained ownership of our new car, and we were dining at the home of our friend, Mme. De Franqueville, who lived on the Rue Moncet. At 10:00 p.m., we said our good-byes because I didn't want to go to bed late. No car! It had been stolen . . . Jean was born on July 7. We were at the peak of joy. I'd only stayed in bed for eight days. Furthermore, I didn't stop working during my pregnancy. I kept giving lessons. One of my students, Diane de Rothschild, hadn't even been aware that I was pregnant. It's true that I didn't do anything to show that I was expecting a child, as some young women do today. I wore dresses with low waistlines, because that was fashionable then, and I can recall that I'd given a concert in Geneva wearing this type of dress at a time when I wasn't expecting a baby! One day, I gave a concert at the Salle Pleyel. I'd played Florent Schmitt's *Rhapsodies*. Schmitt was in the theatre, and he came to congratulate me backstage after the concert. I recall that Robert said to him: "You know, she's six months pregnant!" He was shouting from every rooftop that I was pregnant, because he was so happy about soon becoming a father! Despite his joy with our son's birth, Robert was troubled by the theft of our automobile. We hired an attorney who filed a stolen vehicle report with our insurance agent. Then, by an extremely odd stroke of luck, the insurance agent was faced with an unusual story. One of his other clients had visited him to insure a completely new automobile that had been purchased second-hand for an incredibly low price. This turned out to be our car.

Ultimately, the thief, who was no first timer, was arrested. Moreover, he wasn't unknown. He was wild about driving automobiles and had been showing off driving a car down the steps at the Gare de Lyon. Afterward, this type of feat was often seen in films, but, at that time, it was somewhat of an innovation. The thief was sent to prison, in Fresnes, where he was obliged to acknowledge that he'd indeed stolen Mr. Casadesus' automobile and that he didn't have any objections to its being returned.

We therefore regained our car, and we immediately took our luggage and our son, to go and settle down in Samois, near Fontainebleau, where we'd rented a very charming house. At last, two or three months of a real vacation, where Robert could work undisturbed, composing and going swimming in the Seine every day.

He always prepared his recitals during the summer. He'd have nearly ten different programs completely ready. Each year, he included new works.

Jean was born in the year when Lindbergh completed his Atlantic crossing with the *Spirit of St. Louis*. Newspapers were describing nothing other than this feat. This period was also the time when Charles Nungesser and François Coli were killed. Everyone was fascinated with these new adventures in aviation, and there was also great fearfulness in relation to these knights in the sky, because, unfortunately, these experiences often ended tragically. Lindbergh's great advantage was that he'd flown in the New York-Paris direction. Furthermore, even today, it takes an extra hour when someone flies in the France-U.S. direction. In any case, Lindbergh's crossing of the Atlantic was among the most important events in the history of travel. In that time, the idea of crossing the Atlantic in an airplane would never have entered our minds . . . and we wouldn't have imagined that someday we'd also be doing the same thing.

My husband read extensively, especially during long train trips. Robert was fascinated by André Gide. Robert didn't know him, but Gide's secretary was one of my students. She told me that Gide practiced the piano every day. In addition, he'd written articles about Chopin, whom he regarded almost as a classic. He detested the lengthy rubatos that some pianists added in performance. It's amusing, because this man who seemed to be whimsical by nature detested exaggerated whimsicality displayed by others. He believed that it was necessary to follow the text as it had been written and to immerse oneself in it.

Robert adored Romain Rolland and Jules Romains, and especially Jules Renard's *Journal*. We'd learned that Jules Renard strongly disliked the music that Ravel had created for his texts. He thought that his poetry was sufficient per se and that there was no need for putting music around and above it! That made Robert furious, because he admired Ravel's music so much. In his reading, Robert hadn't overlooked Debussy's writings about music. His profession demanded it!

Robert taught courses in Switzerland on a very regular basis. In fact, he went there to listen to the students of Miss Bourgeois, in Geneva. It's flattering for a teacher that a musician pursuing a career as a soloist would take the time to listen to her students. She always gave a dinner in our honor and unfailingly offered chocolates to Robert. One day when we'd given a two pianos recital at the Salle de la Réformation; I received an enormous bouquet of flowers, with an enormous box of chocolates dangling from the bottom. For a moment, I'd wondered why the bouquet weighed so much! Quite simply because Miss Bourgeois had added a kilogram of chocolates . . . for Robert!

She was an excellent piano teacher. She immediately taught modulation—in other words, how to shift from major to minor—to children who were just beginning.

Robert also listened to many students taught by Émile Jaques-Dalcroze.[1] We'd never met him, but Robert admired him greatly. He believed that Jaques-Dalcroze was an extraordinary person. The work that he was doing with rhythm, with bodily expression, and with listening skills was truly remarkable.

After Jean's birth, I was extremely busy, like all young mothers. Even though I had some help, between the lessons I was giving, managing a house, my own personal piano practice, and my son, it was a lot. Aunt Rosette helped me considerably, too, but, as I've already said, she didn't like extremely young children so much. She was only interested in children above the age of four. Then she was amazing. She's the one who taught Jean his notes.

For a few years already, Robert's reputation had kept growing. He'd told me that, in 1919 to 1920, one of his students whose mother hosted all artists, said to him one day: "If you wish, I can get you an audition with Arthur Rubinstein." Rubinstein was ten years older than Robert, and he was already an established pianist in Paris. Rubinstein had listened to Robert, and afterward he supposedly said: "He's exceptionally talented, but, for my part, I wouldn't advise him to give public concerts for approximately ten more years. He'll feel more at ease when he's ten years. older." At that time, the family believed that, even if Rubinstein hadn't been envious, he just didn't want Robert to rush into the profession. Horowitz and Rubinstein often performed at salons during those years.

Almost during the same period, just after World War I, Miss Champion, in whose home Robert had already been giving courses, wanted to resume her public courses. Her students were primarily amateurs. She had a studio on the Rue d'Amsterdam, and she absolutely insisted on having Robert as a teacher.

In fact, Robert was expected to become a successor to Raoul Pugno, who died in Moscow in 1914 during a tour. With considerable pride, Robert had agreed to this extremely flattering appointment as a successor. He'd be giving courses nearly every two months. This honor was extremely important for him.

Miss Champion was a small elderly woman who was close to sixty-five years old. She was said to be a typical spinster, but she must have experienced passions during her life. She adored Pugno. She adored him so much that her parrot very frequently prevented everyone from playing or conversing as it shouted: "Rrrraoul! Rrrraoul!" Pugno's first name was Raoul! Imagine the knowing smiles among her audience.

# NOTE

1. Émile Jaques-Dalcroze was a Swiss composer, esthetician, and teacher (1865–1950). He was a friend of Bruckner and Strauss, and he invented a teaching method. He was the founder of the method of teaching rhythm that bears his name and is still taught throughout the world.

*Chapter 6*

# Building a Repertoire
# Intended for Tours

## *Our First Trip to Russia*

As we return to the beginnings of my husband's career, Robert played the *Second Book* from Debussy's *Préludes* at the 1924 Decorative Arts Exposition at the Place des Invalides. This composition was played infrequently at that time. Therefore, this was a quite noteworthy event. No one was familiar with this work. The *First Book,* which includes *La cathédrale engloutie* and *La fille aux cheveux de lin*, was performed more often. Those were Debussy's two best known works. *Les Danseuses de Delphes* or *Voiles* were seldom performed. *Feux d'artifice*, which is the final prelude, wasn't performed at all. *Arabesques* or *L'Île joyeuse* were performed, while *Masques* was never performed. At the Conservatory, we were told to practice *L'Île joyeuse* or the *Suite pour le piano*, which dated from 1904 to 1905, whereas the *Préludes* are from 1912. During the war, there weren't many performers to play Debussy's or Ravel's works.

Robert contributed to making the *Second Book* better known. *La Puerta del vino* is marvelous. People were completely surprised to hear this music that's so colorful and so Impressionistic. Indeed, some of Debussy's works were only revealed approximately three decades ago. The *Études* were never played. When Robert recorded all of Debussy's works for Columbia Records, they didn't want this work to be recorded because it was considered too difficult and too avant-gardist. . . . That was during the 1950s! The *Études*, which are works from the end of Debussy's life and are strikingly remarkable, have only been played for the last twenty years. Therefore, as you can see, Robert was often criticized for not playing modern music. . . . That's mistaken. He played the music of his own era to a tremendous extent. As the pianist Claude Helffer has quite correctly said: "For each person, music from his own era!

We're exposed to avant-garde music from our own era. Casadesus was also exposed to his era's "avant-garde."

Twenty-five years ago, we recorded Bartók's *Sonata for Two Pianos and Percussion* and Debussy's *En blanc et noir*, which were hardly ever performed at that time. We also recorded Milhaud, but we didn't venture any further.

Robert liked to begin his recital programs with Scarlatti, Rameau, or Mozart. He was among those who appreciated Rameau and who believed that he was an essential figure in the history of music in France. An unusual remark was made to him one day after a recital. A journalist who'd greatly admired Robert's performance asked him: "You played Rameau marvelously, but it actually involves a transcription, doesn't it?" Robert replied, "Not at all. I played exactly what's written in the edition that was reviewed by Saint-Saëns." Rameau possessed all of this "pianistic" abundance that may have been useful on the harpsichord. He truly created a technique that was different from Couperin's. As for Couperin, he used embellishments more often, with less mordents. Indeed, with Bach, the organ is present as the foundation, and, with Rameau, it is the harpsichord and the future piano. Bach wanted to create *French Suites*, and he was therefore aware of what was being done in France by the Couperins or Lully and in Italy by Scarlatti, who belongs to the same period.

In 1934, Robert gave a recital that was entirely devoted to Scarlatti. He was going to record these sonatas on the following day, and he experienced severe nervousness because he said that they were extremely difficult to play. He adored this music.

There's no question that it's easier to begin a recital with Mozart than with Rameau or Scarlatti, who require an extremely rapid and agile technique, although this isn't obvious when a pianist's hands are cold. When a pianist has stage fright, which is often the case before a concert, his or her hands will always be cold. Sometimes, Robert would say, "My stomach hurts." I can recall that they'd spoken about this with Arturo Toscanini, who'd said to him: "Oh, I know about this bellyache before concerts! Me too, I have stage fright when I walk onto the stage." Usually, Robert's stage fright disappeared as soon as he started playing. Once, however, he was obliged to play one of Mozart's concertos with frozen hands for its entire length.

In a concerto where you don't play during the long orchestral *tutti*, it's exceedingly difficult to get warm. You must stay impassively waiting for your entrances, and your hands also stay cold, unless you wear white gloves as Liszt did, although he took them off just before his first entrance. . . . That must have been very comfortable and also very elegant!

One evening, we attended a recital by Paderewski at the Théâtre des Champs Elysées. It was in the 1930s. He'd included Chopin in his program, of course, as well as Beethoven's *Appassionata.* Before the concert began, he found it necessary to carry out a ritual. The hall was kept dark, but he didn't come onto the stage. Sometimes the audience would wait like this for five or six minutes, to such a point that people would end up asking whether Paderewski was going to give his recital. He created a certain suspense in this way. He waited until there was no longer any noise in the hall, so that the audience would be fully attentive. Finally, he deigned to enter, to sit down, and to begin playing the *Appassionata.* Magnificent playing and a superb interpretation. Suddenly, in the very middle of Beethoven's famous sonata, an umbrella fell. Paderewski stopped abruptly and left the stage. We waited for at least ten minutes before he returned. He came in again and stared at the audience seemingly saying: "You were noisy, and that completely ruined my concentration."

We were quite surprised by his Chopin. He took astonishing liberties, and he accentuated the rubatos. This highly affected and extremely mannered way of performing pleased the public.

As for us, we were extremely disappointed with his way of interpreting Chopin.

It must be acknowledged that Robert possessed a concept that was entirely different from Paderewski's. The Poles adored Paderewski's way of approaching their national music. It is true, however, that this was hardly pleasing in France. The French felt that he didn't play with enough nimbleness or with enough subtlety. On the other hand, Robert played the four *Ballades* frequently. He even recorded them on several occasions. Furthermore, he said in this regard: "It isn't because Chopin had a subdued way of playing that calls for interpreting his music in a subdued way, as suggested by the comments from his time that can be found, insofar as his fragile constitution didn't allow him to play more powerfully. There's heroism in his music. He always fought against Russia . . . Apart from the two piano concertos perhaps, the *Polonaises,* the *Scherzos,* and the finales of his *Ballades,* which were composed according to poems with heroic texts, possess a dynamism that isn't sickly in any way." In any case, Robert's way of playing Chopin was overwhelmingly supported by the composer's countrymen. It wasn't so long ago that Witold Lutoslawski was still saying to me: "We adored Casadesus and his way of playing Chopin."

Moreover, in 1949, the Poles asked Robert to give a recital in London on the occasion of the celebration of the composer's centennial. The Royal Albert Hall was packed, and the program was entirely devoted to Chopin, as you can imagine.

Robert, who went to Poland each year before World War II, never wanted
to go back. All the people we'd known there had been killed during this
monstruous period.

From 1924 onward, Robert went to Switzerland each year. He'd complete
a tour of the three largest cities with Ernest Ansermet and his orchestra. In
1926, he also gave a recital in Vevey. This recital had been organized by
young people who were less than thirty years old and who absolutely wanted
to give a dinner for him after the concert. They chose one of the most beautiful apartments overlooking Lake Geneva, but because they felt that the furniture didn't possess the required quality for such a dinner, they proceeded with
an actual refurnishing by bringing in more valuable furniture so that the setting would truly be remarkably elegant. They were hoping that Robert could
admire beautiful Swiss antique furniture during his dinner. . . . We found this
degree of attention extremely touching, and Robert never forgot it.

These young people had heard Robert in Geneva and Lausanne, and they
wanted to have him come to Vevey at their expense because they liked listening to him so much.

Robert also enjoyed Holland tremendously. The public there was very dis-
cerning, and, above all, there was the magnificent *Concertgebouw* orchestra.
He performed there throughout his life. Whenever he was in Amsterdam, he
visited the Rijksmuseum. He adored Rembrandt's *The Night Watch* and the
Frans Hals paintings. We had excellent friends at whose home we frequently
stayed. They pampered Robert. They had an adorable house in Haarlem, with
an impressive height and a pointed roof, although it wasn't heated. . . . We
stayed in a room on the second floor that was reached by a bitterly cold stairway. The ground floor was heated by a large stoneware stove, and the rooms
were heated by additional electric heating. The bone-chilling cold didn't keep
us from playing in a quartet with the owner! He played the second violin part.
There was always a kettle humming on the stove, ready for making a good
cup of tea or coffee. We truly had the impression of living in the era of Frans
Hals, in the period when this delightful frozen house had been built.

In Haarlem, at the Frans Hals Museum, which is located, as you know,
in the old almshouse, Robert always admired the hands of individuals who
were painted with so much authenticity. In his opinion, the hands were very
often more expressive than the faces, which were always somewhat the same,
encircled by their large hats and their fluted or stiffened collars.

In 1928, we went to Vaux-le-Pénil near Melun for a long vacation after an
automobile trip to Brittany. Robert was working intensely on composition.
He made notations in his datebook practically every day: nine to ten hours of
composition. During his long train trips, he also transcribed Mozart quartet
and quintet scores, so that we could play them four hands. He adored this.
He always wanted everything to be exact, without missing any notes. Some

piano scores eliminate difficult portions of original compositions that require crossing of hands. Robert nevertheless proceeded in a way that allowed the original works to be respected completely. Even with Beethoven's *Quartets* that had already been transcribed, he insisted upon redoing them.

During this period, Robert composed at the piano. He also worked at the table in hotel rooms, especially when he was traveling. Furthermore, he customarily said that it's possible to compose chamber music at a table, whereas piano compositions can only be created at the piano. In any case, that's how it was.

Usually, he played his compositions for me, and he kept me up to date. I was always ready to admire him, even if what he'd written was beyond me. It must be said that I didn't have enough knowledge of composing to offer criticism. I was more inclined to find his music a bit too advanced. . . . What seemed too modern to me in that time doesn't seem that way at all today! There's no question that music has evolved at a very fast pace in fifty years.

In January 1929, we traveled to Florence to give a concert, and this allowed us to discover Italian painting in its birthplace: Del Sarto, Masaccio, Botticelli, Raphael, Fra Angelico, etc. Obviously, we visited the Palazzo Pitti. In Milan, we heard *Tosca*, at La Scala. We continued to Verona and Padua. Because there were two free days, we decided to go to Venice. From Padua, we took a small electric train along the Brenta River. The trip took four hours! We left Padua at 8:00 a.m., and we reached Venice at noon. Of course, we visited the Piazza San Marco, the Campanile, and the Doges' Palace. The weather was cold, and the sky was overcast. Not a trace of sunlight. . . . We rode in a covered gondola that was completely black, and I must say that this black gondola floating on murky water didn't charm us. We were even rather disappointed with the dull light and all the canals where enough trash was floating to make an entire meal. . . . Our discovery of Venice didn't spark our enthusiasm! We returned to Venice many times thereafter, and this unique city ultimately manifested its charm to us. In due time, we were captivated by the magic of this exceptional place. On this first trip, we were at least enthralled by paintings and by the mosaics in the basilica of San Marco. Our homeward trip was by train, via Milan, Genoa, and Cannes. We stopped in Toulon for a recital by Robert. By chance, Jean Cras,[1] the naval officer-composer, was in port with his squadron. He invited us aboard his vessel and showed us his collection of flutes from the four corners of the earth. We were quite moved by his welcome. He was fascinated with flutes, and he composed several works for this instrument that goes back to the dawn of time.

During this stopover in southern France, we visited Antibes and le Vieux Nice, where we discovered mimosas. Today, all that seems obvious and commonplace, but, sixty years ago, this wasn't so in any way.

At the beginning of February, Robert gave a concert in Brussels, at the new Palais des Beaux-Arts, which had just been opened. This new venue offered extremely good acoustics.

In the same year, we spent our first seaside summer at Lancieux. This was an important event for us. We were delighted that our little boy could have fun in the sand and could play with a young cousin. Robert alternated between swimming and composing. On certain days, he spent eight hours composing continuously. This is the year when he composed his *Piano Concerto*. We also took long automobile trips, and we discovered Brittany and its roadside shrines that fascinated Robert so much.

In August, in the Netherlands, with Karl Schuricht as the conductor, he performed at Scheveningen, the famous beach near the Hague. He returned every summer until the war. In earlier times, Robert Schumann had also given concerts there.

In early September, we left for Biarritz. Robert would be taking part in a Ravel concert that took place at the Casino. He played *Ma mère l'Oye* four hands with Ravel, as well as other piano compositions. Philippe Gaubert and Madeleine Grey were also included among the performers. At the appointed time, there were only fifty persons in the hall, which could accommodate six hundred. I frantically went to tell Robert, who was getting ready in a dressing room: "You can't play before so few people. Ravel's going to be mortified." Without any hesitation, Robert replied: "No, no, Ravel doesn't want to cancel it! We're going onstage in five minutes." The emptiness of the hall must have also astonished the Mayor of Ciboure, who was a friend of Ravel. He didn't understand that there could be so few people to hear Ravel after the success that he'd just encountered in the United States. It was shameful that France would show so little enthusiasm, or even curiosity, for such an artist. The mayor had decided to devote a day to Maurice Ravel during the following year and to spare no efforts for making this event a success that people would talk about.

We took a train again to join our son who'd stayed in Saint-Malo. Then, we returned to Paris at the end of September. Afterward, Robert completed a tour in England before we'd be taking our first trip to Russia.

On October 14, 1929, at 10:00 p.m., we left the Gare de l'Est en route to Warsaw, which was the first stage in this extensive and long trip. We reached Köln at 8:00 a.m. and Berlin at 5:00 p.m. At 11:00 p.m., we left Berlin, traveling toward Warsaw, where we arrived on October 16, at 7:00 a.m. We didn't leave for Moscow until October 17, at 7:00 a.m. In those times, going to Russia involved a veritable expedition!

In Warsaw, at the point when we left our hotel, Robert discovered that he'd lost his passport. We dashed to the French Embassy to apply for a new passport. With considerable luck, he obtained one very quickly, but this delay, as you may suspect, made us miss the train for Moscow. This meant that we had to take another train that was much slower, and, moreover, it was much less comfortable. The cars were wooden, and so were the seats, which were therefore hard. A total lack of comfort. Fortunately, each wagon had an attendant for serving tea, which at least allowed us to have a hot beverage. There were only two wretched cups for the entire car, however! I went through heroic contortions to drink a little scalding tea without putting my lips on the brim of the shared cup! Moreover, there was absolutely nothing to eat, because travelers had to bring their own supplies for the trip. In our case, however, we didn't know this. . . . at one of the numerous stops—in Smolensk, as I recall—Robert disembarked to find some food for us in the station. I had a horrible fear that the train would leave without him. I must say that I was terribly distressed by this improvised trip. . . . Robert finally returned, bringing sandwiches on black bread that were stuffed with pieces of fatty pork! He'd also bought a bottle of mineral water that we weren't able to drink, because its salt or iron content was so high. I don't remember anything more, but it was horrible! In a word, this trip was very arduous. When we arrived in Moscow, we spent two hours delayed in Customs. All of our baggage was carefully inspected from top to bottom. We even saw a Russian who'd bought little berets for his children have these ill-fated berets shredded with a knife because it was illegal to import these items that were nonetheless harmless. We were shocked. This seemed so senseless. We'd already been frightened by the barbed wire fences that ran along the border. . . . When we arrived in Moscow, we were met by officials from the "Persinfens," the orchestra that Robert would be performing with, which had been Koussevitsky's former orchestra. The violin soloist, a certain Mr. Konstantin Mostras, was accompanied by one of his comrades and by a representative from the French Embassy. Upon leaving the railway station, we were astounded to see that all the men wore caps and that the women wore scarves. No hats! Robert and I were the only people wearing hats. We must have created quite a sensation. We truly felt as if we were standing at a factory exit gate. . . . We went as quickly as possible to the conservatory where Robert's first concert would be given on the following day, so that we could try out the piano. When we entered this beautiful hall where the walls were adorned with composers' portraits, I was surprised to find Debussy's portrait. . . . Ravel's was missing, however. Nevertheless, Ravel was well-known in Russia, but obviously not well enough at the time when the conservatory was built, in other words just before the Revolution.

This theatre offered excellent acoustics. We found it very moving to be there. Robert was enthusiastically received. I think that he may have played Beethoven's *Emperor Concerto*, and I can recall that, afterward, he was asked to perform several encores.

Robert had also played Fauré's *Ballade*, which required a certain number
of rehearsals; although this conductor-less orchestra had been relatively successful with Beethoven, who was often included in its programs, it was more
difficult for Fauré, whom it had seldom played and with whom it was certainly far less familiar. The violin soloist, the second violin, and the first cellist performed across from their fellow orchestra members, with their backs
completely turned away from the audience, and I assume that they're the ones
who communicated entrances to their colleagues.

During this "extended" trip, the pace was quite fast, and once or twice we
had to give a concert at 8:30 p.m. and then leave for the next city at 2:00 a.m.

In Moscow, we stayed at the Hôtel Metropole, which was falling into
disrepair. There was no maintenance whatsoever. The furniture was massive,
and the armchairs had such huge armrests that a person could spread the
fingers on his or her hand without going beyond the edges! Something else
surprised us, however: we ate very well there! The *borscht* was delicious, and
they even served us stuffed spring chickens. Breakfast, however, was rather
Spartan: tea, sugar, milk, and bread, although without butter or preserves.

We'd been warned that there were microphones installed in our rooms.
Initially, we also paid attention to what we said, and then we very
quickly forgot.

They came to pick us up at the hotel in a Lincoln to drive us to the concert
hall. This was a Lincoln convertible. . . . Russian officials only used convert-
ibles, and only the embassies used closed cars. That suggested a somewhat
bourgeois appearance. In fact, extremely few cars could be seen on the
streets. Only officials possessed automobiles. Furthermore, these vehicles
were always driven by chauffeurs. I've especially retained a memory of
sleighs traveling on Moscow's streets. People were buried under fur blankets,
and the drivers wore enormous overcoats and *shapkas* that nearly covered
their eyes.

During our visit, we had enough time to discover the museums. We also
undertook a rather odd visit: it was to a private home that had been decorated
by Matisse, and the guide was none other than the former owner, who'd been
obliged to donate his estate to the Government. He seemed quite contented
with still being able to stay in his home, even in the capacity of a curator. At
least, he could still enjoy his Matisses! This situation greatly surprised us. We
were invited to visit the Kremlin, and we were extremely impressed by the
silverware collections that could be seen there. There were enormous pieces
that were too ornate for our tastes but were luxurious, nonetheless. During
our stay in Moscow, Mr. Mostras' wife served as our interpreter. She spoke
French perfectly, because she'd been brought up by a French governess.

We were slightly on guard in our discussions with her because we didn't
know whether she was in favor of the regime or opposed to it. She didn't

reveal anything of her true feelings. She was a charming woman who'd certainly experienced a completely different way of life in the past. The Mostras family lived in one of the rooms of their former apartment that they were now sharing with other families. Mme. Mostras had hired one of her former servants who was more than seventy years old. This dear old soul had to sleep in the hallway on a bed that needed to be unfolded each night, because she didn't have a room. One day, the Mostras family invited us to lunch, and we thought that they must have saved the week's supplies to offer us a meal that was worthy of the name. Food was extremely precarious during this period. During this meal, there was one detail that led me to believe that Mme. Mostras wouldn't be in favor of the new regime, because I observed an icon hidden in her cabinet when she opened the door to fetch something. I knew, of course, that, since the Revolution, it was forbidden to display these idols that had belonged to the past, but it was clear that, concealed within a piece of furniture, the icon wasn't disrupting established order and would still allow worship in the usual way.

Russians are naturally very generous people who enjoy honoring their guests, and I was extremely moved during this trip to receive a champagne glass in one place or a silver spoon somewhere else from people who certainly didn't possess very much, although they wouldn't hesitate to offer you something that was possibly their only reminder of a bygone era.

Mr. Mostras also taught music, and Emil Gilels' sister was one of his pupils. As you know, she was an excellent violinist. I also recall that Emil Gilels had attended Robert's recital at the Moscow Conservatory. Robert had noticed this red-haired boy in the first row! Gilels had just turned seventeen, and he'd arrived from Odessa, his birthplace, in order to continue his piano studies. Subsequently, we often saw him again in both Europe and the United States.

During our stay in Moscow, we went to the theatre frequently. We therefore had an opportunity to see Eugene O'Neill's *All God's Chillun Got Wings*. We also went to the Kamerny theatre, where we saw remarkable actors. We'd met some of these actors who explained that, in Russia, there wasn't any specialization, and that they needed to be capable of performing not only comedies but tragedies. This method gave them extraordinary flexibility and a perfect sense of adaptation.

We attended a performance of Charles Lecoq's *Giroflé-Girofla*. The Russians greatly enjoyed French operettas during that period. I must confess that we were slightly disappointed by the ballets despite the excellent reputation that they'd acquired. The theatre itself seemed to be of far better quality.

Another recollection comes to mind. I was extremely astonished by the odor of rotten apples that was pervasive when we entered the Conservatory. Afterward, it was explained that this originated from the fact that students ate apples between classes and then tossed away the cores in the corridors.

Because cleaning wasn't done every day, the cores rotted where they fell! In fact, Muscovites were only eating one meal per day in the evenings, so that they needed to stave off hunger during the day.

During our travels, we were able to observe that this city was in rather regrettable condition: the outer surfaces of houses were deteriorating in clumps, and the façades displayed a mournful and neglected appearance.

The response to the concerts was enthusiastic. The audiences applauded unhesitatingly, and they came up onto the stage to give us ovations. We were almost carried away in triumph! We were incessantly asked for additional concerts: for the artists' club or for the writers' club, where we happened to meet a white-haired elderly lady who was none other than Tolstoy's sister.

Because actors couldn't attend evening concerts because they were performing too, Robert was asked to give afternoon concerts, especially for them. As a way of thanking us, we were given an enormous samovar where the following text was engraved: "To the great artist Robert Casadesus, from the instructors, associates, and students of the Moscow Conservatory, as an expression of their recognition and admiration," followed by their names.

After Moscow, we traveled to Leningrad. It took a night on the train to make the trip. We discovered the Neva River, the façades of the Hermitage that border the river, the midnight sun that hails the presence of summer, and the thousand and one canals that make Leningrad a type of northern Venice. Of course, we visited the Hermitage Museum and the Russian Icons Museum. We were enthralled by this city's beauty and charm.

The concert took place in the Nobles' Room at the Hermitage Museum. We were told that there were always three or four seats that were reserved for sailors. That evening, the poor sailors who'd received tickets and who'd taken seats in the first row were so bored while Robert was playing the *Appassionata* that they began chatting. I can tell you that this got seriously on my nerves while the rest of the audience was listening so attentively. I'm sure that you can't imagine the brand name of the piano that Robert played in Leningrad . . . *Red October.*

That amused us considerably! I hadn't thought about the symbolism of red in Eastern Europe, and I'd brought along a red performance gown. Because I was hesitant about wearing it, I was told that nothing could please the audience more than if I were to wear this color that was so profoundly associated with the Revolution.

When we left Moscow, we were accompanied to the train station by a crowd of people whose arms were filled with flowers. It was very touching.

After our return to Paris, we went to the Opéra-Comique to hear Emmanuel Chabrier's *Le Roi malgré lui.* We saw Ravel there, and he didn't curtail his praise of this opera. Nevertheless, he added that he would be delighted to rearrange certain passages that deserve richer and more abundant orchestration.

He was intending to write to Mme. Breton-Chabrier, who was Chabrier's daughter-in-law, to discuss it with her. Moreover, he was prepared to undertake this endeavor without any compensation.

In November of the same year, Robert completed a tour of Spain that took him to Irún, Oviedo, Madrid, Bilbao, Zaragoza, Seville, Valencia, and Barcelona. Notwithstanding an extremely demanding schedule, he found free moments to compose between his concerts. He treasured the memory of snow in the Sierra Nevada, which created landscapes with unreal beauty. Of course, he didn't fail to visit the Prado Museum in Madrid. He adored Goya and his incisive but occasionally harsh and pitiless vision.

In January 1931, we were booked for a series of concerts in Algeria. We sailed from Port-Vendres to travel to Algeria. We left at 10:00 a.m. and we arrived the following day at 8:00 a.m. The concert took place at 5:00 p.m.

This was the first time that Robert had gone to Algeria. For my part, I was delighted to return, because I'd lived there for seven years, between the ages of two and a half and nine. My father and my mother were attracted by this country since one of my father's sisters was living in Oran. Her son was an attorney. After my father had been appointed to a position in the Customs Administration, he moved to Algiers. That's where I learned the piano from my mother, who was teaching at the Conservatory. When I was seven, I won my first prize. I'd obtained recognition, and I can recall that I liked being applauded. . . . Indeed, I think that I always wanted to pursue a career.

In Algiers, we met my mother's brother, who was the orchestra conductor at the Grand Théâtre. In those days, artistic life in Algeria was extremely active. I can recall that we met the violinist Jacques Thibaud in Oran, where he too was completing a tour in Algeria. Our itinerary took us as far as Tunis, and this allowed us to visit Kairouan. As we were returning, we stopped at Biskra, and, therefore, we were able to discover the desert and its oases.

We returned to France on a freighter that was piloted by one of my mother's former students. The captain let me steer the ship, which was very flattering to me! I can recall that the sea became turbulent as soon as we approached the Golfe du Lion. That area is always fearsome.

When we arrived in France, we immediately went to Monte-Carlo, where Robert was giving a concert conducted by Reynaldo Hahn. He was an unusual individual who was highly intelligent and highly cultivated, although he displayed supreme disdain for the public. He observed the world with an air of haughty superiority and always appeared to be "deigning to conduct, and deigning to offer music to these geese-like throngs in front of him."

He contributed enormously to popularizing Mozart. Elderly women were most fond of him and he achieved genuine public success. He was always very well-dressed . . . he'd adorn himself with an enormous pocket square that conspicuously protruded from his chest pocket—it also looked extremely arrogant!

We spent very pleasant times in Hahn's company. Robert admired him and said that he was an excellent musician. He knew how to make an orchestra perform. I can't say that he was an extraordinarily great conductor, but he possessed a form of authority that let him dominate scores, as well as musicians. His art songs enjoyed immense success. I believe it can be said that he influenced Francis Poulenc to some extent. They belonged to the same breed of musicians.

## NOTE

1. Jean Cras (1879–1932), left behind charming works that, unfortunately, are not well known.

## Chapter 7

# 1931

## *En route to South America*

On May 6, 1931, we sailed from Bordeaux on the liner *Massilia* for our first Atlantic crossing. This represented a true adventure for us, and, to some extent, it resembled an expedition into the Southern Hemisphere's seas.

Because we'd be away for three months, we decided to bring Jean with us. He was a very well=behaved child and was very obedient. We knew that it wouldn't be a problem for him to be with us, and I can confess that I was more at ease than if we'd left him in Paris, even with a proper caregiver. I'd explained to him that I was going to be very busy, that I was going to be playing the piano, and that, during the crossing, he'd have to stay with the governess while we'd be going to lunch, because children weren't allowed in the adults' dining room. He did so without complaining.

The crossing lasted sixteen days. The Pleyel Company had set up a piano in our cabin, and it provided a technician who was expected to accompany us throughout the trip. Mr. Coulon offered invaluable assistance, because, in addition to the work that he performed with noteworthy skill, he served as a companion for Jean when we were practicing. He was an extremely kind man who quickly became a friend. He's the one who taught Jean how to recognize numbers and how to play lotto. On May 7, we were en route. A stopover for several hours allowed us to take a quick tour of Lisbon. I recall that we bought cherries for Jean, and that was a first of the season delight for us.

You know about life aboard ocean liners. People become acquainted, and that's how we met the singer Ninon Vallin, whom we didn't know. She was also traveling to South America for a series of recitals and opera performances at the Teatro Colón in Buenos Aires. We also met a Brazilian couple that was traveling with their thirteen year old daughter, who very quickly became Jean's partner for games. In addition, we visited them later in Rio de Janeiro, where they lived.

Our daily lives were quite well organized. In the morning, Robert practiced on the piano in our cabin after having done a few exercises in the gymnasium. In the afternoon, he relinquished his position to me and took advantage of this moment of freedom to take Jean for walks on the bridge or to see Guignol performances. I recall that it was unendurably hot in the cabin, because, obviously, air conditioning didn't exist yet. The cabins were equipped with fans that merely churned the hot air . . . and we were literally smothering. In the evening, we went to the cinema, or we attended shipboard shows.

As you can imagine, we didn't escape the ritual crossing of the Equator, and, in fact, Ninon Vallin served as our godmother. I must point out that this "crossing" of the Equator disappointed me slightly. I'd expected a radiant sun requiring wearing of a sun hat . . . and we only had a gray sky and thick fog that obscured the horizon. One thing fascinated me, however: the schools of flying fish that leapt around the vessel. They arrived in successive waves . . . it was amazing!

Ninon Vallin was a charming woman who was rather buxom, like many female singers in those days, although this didn't prevent her from being successful with men! She gave an impromptu recital, and she asked Robert to provide accompaniment, which he did with pleasure. She was in extraordinary vocal form, and the passengers appreciated this surprise concert according to its true value . . .

Upon our arrival in Buenos Aires, we were welcomed by the impresario who'd organized Robert's tour.

Robert immediately asked how everything was going to proceed, because we'd only received very few details before our departure from Paris. The impresario responded with some embarrassment: "I'm wondering whether you're going to have much of an audience. You aren't well-known, and I think that I should change the terms of the contract. Otherwise, I won't meet its objectives." Robert's response was immediate; he replied without hesitation: "If you won't uphold the terms of the contract, we'll be leaving as of tomorrow. I'll pay for the trip, but I don't want you to change one line of the contract . . . " Robert was right in standing up to this gentleman, because everything proceeded very favorably thereafter. Indeed, there wasn't a large audience for the first concert, but the reviews were excellent, and there weren't any problems with subsequent concerts. Robert always played to a full house.

This tour that consisted of approximately ten concerts also took us to Montevideo and to Santos.

In Buenos Aires, we were fortunate enough to attend Lily Pons' first performance in Argentina. She sang *Lucia di Lammermoor* under the baton of Otto Klemperer, who regularly conducted at the *Teatro Colón*. The performances were of an exceedingly high quality, and Klemperer was regarded as a star in

South America. I recall that, during the first act, she unfortunately slipped for a moment, and the audience uttered a disappointed "Oh!" Without allowing herself to lose her poise, she pursued her path unfailingly, somewhat like a trapeze artist striving to ignore the void beneath her. The Argentinian audience was an audience of connoisseurs. It only had one flaw: people ate candy during the performance, and it was impossible to escape the rustling of wrappers that had contained it. This annoyed me! I considered it to be extremely disrespectful and irritating for the performers who were being distracted. Another Argentinian practice also shocked Robert and me. We observed that a large portion of the audience left the concert hall before the end of shows or concerts. I inquired about this "custom" that came close to rudeness. The reason was simple, but surprising. Chauffeurs couldn't park their vehicles in front of the concert halls' doors for a long time, and their passengers needed to reach the cars as quickly as possible, so that leaving the hall ahead of other persons was the only solution.

Whenever we could, we went to hear Ninon Vallin. She had an extremely natural and instinctive voice, and her projection was perfect, with a high level of musicality. We'd heard her in Massenet's *Manon*, which was one of her great roles. During our stay, Debussy's *Pelléas et Mélisande* was on the schedule for the *Teatro Colón:* Georges Thill sang the title role. One evening, when he had a cold, he was replaced by André Gaudin, who was none other than a cousin of ours. This coincidence amused us . . . Speaking very directly as she always did, Ninon Vallin had told us in regard to Thill's cancellation: "I find it impermissible that he let himself be replaced. A singer should sing even if he has a cold!"

We also attended an exceptionally beautiful performance of Wagner's *Meistersingers*, with Klemperer conducting once again. We had the opportunity to meet the violinist Jan Kubelik, who was the father of the conductor Rafael Kubelik. At that time, he was as well-known as Eugène Ysaÿe.

Robert was enormously successful at the *Teatro Colón.* Unfortunately, I can no longer recall which concerto he played, but I do remember very precisely that our friend Ernest Ansermet was at the podium. He also appeared regularly in this celebrated hall where extremely prolific artistic activity reigned. We also heard the pianist Ricardo Viñes, who predominantly played Spanish music. That was the only time that we ever heard him. It was being said at that time that he couldn't return to France, because he didn't have a cent in his pockets . . .

It seemed that he'd gambled away all his fees and that his friends had to pay for his return ticket. He was unfortunately possessed by the demon of gambling, and he never overcame it.

This trip was especially fascinating, and full of unexpected occurrences. To reach Montevideo, in other words to cross the mouth of the Rio de la Plata, a night aboard a ship was necessary. Montevideo was regarded as being a red city that was less snobbish than Buenos Aires, which was the affluent city. On our vessel, we met Arthur Rubinstein, who was also giving a series of concerts in Uruguay. We dined together, and I can recall that, at the end of the meal, he was astonished that we were already going to bed. "As for me, I'm going to be gambling!" he said with an amused expression. Truthfully, at that time, he was capable of playing cards all night. I'd been astonished, because I'd heard him play Albéniz' *Navarra,* which is an extremely difficult work that abounds in small details and counterpoints, when I noticed that he didn't play all of the notes. Because I was also practicing *Navarra* at the same time, I was quite familiar with it, and it was truly surprising to me that a pianist of such standing could engage in omissions of this kind. He played the theme in a marvelous way, with extreme elegance, but that apparently didn't prevent him from skipping some notes . . .

Rubinstein achieved enormous success with the public and it was said everywhere that he played Spanish music like no one else. He claimed that he practiced the piano very little. To tell the truth, he was extremely gifted. Later, his wife contributed significantly to his career, sparing him from many constraints so that he could devote himself solely to piano playing. His marriage truly transformed him. On account of his wife, he became a true aristocrat. She was also an aristocrat who was the daughter of a Polish conductor who conducted a concert by Robert in Warsaw on one occasion. She was extremely familiar with the intricacies of the profession, and she possessed an amazing flair that allowed her to manage her husband's career with exceptional efficiency. The wife's role is certainly fundamental for an artist.

In terms of speaking briefly about Robert's colleagues, I can recall that José Iturbi, who was an excellent friend of ours, ventured into film in a parallel way with his career as a pianist. He'd played Chopin in a film devoted to the famous Polish composer's life. In fact, this was detrimental to his career as a pianist. The public had also been shocked that a pianist could perform in film roles.

As I go back to our South American tour, I recall that we took a ship to travel to Santos in Brazil. Jean accompanied us there. He was a very sensitive child. At that time, I was practicing Schubert's *Musical Moments*, and, one day, I saw that he was crying while he heard me playing. I asked him what the problem was, and he answered in his little voice: "I don't know, Mama!" Because this had happened once before, I realized that it was the music that had affected him. At that moment, I couldn't keep myself from thinking that perhaps he too would become a musician. It's obvious that he was very responsive to music and, when I took him to listen to music in public gardens—at that time, music kiosks often welcomed military concerts—he was always extremely happy and would listen very attentively.

We were surprised to find that many of the concert halls where we were playing were out in the open. That was undoubtedly on account of the heat. This was not always advantageous because, when there were high winds or tornadoes, which occur frequently in this region, the wind rushed into the hall and onto the stage as well. I remember that I experienced some problems with the wind rushing under my gowns while I was playing. . . . One day when we were giving a recital with Robert, I finished a sonata shivering all over. During the intermission, Robert asked the hall's manager to find another gown for me at our hotel, as well as a glass of rum in order to enable me to finish the concert!

The open-air markets were filled with a striking charm. The cargo vessels that sailed for Europe were loaded with bunches of enormous green bananas while we were eating extremely small bananas that were known as *cadoros*, or golden bananas. . . . This is a tiny variety that's the size of a person's little finger. Absolutely delicious. A veritable piece of sugar. We also ate pineapples that people cored for us and that we'd bite into with gusto.

I have another memory that touched us profoundly: when we were getting off the train in Santos, we were greeted by a band playing the *Marseillaise*. We were deeply moved by this welcome.

From Santos, we left for Rio, where we spent approximately ten days. We stayed on the Copacabana beach, which, in that time, only offered a few scarce hotels scattered among the pines. It was wonderful! We'd organized our lives very effectively during those ten days: swimming in the morning, concerts in the evening. We received warnings about swimming, because the sea, which seemed so calm, was infested with crocodiles, and it unfortunately happened that imprudent swimmers could be torn to shreds.

In Rio, we visited the Alzevedos with whom we'd made the crossing as we traveled from France, and they very kindly offered to lend us their boat to go to the *Ilha de Paquetá*, so that we could avoid the horde of tourists who relied upon the regular boat. . . . We very gladly accepted their offer, and we found ourselves aboard a splendid vessel the next day. Their boat possessed a truly striking appearance, and all of its copper items gleamed. Another couple whom we'd met in the Azevedos' home accompanied us. After visiting the island, we began our return trip. It must have been 4:00 p.m. I'd forgotten to mention that we'd left Jean at the hotel in the care of a nice Russian lady who'd been recommended by the French consulate. Our journey had begun and, all of a sudden, the engine failed. The pilot, who looked embarrassed, told us that he didn't have a lantern to signal our presence. Meanwhile, night was falling because it was wintertime. Not only was there no lantern, but there weren't any oars or sails.

In that location, the current is rather strong, and we'd started drifting. At one point, we were overtaken by the regular boat that was filled with tourists.

We began shouting with the hope that they could understand that we had a problem, but shouting, screaming, or waving our arms in every direction was of no avail because no one heard us, and no one noticed us. The night was becoming increasingly darker. As you can imagine, we started to panic because any ship could have rammed us. . . . I honestly believed that our final hour had arrived, and I couldn't stop thinking about what would become of our poor little Jean if something happened to us. . . . After a moment that seemed horribly long to us, we came into sight of an island that was a type of fortified citadel. A commanding voice immediately shouted that docking there was forbidden. In fact, this island was a military base. The sentinel readily understood that we were having some problems, and he allowed us to disembark. We were thoroughly frozen, because, quite obviously, we didn't have any warm clothing with us. The servicemen offered us a good cup of coffee, and then they took us back to continental Brazil on one of their launches. It was three o'clock in the morning. . . . Later, people told us that what had happened wasn't exceptional at all because it wasn't uncommon for these beautiful vessels to lack the absolute necessary minimum resources for sea travel. In spite of that incident, I can say that I would have gladly prolonged our stay in South America, because life there was truly very pleasant.

## Chapter 8

# 1931

## *Finding Adventures in Each Corner of a Country*

As soon as he arrived in Paris, Robert was busy with his concerts again. On October 5, at the Théâtre Sarah Bernhardt, he played for the first Parisian performance of his *Concerto Nº 1 pour piano* with Gaston Poulet conducting. Robert was accustomed to saying that he felt an overwhelming emotion when he interpreted his own compositions. It's true that a person knows his or her own works to the most profound extent, although it's necessary to maintain a certain distancing when interpreting them. . . . It's a strange combination.

On October 18, there was another concert in Paris with the Pasdeloup Orchestra and with Rhené-Baton conducting. Immediately thereafter, Robert left for another tour: Warsaw, Lodz, and Bucharest, where he met the conductor George Georgescu, with whom he'd never worked. The orchestra was of the highest quality, and Georgescu enjoyed a wonderful reputation. Today, he's hardly ever mentioned. It's a shame because he was an extraordinary figure, an excellent conductor, and a dedicated musician. In those days, Bucharest was magnificent and culturally highly active. Robert gave several concerts there as recitals and as well as with orchestra.

I joined Robert at the end of his Central European tour. I was seven months pregnant, and I can recall that it didn't go very well. I'd been unwise to undertake such a journey. In Vienna, I had to rest in bed, and I believed that I couldn't continue the trip. I nevertheless boarded another train for Bucharest, and I needed to seek bed rest once again because the tour was far from ending. . . . In fact, we traveled as far as Costanza, where we needed to take a ship to go to Istanbul. After crossing the Black Sea, I was surprised by our arrival in the Bosporus, which is undoubtedly one of the most beautiful places in the world, with its low-lying mist and its mosques that rise above the city's roofs. This city, with its black wooden façade houses and their *mashrabiyas*, is endowed with immense charm.

Quite obviously, we visited Saint Sophia, the Blue Mosque, Topkapi, and the Grand Bazaar with its jewelers and its specialized artisans, such as zinc workers and copper engravers, its stalls with fruits and vegetables, and its spice market where the intermingled scents of saffron, coriander, and cumin announce their presence long before you arrive.

Having read Pierre Loti's accounts, we were expecting to see veiled women dressed in black. Disappointment. None of this exoticism that he could describe so wonderfully. . . . In contrast, there was a modern city undergoing full expansion, with an extremely European appearance. We were far from the Constantinople where the sultans, who lived at Topkapi at the end of the last century, were accumulating treasures that can still be seen today. Ataturk was proceeding with building a twentieth-century Turkey. In Istanbul, we had a few problems with the agent who organized the concert. When we met him, he very precisely stated to us as he offered us a cup of delicious Turkish coffee: "It won't be possible for us to pay your fee after the concert, but we've arranged with Mr. Feder in Athens. He's the one who's going to pay you after your concert there." We boarded a boat again and crossed the Sea of Marmara, which was an immaculate blue, so different from the Black Sea, and so narrow, with its superb landscapes bathed in a soft light that was floating above us. We felt the extraordinary sensation of being on the hinge joining Europe and Asia. Then we entered the Dardanelles Strait, a sea corridor that led us to the Aegean Sea. We landed in the picturesque port of Piraeus. Then we went to the agent whom we informed that he should pay us for the concert in Istanbul. . . . He replied that he hadn't received any instructions from his colleague in Istanbul. Indeed, we'd been cheated by the Turkish agent. . . . At least we'd experienced the pleasure of discovering Istanbul! We quickly forgot this incident, but we began to wonder about Eastern ethics.

The obligatory tour of Athens: the Acropolis, the Agora, the ancient theatre. We were fascinated by restoration of vases that had been discovered in a thousand fragments and were reconstructed by clever archeologists like veritable puzzles.

After our stay in Athens, where Robert received an enthusiastic welcome, we went to Brindisi by sea, which allowed us to admire the Gulf of Corinth and the entrance to the Adriatic. The Gulf of Corinth is extremely impressive. It is so narrow that it seems like two ships literally couldn't pass each other and that the shore could be touched by just extending an arm.

From Italy, we returned to Paris by train, because Robert was giving a concert at the Salle Pleyel.

The end of 1931 was devoted to a tour in England and in Holland.

That year, Robert had also been working with Georges Enesco on Guy Ropartz's *Trois sonates*, which they subsequently played before him in Strasbourg, where he was the Director of the Conservatory. We also had an opportunity to hear the pianist Harold Bauer, to whom Ravel's *Gaspard de la Nuit* had been dedicated. He possessed a marvelous touch.

We also saw Ravel again at a dinner in the home of our friends the Fourniers. Mr. Fournier was an amateur cello player, and he'd married the violinist Carmen Forté, who was relatively well-known at that time. Enesco also attended this dinner. As after-dinner coffee was being served, Enesco joined Robert and Mr. Fournier, and they played Ravel's *Trio*. Ravel was still absolutely delighted with the success that he'd obtained in the United States. The dinner had been exquisite. There were cherries for dessert, and, as I recall, Ravel told me that these fruits were a true "oral delight." The expression amused me. . . . While the three musicians who were friends played Ravel's *Trio,* he didn't cease pacing the floor. He seemed extremely nervous, and he'd only repeat that this trio resembled something from Lalo or Saint-Saëns. . . . People would have said he was afraid that it wasn't really by Ravel. . . . I was extremely astonished by this completely unusual nervousness, and I wondered whether he was ill. . . . Were there signs that could have been precursors of his illness? That was also the year when we became acquainted with the publisher Robert Juillard. He'd married one of my childhood friends. He was a man who was barely thirty years old, and he was very dynamic and highly imaginative. He'd just created *Editions Sequana*, which offered book sales by subscription. Robert was a subscriber because he read a lot during his long train trips. He enjoyed this collection whose authors included Georges Bernanos, Vladimir d'Ormesson, Henri Daniel-Rops, François Mauriac, Denis de Rougemont, and Georges Duhamel.

The year 1932 began with a series of concerts on the Côte d'Azur for Robert and with the birth of our son Guy on January 23.

On the eve of this important event, Robert had been performing in Monte-Carlo, and he was calmly aboard a train on his return trip while I was giving birth. Robert's father went to meet him at the railway station to announce the birth of his second son. At that time, I believe that I was slightly disappointed not to have a girl. Robert, however, was delighted with the arrival of another boy, and he was especially proud when he went to declare his son's birth at the mayor's office.

Shortly after Guy's birth, I accompanied Robert on his second tour of Russia, and I hired a young Swiss woman to take care of the baby in my absence.

During our stay in Moscow, we went to the Bolshoi several times, where we heard truly exceptional singers. This time, we had an opportunity to visit the French Museum and its splendid collection of works by Matisse and Degas. From Moscow, we traveled to Kharkov and Kiev.

In Kiev, we had a strange adventure that affected me deeply. Upon descending from the train, we were approached by a man who spoke French poorly and who stammered "Do you speak French? Philharmonic?" and then gestured for us to follow him. Because we thought that he was the person assigned to greet us, we followed him without too much hesitation. He led us to a type of government building and directed us to the first floor while saying "Card, card!" Then another person gave each of us a card. We understood that this was a food card. After this procedure was completed, our guide led us into a store where there was only minimal merchandise on display in the aisles: some chocolate bars, some packs of cigarettes, and some bundles of cloth. That was nearly everything. Then, as he winked at me, our guide made me understand that I should buy some chocolate. Afterward, he proceeded to cut five meters of fabric for a man's suit. . . . the salesperson, as I can recall, had touched the lapels of my husband's suit to enable us to understand that it was of better quality than the fabric that he'd just cut for us.

We paid for our purchases, and I'll confess that we were beginning to find this situation odd and especially unpleasant.

En route to our hotel, we saw long lines waiting in front of stores and particularly in front of bakeries that nonetheless didn't seem to lack bread. When we arrived at our destination, our guide took his packages of cloth and reimbursed us for our expenses, while unceasingly uttering the word "concert" . . . Then he departed, and we never saw him again. We attempted to arrive at an explanation for this strange encounter, and we ended up telling ourselves that this well-informed man had found a clever way to beat the system. . . . Nevertheless, we couldn't determine how he'd learned that we were musicians who'd arrived to give a concert.

Before our departure from Paris, we'd been advised to bring some provisions because running out of food could be a risk. We were told that people were dying of hunger in the Ukraine, but that there were no problems in Moscow . . . which turned out to be false. . . . I can recall that we ate borscht with nettles because it was the season for nettles. It's clear that there was a real problem with food supplies. I can recall seeing people huddled around samovars on the platforms in railway stations. Others were selling their meager vegetables or a few dairy products. A rather oppressive atmosphere reigned.

We were also told that everyone was dreaming of going to Moscow, with the belief that they'd find a paradise there. In fact, only workers who were likely to find jobs were being allowed by the authorities to travel to the capital. Authorizations were only issued sparingly, and, in railway stations, we observed soldiers poking their bayonets under the cars to determine whether unauthorized passengers were hiding there.

During these long train trips, the conductors locked us in our compartment at night, under the pretext of preventing theft while we were asleep. I must say that we were horribly alarmed by the idea that we couldn't get out if anything whatsoever were to happen.

Robert gave two concerts in Kiev. We were surprised to observe that one of the pianos was white. We believed that this piano may possibly have come from a wealthy owner who indulged in this luxury in an earlier era. Robert liked to tell this story, because it's the only time in his life when he played upon a piano of this color . . . in public.

After our departure from Kiev, a lady absolutely insisted upon inviting us to her home. Obviously, she only occupied a portion of her former property, and she'd converted its covered terrace into a room. In one of the corners, she'd created a semblance of a living room, where she served us heaps of delicacies that she'd specially prepared for us. We were quite affected by this welcome, which was a reminiscence of a distant past.

It would be pointless to tell you that we were deeply moved by hearing the famous bells of the Great Gate, which had inspired Mussorgsky's *Pictures at an Exhibition.* A representative of the Soviet Ministry of Culture made it possible for us to visit a vintage home. He was a highly cultivated man who spoke French extremely well and had been educated in Paris. After the Revolution, he even returned to Paris and revisited the apartment where he'd lived. He emphasized the charm of tradition, beautiful homes, and antique furniture that was lovingly preserved. . . . His statements surprised us during the visit because he didn't refrain from showing us all the harm that had taken place during the Revolution, including holes in the ceiling to install heating, which had damaged the antique woodwork. . . . It was surprising to hear an official openly criticizing the damage caused by the Revolution. . . . Before we left Moscow, we met Mme. Mostras again, at a luncheon.

As had occurred during our earlier trip, we received charming gifts from our hosts: two delightful champagne glasses, and an enormous broach that was adorned with garnets and dated from Napoleon's era. Once again, these people who didn't know us, offered us their heirlooms.

This time, without knowing how to thank all these people, we left them the contents of our suitcases, which would certainly be useful to them. Mme. Mostras herself let us know that her husband would be glad "to wear Mr. Casadesus' overcoat" and that this would allow needy students at the Conservatory to be given money that he'd saved for a coat. I don't know why she offered this clarification . . . was she possibly ashamed of having asked for my husband's overcoat to be given to her? During this trip, I'd bought Persian lamb and fox furs. I think that they'd already been worn because they very quickly became shabby looking.

The French ambassador offered me an amber necklace. I'd hesitated to buy emeralds because people had warned me that they were often fakes. On the other hand, I did proceed with buying icons according to the ambassador's advice.

Upon returning to Paris, we attended a Debussy festival that took place at the Théâtre des Champs-Elysées. We also heard Fritz Kreisler's performance of Beethoven's *Violin Concerto*. He displayed extraordinary ease in handling the bow. That's one of the most important aspects in a violinist's performance, comparable to the left hand for a pianist. Kreisler showed a refined sensitivity, and his interpretation of Beethoven simultaneously offered elegance, grandeur, sumptuous sound quality, delicacy, and power.

Afterward, we saw him again in the United States rather frequently.

In 1932, Jean, who'd just become five years old, started learning the piano. That summer, we spent our vacation on the Côte d'Azur, at Beaulieu-sur-mer, where we enjoyed swimming in the sea. Robert spent a lot of time composing during this visit. We also took a trip to Mallorca. At this time, Palma resembled a city resting on the water, when we arrived in the early morning hours and could see the shore. It was stunning. The roofs appeared to be flush with the sea. No trees could be seen. The city had a superb golden hue. It was especially beautiful. In 1972, the painter Joan Miró told us that the island had been completely disfigured when skyscrapers were built. . . . His house had now been submerged amid buildings. Fortunately, he'd been able to save his garden during this transformation-massacre, and that allowed him to distance himself from these horrors. . . . He was furious at seeing his island sinking into such a state of ugliness.

During the time of our visit, all the houses left their doors open. It was possible to observe simple, charming interiors with attractive straw chairs, and beautiful fabrics that were still woven by hand. Local art reflected extremely good taste. In Valdemossa, we visited Chopin's room, or cell, in the convent that became famous on account of its illustrious tenant during the preceding century.

A person can understand that this stay was highly detrimental for him, especially during the winter when it's so cold and damp. He didn't have anything other than a brazier for staying warm, which wasn't particularly advisable for a person suffering from tuberculosis.

It seems that the island's inhabitants were hostile to his presence because they feared that he'd contaminate the population.

Robert was asked to give a recital devoted to Chopin, and he quite willingly agreed. In those days, concerts were given near the cathedral in Palma de Mallorca.

On our return trip, we visited Barcelona before arriving in Beaulieu-sur-mer, where Jean was waiting for us.

On the coast, we went to visit the Salomon Reinhardt villa, which was a faithful reproduction of Greek architecture. At this villa, we encountered an upright piano with a keyboard that could be folded up. It occupied an extremely small space, and it didn't clash with the décor. Robert and I were fascinated by this ingenious concept. Mr. Lyon from the Pleyel Company was the inventor, and, when we returned to Paris, we ordered one of these pianos for our apartment on Rue Vaneau.

In October, Robert conducted his *Concerto pour violon*. Henri Merckel, a violin soloist with the Société des Concerts Orchestra, was the performer.

Robert conducted extremely infrequently. In fact, conducting never tempted him in the way that it tempts some soloists. He felt stiff and . . . ill at ease. For conducting, a certain ease in the shoulders or a certain flexibility is needed. My mother's brother, who was a conductor, as you know, always said that a conductor's hands are also highly important. There are some who make too many gestures, and others who hold the baton very stiffly. Moreover, when a person observes conductors, it can be immediately seen who possesses ease and who doesn't, even when someone is a neophyte. It's the same for how a bow is held by a violinist.

In the autumn, we went to hear Mary Garden in *Pelléas et Mélisande* at the Opéra-Comique. She'd performed in the title role in 1902, and, although she was no longer quite young, she still conveyed all its musical subtlety. We enjoyed this version where the casting was practically the same as that of the premiere under André Messager's direction. Mary Garden was slightly stouter, but she was still splendid.

During that year, we also attended the theatrical debuts of Robert's cousin, Gisèle Casadesus, who was the daughter of Henri, the founder of the Société des Instruments anciens. She was exactly eighteen years old, and it could be seen that she possessed all the talents of a born actress.

The following year, the Société des Instruments anciens completed a tour of the United States that would be enormously successful.

It was also at this point that we met the Portuguese conductor Freitas Branco. He was a strikingly handsome man. He'd married a French pianist who was as blond as he was swarthy. They made an extraordinary couple. He conducted French music with exceptional talent. For example, he displayed a perfect familiarity with Ravel's *Alborada del gracioso*. He didn't do anything extraordinary was always mindful of the equilibrium of a composition.

In April, we left for our first tour in Egypt. We embarked in Venice, and we landed in Haifa three days later. At first, we went to Beirut, a city undergoing a full expansion and proud to display the façades of its banks, which occupied an entire district. At this time, Beirut was a powerful financial market, just like Tangier. The city was delightful, with a bay that resembled Nice's Bay. The very luxurious hotels were located along the seafront. Everything emanated affluence and comfort. When we arrived, we were offered delicious candied fruit according to the Oriental custom of welcoming visitors.

The first concert was given at Saint Joseph University, and the second took place at the American School.

We visited Baalbek and Byblos. The cedars were worthy of their reputation. It has been said that, in Antiquity, cedars were sent from here to Greece and Italy. It was these Lebanese cedar trunks that were so straight and so tall that they were used for building colonnades for temples.

Father Heiddie, the vicar whom we knew in Paris and who taught Robert the catechism, had lived in this country. He'd been born in Egypt with French parents, and he'd been educated at the French school in Cairo. He told us that he would ride over his lands on horseback. At that time, a priest was a veritable sultan! He also told us that the Lebanese had done everything for the French to deliver them from Turkish domination, and that the first thing that the French decided upon was to impose taxes upon the population . . . whereas the Turks hadn't obliged them to pay any taxes! He'd concluded that the Turks were more generous than the French.

Christian influence was omnipotent in Lebanon, and Robert and I believed that this would threaten to pose problems sooner or later.

Americans also had an extremely large colony in Beirut and a very beautiful university.

We left Beirut by tour bus to travel to Tel Aviv. We went to Jericho, the Dead Sea, and the sources of the Jordan River. Upon our return from this trip, Robert was composing abundantly. He was very moved by the journey. Seeing the places where Christ had lived . . . this land that was laden with the history of our civilization moved him deeply: the Dead Sea, the hallucinating scenery, the color of stones, the sky that blended with the desert's pebbles, the boulders, the harshness of its landscapes. . . . We couldn't refrain from plunging our hands into the Dead Sea to confirm at first hand that it was salty! At that time, there wasn't any civilization there. It was a desert filled with stones.

In Jerusalem, Robert performed Beethoven's *5th Concerto,* which is known as *The Emperor Concerto.* This was the first time that it had been performed there. The Jerusalem Orchestra included excellent strings. It had been founded by Hubermann. All the instrumentalists came from Europe or from Russia. Some of them had settled in Palestine after the 1905 Revolution. The woodwinds, who were also of notably high quality, were English. As you know, Palestine was a British protectorate at that time. Robert was delighted to find an orchestra of this quality.

During our stay in Jerusalem, we didn't fail to go to the Wailing Wall and the Mosque of Omar.

The entire trip was fascinating. We traveled by tour bus, and I can assure you that the roads were more like dirt roads than highways.

From Jerusalem, we went to Cairo, where Robert gave a concert, as he also did in Alexandria. Subsequently, we traveled to Ismailia, where there was a rather large French community that was essentially composed of personnel who worked on the Suez Canal. We'd have thought that we were in Europe.

In Cairo, we were the guests of an Egyptologist, Mr. Terrasse, who enabled us to visit the Museum. Tutankhamen's treasure had just been discovered. We felt as if we were entering a living room in a "Napoleon's Return from Egypt" style.

We made the traditional visit to the Pyramids. The influence of the Nile was strongly felt because it accounted for everything that existed, so that upon leaving the river and the flood zone, a person would arrive in the desert. The boundary of the area fertilized by floods was distinctly visible, and, beyond it, there was endless sand. The demarcation was clear.

We traveled down the Nile, and we saw Philae, the famous Philae whose bas-reliefs had been destroyed under Justinian, so that crosses could be carved in this location. From Aswan, we traveled to Luxor by train. Afterward, we crossed the Nile to reach Thebes on the other bank. We discovered the famous Valley of the Kings with its frescoes, the colossi of Memnon, Tutankhamen's tomb, the tombs of nobles, the Valley of the Queens with Nefertiti's, and Ramses' tombs, and the Medinet Habu temple.

We also visited the Temple of Karnak, and we met another French Egyptologist, Mr. Chevrier, who was working on the excavations. His wife took us to the work area, where we witnessed something extraordinary: the archeologist himself, lying upon the sand and extracting the head of Amenhotep IV. Observers would have thought that he was delivering a child. This was so thrilling after so many centuries!

A small village was located a hundred meters from us, and the archeologist informed us that the excavations couldn't continue because it would be necessary to expel the villagers and that this could possibly take fifty years.

We then returned to Cairo, where Robert gave a recital again. The audience was extremely cosmopolitan, and it partially consisted of university faculty who were staying at English, French, and American universities. During this period, the English often spent the winter in Egypt. The hotels were splendid and quite luxurious, while offering extremely high-quality service. After a recital in Alexandria, we then boarded the *Champollion* to return to France.

As soon as he arrived in Paris, Robert began composing. This trip had profoundly inspired him.

This period of intense work was interwoven with visits to art exhibitions. At this time, we went to an extremely beautiful retrospective of Utrillo's work. We also heard Wilhelm Backhaus, who'd received advice from Brahms. . . . Robert admired this brilliant Beethovenian with a sober and pure way of performing.

Robert and I gave a recital at the Salle Gaveau, and I can recall that Albert Roussel attended it.

We saw Berlioz's *Damnation de Faust* at the Opera, and we returned to attend *Pelléas*. Robert adored *Pelléas* and never grew tired of it. He considered the interludes sublime. In his opinion, Yniold's voice was an angel's voice. Robert only liked certain operas, such as those of Mozart and Richard Strauss. . . . He especially liked them on account of the music. In that period, emphasis wasn't given to stage design in the way that it is today. It was possible to see quite clearly the backdrop depicting mountains beginning to move on account of a draft, yet the audience paid no attention to it. Indeed, in those days, audiences were only interested in the music and in the quality of the singers' voices. The era of images hadn't emerged yet.

At the beginning of July, we finally took our vacation in Brittany in a very charming house that we'd discovered at Easter. A tennis court was available for us, and I began teaching Jean how to play. He'd just turned six years old. As he did every summer, Robert gave a series of concerts in Holland. When he returned, he spent long hours on orchestration, as his datebook indicates. At this time, he was working on his first symphony.

# Chapter 9

# At Work

When Robert was composing, he often spoke to me about themes that he was discovering. After a morning of composing, he'd play what he'd written. He'd explain to me how one passage or another had been created: reintroduction of the theme or the orchestra's entry when a concerto was involved. For example, he clearly indicated the entry of woodwinds or flutes. Robert greatly loved the sound quality of woodwinds. When he attended a rehearsal of one of his works, he always emphasized the woodwinds' entry. He wanted them to be heard. Furthermore, when he was playing a concerto by Mozart, he always said that he was in a dialog with the oboe or the flute—that's often the case in concertos—and that he consequently needed to recreate the woodwinds' sound quality at the piano.

Robert detested spasmodic playing and jolting interpretations.

Some editions should be verified in relation to the original manuscripts because linking indicated by a composer has often been incorrectly reproduced by the publisher, to such an extent that the line for a phrase no longer has anything to do with what the composer had intended.

Robert strongly emphasized rhythm. He said that it was essential. Some performers adopt a hellishly speedy rhythm that prevents any form of breathing. Now, for Robert, breathing was fundamental. To understand a phrase and to be able to sing it according to a singer's way of breathing, a sustained breath without truncating the phrase is extremely important for interpretation. The singer, who must keep taking breaths, is capable of achieving perfect phrasing. For a pianist, it's enormously helpful to take it into consideration in relation to tempo. It's necessary to imagine voice inflections. A crescendo should be achieved gradually, never leaping. One must think about linking. Flexibility of the wrist is fundamental for obtaining beautiful sound quality; the arms should move freely too. Octaves must be played with a relaxed wrist, with only rare exceptions. In this way, a pianist must think about pausing before leaping, and sound quality will be considerably better. That seemed to be a very valid principle to me, and I've always cited it to my students.

Certainly, everyone experiences music in a different way. It's often said that Italians have a warmer and more dynamic way of interpreting music than people from Northern Europe. Robert himself had certainly inherited something from his Catalan and Swedish ancestry! It's clear that his sense of rhythm emerged strongly when Spanish music was being played. He often said: "It's obvious that you don't have any Spanish blood in your veins. You don't have their rhythm or the sense of accentuation like people do in Catalonia . . . even if Catalonia isn't Spain!"

Robert always felt quite free in relation to his interpretations, even though he remained respectful in terms of phrasing. You know, however, that a line can blossom as easily with fervor as with a diminuendo.

Silences also possess great importance for interpretation. Some persons prolong them, while others shorten them. Robert was extremely sensitive to this. He always maintained scrupulous care in following manuscripts, but they can be rendered unenthusiastically or by putting one's whole heart into them! I believe that this was Robert's entire secret.

He was capable of totally communicating what he felt. I've rarely met pianists who can impart so much human warmth to an interpretation. It isn't a matter of playing loudly to communicate power, for example. It's also necessary to add beautiful sound quality. Indeed, Robert knew very well how to do it.

The piano must be handled very cautiously because there's a risk of its very quickly being turned into a sewing machine. . . . Sound quality arises from the intensity that's conveyed by the weight of fingers upon keys, as well as from intensity coming from the arms. A person plays with his or her entire body. In the beginning, Robert moved frequently while he played, and then, as he grew older, he modified his body's movements. That too can be practiced.

In his early years, Robert maintained three different recital programs that he used in alternation. Usually, he began with Scarlatti, Rameau, or Couperin, and then he moved on to Haydn or Mozart, frequently playing two sonatas from one of these composers. Subsequently, he'd play a composition by Beethoven, and he'd end with Schumann, Liszt, or Chopin.

He'd thought about playing Paul Dukas' *Sonate*, which he greatly admired, but he declined to do so because he believed that a sonata that lasts an hour requires too much attention from the audience. It was the same situation in relation to Schubert. He played many of Schubert's compositions for his own purposes but was reluctant to include him in his recital programs. He only played the *Sonata in A major*, which is shorter. Robert was extremely careful in preparing his programs. We discussed them together. Usually, he always varied the composers featured in his programs. Extremely rarely, he devoted an entire recital to a sole composer, as was the case with Ravel and Chopin. He said that, if the intent is for the public to understand Debussy, Fauré, or

Ravel—he was thinking of American audiences in particular—it's necessary to include the most noteworthy classics: Beethoven, Chopin, or Mozart.

One day in New York, a concert promoter said to him: "You certainly have a knack for creating your programs because you let people who are late come in, since you often start with a short composition." Yet Robert didn't forego placing a long work at the beginning from time to time.

On thing is certain. Robert always prioritized playing French music. This wasn't on account of chauvinism but simply because he deeply loved French music. Indeed, for a soloist and, moreover, for any musician, the aim is to communicate with the audience. If you only play for effect, sharing doesn't occur. To communicate your love of a score to listeners, considerable humility and selflessness are needed. An artist can feel it very intensely when there's communion with the audience. If you don't perceive this exchange, it's because you haven't performed well.

I must say that, throughout our lives, we had favorable working conditions. We didn't get in each other's way because we had a couple of rooms soundproofed. Robert worked in the library where we'd set up two pianos, and I worked in the living room . . . or vice versa. Robert always played his programs for me before putting them into circulation, especially when he was including a new composition. That had been the situation with Ravel's *Gaspard de la nuit*, because, in the diabolical *Scarbo*, the same measure must be repeated eleven times, ten times, nine times, eight times, etc. There's a risk of missing a note, and Robert wanted to be sure that he hadn't memorized a phrase erroneously.

My husband insisted on being faithful to manuscripts. In 1927, he went to London as an advisor for the Ganche edition of Chopin's works. In the *2nd Sonata*, there's a phrase where one measure is completely changed, both in terms of its notes and its alterations. I believe that Ganche had worked from the edition given to him by Jane Sterling, which was the last one reviewed by Chopin. Were there missing items? Was there a torn page or, indeed, was there a variant introduced by Chopin himself? The result wasn't entirely disagreeable, but the phrase was totally transformed. After having worked on this new sequencing—that bothered him because he was accustomed to doing it another way—Robert performed the sonata in concert and, at that time, it was believed that he'd made a mistake. . . . I therefore advised him to continue playing the earlier version, the one to which the public was accustomed.

It's quite strange, this force of habit running against the authentic version.

If you start taking on the role of purist, it will never end! Even in the Ganche editions, errors with sharps can be found. Unfortunately, there are always errors that pass through, even if careful proofreading has been done. Yet errors are nonetheless infrequent.

It seems that there are errors in Ravel's *Miroirs*. This music is so subtle and so refined, however, that it's possible to wonder whether it may be an example of its creator's vanity or a variant reflecting Ravel's intentions. From playing and replaying this work, I arrived at the conclusion that it had to remain as is. In any instance, Ravel told my husband that there was a printing error in *Scarbo*, and Ricardo Viñes also said so.

Ravel attributed great importance to tempi. Robert was perfectly familiar with Ravel's tempi because he'd played Ravel's works in his presence. Today, some pianists play *Scarbo* at breakneck speed. That's a mistake. Ravel always said that *Scarbo* is a scherzo. It should be played like a scherzo, with proper control of the three beats. In particular, the nuances must be respected. It must be experienced as a feeling because it isn't always easy to explain. In fact, Ravel intended to create a difficult work, somewhat within the genre of Balakirev's *Islamey*, which had always interested him, as he said. Today's pianists don't always consider the beauty of the theme and the pianissimi. It was Ravel's intention that *Scarbo* would begin with a scratching effect, and he didn't want the repeated notes to be heard clearly. He hoped that it would give the impression that this devilish gnome was appearing and disappearing, and so forth . . . If you're playing at full speed, you won't respect the silences or the devilish spirit, and the pianist winds up sounding like a sort of typewriting machine. It's a pity, indeed, because this work is sublime. One day when I was playing *Jeux d'eau,* Ravel said: "This must be *a tempo*. I wrote that on the score. It should be cheerful and sparkling. There's no need for a *rubato* or romantic effects." He wanted this piece to be a cascade of notes. He wanted it to be like water and to be fluid. He wanted it to be faithful to Henri de Régnier's verse: "This river god laughing as the water caresses him." Ravel repeated: "Don't play it sadly. It's an evocation of the sensual pleasure created by Régnier's epigraph." There's a type of sadness at the end, nonetheless. As there often is with Ravel. It's like the end of the day, or something that's been completed, albeit regretfully. . . . Perhaps Ravel regrets not being this river god whom the water is caressing! There's no need to shy away from this feeling of sensual delight. Ravel wanted it that way, and he indicated everything on the score. When he indicates "expressive," it's your responsibility to add expressiveness and to immerse yourself in his Impressionistic harmonies.

I only rarely made comments about interpretation to my husband. Perhaps for certain works by Chopin. I believed that he started *Ballade No 4* somewhat too quickly. He replied that if it were played too slowly, the beginning would no longer have the same phrasing. That's all!

For Mozart, I never had the feeling that I should say anything at all. It always seemed so beautiful to me. He had such a touch, such phrasing! I don't know whether what I told Robert influenced him. He had such personality.

One thing is true—that I often yielded when he made comments to me, because I felt that he was correct.

When we played two pianos, I often wanted to imitate him, because I felt that he was doing what had to be done. When you're playing two piano or four hands repertoire, it's extremely important to feel things the same way. Never think that it's easy to play as a duo. Not only will a lot of practicing together be needed, but it's also necessary to know how to listen together. Regarding his piano-violin duo with Zino Francescatti, Robert always said: "If we were capable of playing together, it's because we practiced together a lot and because each of us truly listened to the other."

The quality of the piano is also exceptionally important. Robert never played without testing the piano. As we change pianos in every city, it becomes important to test the capabilities of the instrument that will be ours for the length of a concert or a recital. Are the keys possibly stiff? What are the pedals like? What is the reverberation time? All these elements are fundamental. We must adapt ceaselessly. This is the reason why some pianists, such as Rubinstein, Serkin, or Michelangeli, traveled or still travel with their own pianos.

Robert himself believed that it was good and bad at the same time because a piano that travels is affected by the trip. It changes because of being transported, because of the hall where it's going to be set up, and with relative humidity levels, etc. Robert believed that a pianist's career also requires making the most of the instrument that's available to you.

Throughout his career, he had to change piano brands. At first, he played Pleyel pianos. Then the Pleyel Company encountered difficulties. Their pianos were less and less available, while there were more and more Steinways. It was quite uncomfortable to change from a Pleyel to a Steinway because they're vastly different. Then Robert ended up no longer playing anything other than Steinways, until the end of his life.

He was truly born to play in large concert halls. I believed that audience communication with him was much less effective in a room where the atmosphere is so different, even being only two meters from the piano, than in large halls. Robert wasn't a pianist for music rooms. There are pianists who play in too restrained a fashion, and it's a mistake not to tell them this.

I frequently attended his rehearsals, and this allowed me to tell him what it would sound like in the hall. I believe that I was rather helpful in this area. I'd tell him whether a phrase or a chord sequence would come across, or whether the bass was too loud or not loud enough. That allowed him to adjust his playing.

People always rehearse in empty halls, which are extremely different from a full house. For example, in recording, sound coloration can change from one day to the next. Sometimes you say to yourself: "This isn't possible;

the piano was replaced!" And that's hardly so; it's the atmosphere that has changed. It can become more humid, and that modifies everything in terms of sound propagation. Robert had told me that, during a recording that he was making with Zino Francescatti, they were obliged to repeat the beginning of a sonata when they were already in the second movement, because, during their lunch break, the studio's atmosphere had changed, and the color was no longer the same.

Robert always exercised his fingers before working on a piece. At the beginning of our marriage, we played our scales together, along with our arpeggios, and a bit of Czerny exercises. I can recall that, at the time when I was preparing to compete for the Pagès Prize, Robert said: "Above all, do your scales well! Don't wear yourself out but do your scales and your arpeggios." Robert thought that scales were excellent for clearness with the fingers, for speed, and for each finger's independence. That had nothing to do with interpretation. Some pianists give more importance to practicing with octaves. Robert liked feeling well warmed up. Because we'd practiced double notes with Moritz Moskowski, we also practiced scales in thirds. All of this was extremely important, and it was included in a daily regimen that we imposed upon ourselves, especially when we were young. We loved working together. We gained enormous pleasure from it.

I wasn't overawed in any way in relation to my husband, but it was truly a pleasure to work with him. Moreover, the situation was the same afterward when we practiced three pianos with our son Jean. When we played the Bach triple concerto where the cadences succeed each other at each piano, it never occurred to us to play differently from the person who'd preceded our part. Jean always said: "Papa has such a beautiful style!" Moreover, Jean had inherited his father's style and his sound quality. We never considered playing any way other than according to the style that Robert imparted, although this didn't prevent each of us from having a distinct personality.

I never saw Robert experience difficulties with his hands. I had a problem with extension. I had to work on this weakness, so I performed exercises recommended by Isidore Philipp, which Robert had performed when he was quite young. It was important not to overdo them. Ten minutes of "Philipp" was enough.

Half an hour was too much. I've seen students completely ruined by this technique. It's good for a person's fingers to be strong, but, if you lose your flexibility, it's truly a shame. Personally, I place greater emphasis upon wrist flexibility. People aren't knowledgeable about their joints: the wrist, the elbow, the shoulder, the arm. All that is enormously important. Pianists who play "too tightly," with their elbows too close to the body, can't move their thumbs in an arpeggio. That's extremely unfortunate.

Robert never gave lessons in technique. His students said, "He doesn't say very much, but the little that he says helps us with understanding everything." Robert never went into details. He only imparted general contours. For example, he never told someone to execute a thumb movement in a particular way. He mainly spoke about works. He said that it was essential to take all cues from the musical text. Nevertheless, for Beethoven's sonatas, for which there are explanatory texts, as with *Les Adieux*, for example, Robert gave recommendations in the simplest way: "It's necessary for a person to feel what the sense of urgency is, or the jostling of a departure, or a lament, even if it's a lament by a man who must leave his town on account of the Emperor's arrival." There's a form of desperation in the Absence phrase. The triple eighth note becomes sorrowful." Robert wasn't a man of letters. He didn't create a novel to explain music. In relation to Schumann's *Papillons*, he could provide the details of its creation: "This work is composed of successions of small pictures. Essentially, it's already Impressionism." He was able to endow each piece with an extraordinary specific quality. To play, it's necessary to think. Determining tone is a difficult aspect of interpretation. Two rules are quite important: breathing and listening to manage to achieve beautiful sound quality and also knowing that a chord is even more beautiful when it is gently set down than when it is struck. Or, if you prefer, struck from high above. It's better to think about applying pressure rather than about hammering. A note must be pressed upon deeply; otherwise, the sound isn't maintained. If you strike it too forcefully, the sound won't be prolonged.

Many pianists sing as they play. Glenn Gould sang. Rudolf Serkin sings. Alfred Brendel sang, and he no longer sings. Jean sang. He had to be stopped because, otherwise, he would've done it during concerts! Robert and I didn't sing. In our heads, yes . . . but not with our voices!

I've always said to my students: "Without looking at your score, for example, in Chopin's *Ballade No 4,* you have to be able to be able to sing. Do, fa, mi, si, re, do, re, mi, mi, mi, mi." There's nothing more difficult than repeated notes. They mustn't be plucked. They must be linked, yet, at the same time, they must exist individually."

All of us have fingers that are so different morphologically. On each person's hand, there are strong fingers and weak fingers. It's necessary to know how to establish a balance among them. This balance must occur in phrasing. Fingerings are important, without truly being important. . . . Sometimes, we happen to have a finger that's too strong in any given phrase, but we can manage to find the proper intensity simply by changing fingers. Striking the note isn't the same with the ring finger versus the thumb. Only when a person thoroughly knows the instrument is it possible to achieve these nuances. I give my students the fingerings that I've used myself, but I always tell them: "Practice this fingering for twenty-four hours, and, if that doesn't satisfy you, change it."

There are fingerings from Chopin that are marvelous. In my opinion, there's no reason to hesitate in using them. I believe that, when we're lucky enough to have the fingerings indicated in the score, no one should forego them. Ravel and Debussy didn't emphasize fingerings that much, although Debussy could have. . . . As for the pedal, it's something even more difficult. The pedal should never be applied on the beat, but only half a second later, because, if it's used on the beat, you'll retain the preceding harmony.

Robert always had many more female students than males. That was also true for me. During this period, there were a lot more females than males who were studying piano at the Conservatory.

Robert wasn't what anyone could consider strict with his students, although, when he wasn't interested in someone, the person probably felt it. He didn't try to conceal his feelings, and he never engaged in pretense. He was extremely knowledgeable about his students' potential value. For example, for Claude Helffer, who was one of his favorite students, he considered it regrettable that his parents obliged him to enroll in the École Polytechnique when he was so wonderfully talented for the piano. Robert believed that Helffer should devote himself entirely to it.

For my part, in my teaching, I've been more aware of details than Robert was. That's extremely feminine, you'll tell me! I often took on Robert's students and made them practice before he'd take over to hear them play an entire work. I prepared them for him. I always tried to explain to students what they could do to overcome difficulties with technique. Robert didn't do this at all.

There's another detail about Robert's working. He read scores in an extremely attentive way. That's also a way of practicing the piano. He frequently practiced works for nothing other than his own purposes. The last work that he was practicing just before his death was Bach's *Goldberg Variations*. This score was on his piano. . . . He considered them superb. They'd been written for two keyboards on a harpsichord, which rendered them terribly difficult on the piano. He believed that the difficulties were an excellent exercise for everything else.

Gaby at 19 in rue Vaneau apartment 1920. *Courtesy of Gabrielle Casadesus Estate.*

Gaby and Robert wedding in Paris 1921. *Courtesy of Gabrielle Casadesus Estate.*

Gaby and Robert at the American Conservatory in Fontainebleau 1921. *Courtesy of Gabrielle Casadesus Estate.*

Gaby and Robert on tour in Russia 1929. *Courtesy of Gabrielle Casadesus Estate.*

European tour by train 1930. *Courtesy of Gabrielle Casadesus Estate.*

On French Line ship *Lafayette* with Arturo Toscanini 1936. *Courtesy of Gabrielle Casadesus Estate.*

Gaby working on a composition by Robert 1938. *Courtesy of Gabrielle Casadesus Estate.*

Present Day Club Princeton N.J concert Gaby with Albert Einstein 1942. *Courtesy of Gabrielle Casadesus Estate.*

The Casadesus family in Princeton—Robert, Guy, Gaby, Therese, Jean (left to right) 1945. *Courtesy of Gabrielle Casadesus Estate.*

Gaby as performing and recording artist 1940s. *Courtesy of Gabrielle Casadesus Estate.*

The Fontainebleau Schools summer 1945 in Great Barrington, MA. *Courtesy of Gabrielle Casadesus Estate.*

The first family of the piano recording session with Eugene Ormandy, 1961. *Courtesy of Gabrielle Casadesus Estate.*

Gaby, Robert and Jean backstage after performance of Mozart three piano concerto, Philadelphia 1965. *Courtesy of Gabrielle Casadesus Estate.*

The first family of the piano at Osaka Festival (Japan) 1968. *Courtesy of Gabrielle Casadesus Estate.*

Jury at the first Robert Casadesus International Piano Competition in Cleveland, 1975. Gaby Casadesus in the middle, Grant Johannesen to her right, and Henri Dutilleux—president of the Jury—to Grant Johannesen's right. *Courtesy of Gabrielle Casadesus Estate.*

Gaby and Leonard Bernstein at Fontainebleau American Conservatory summer 1987. *Courtesy of Gabrielle Casadesus Estate.*

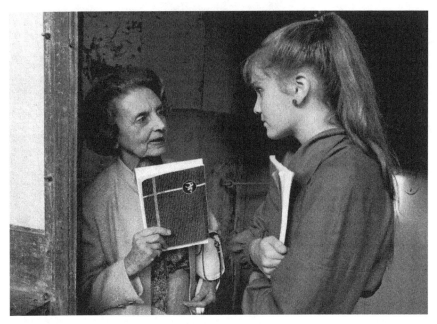

Gaby with one of her students at Fontainebleau American Conservatory 1987. *Courtesy of Gabrielle Casadesus Estate.*

Gaby giving a masterclass in the Jeu de Paume at the American Conservatory, 1988. *Courtesy of Gabrielle Casadesus Estate.*

# Chapter 10

# Discovering the New World

In 1934, at the American Conservatory of Fontainebleau, Robert became the successor to Isidore Philipp, who'd reached retirement age. In addition to overseeing piano classes, he gave master classes twice each month.

That summer, we leased a house in Auvergne. We had a superb view of the Forez region's volcanic hills and mountains. We picked raspberries in abundance, and we ate trout caught in a river that flowed a short distance from the house. Jean began practicing the piano seriously under Aunt Rosette's guidance.

For Robert and me, this vacation was interrupted by trips to Switzerland and to Salzburg, where we gave recitals with one and two pianos. Some of the concerts took place at 11:00 a.m., which was an extremely agreeable schedule for performers, as well as for the public.

As he did every summer, Robert went to Scheveningen. For the concert program, Brahms was offered, and Karl Schuricht, who was also loyal to these summer concerts, was at the podium.

Schuricht liked Robert's way of interpreting Brahms. He appreciated the intensity coupled with expressiveness although without excessive bursts of hyperactivity, and this was one of the characteristics of my husband's playing. There wasn't anything superfluous. That pleased Schuricht, who was accustomed to saying: "When you're telling someone that you love her, you don't need to shout. It's all about the intensity with which you speak the words. Each word."

They truly enjoyed working together. Their "team," as is said in English, was similar to the one that Robert formed later with George Szell. Strong affinities in taste and style, along with strong mutual respect, reigned over their relations. Respect for other persons is a primary attribute for an artist.

The Schurichts very quickly became our friends. One day, he announced to us that his wife, who was Jewish, would need to establish residence in Paris. Subsequently, he often entrusted us with money for her, as a result of our professional interaction, and we'd send it to her upon returning to Paris.

When he came to France, they were often our guests. Then, when the war broke out, Mme. Schuricht was forced to seek refuge in the United States because France had ceased to be a safe haven. At one point, we believed that Schuricht would be leaving Germany in order to join her. Although he was deeply opposed to Hitler's regime, he never had the courage to leave his orchestra in Wiesbaden. He feared that he couldn't reconstruct his career elsewhere. This long separation ended with a divorce. Mme. Schuricht remarried in the United States. This story troubled us deeply because they were an excellent couple, although his lack of courage, in its own way, ruined everything. I believe that he was wrong not to leave because I'm convinced that he could've made an especially successful career in the United States. His talent would certainly have charmed the American public.

The year 1934 is when we took our second trip to Egypt. This time, we visited the entire northern portion of the country by automobile. We also traveled to Tel-Aviv, Haifa, Jerusalem, and Saint-Jean-d'Acre. Robert was just as amazed by the locations that we visited as he'd been during our first trip. It's impossible to remain unresponsive to the blue of the sea, the light that creates gilded hills, and the stars that illuminate the sky and seem so close to us.

As soon as we'd boarded the ship for our return, Robert began composing his *Quatrième Symphonie.* I recall that the sea was very rough between Haifa and Siracusa and that we were glad to return to *terra firma.* Afterward, we made a stopover in Naples, where we stayed long enough to go to Pompeii, which was another site that was quite moving. We even climbed to the peak of Vesuvius, where enormous quantities of fumes were being released at that time. We took a taxi, and then, from the point where the road ended, we ascended on foot to the crater. Someone had lent us shoes with extremely thick soles that protected us from the ashes and the incandescent scree. We were able to advance just to the rim of the crater, and an extraordinary spectacle awaited our eyes there. We were actually able to see the earth breathing. It was an extraordinary sight. . . . This boiling orange and golden yellow material that was red in some locations. . . . Better not to come too close, however, so that we could avoid spewed stones and molten lava flows. It had an awe-inspiring beauty, and the heat was unbearable.

Upon returning to Naples, we took the train in order to reach Monte-Carlo and then Paris, where we spent our Christmas celebrations. On December 29, a major event took place: we departed from the Gare Saint-Lazare for our first tour in the United States, heading to New York via Le Havre, Southampton, and Ireland. On January 6, 1935, at precisely 7:00 p.m., we landed in the port of New York. Two of our old friends from France were waiting for us on the dock.

It gave us such pleasure to see these familiar faces again. Night was falling, of course, and Robert, who feared that all of these skyscrapers towering above us would give him vertigo, experienced the pleasant surprise of discovering the city through a sort of gilded mist, which was one of the most beautiful views of Manhattan that a person can have. Thus, we discovered New York at night, and this first sensation was unforgettable! 6th Avenue was still covered by the elevated metro whose heavy carcass created a hellish noise combined with noise from the automobiles that were traveling beneath it.

This North American tour also included a series of concerts in Canada. The first city that we visited was Ottawa, where we encountered extremely cold weather that we absolutely weren't accustomed to. The cold was so bitter that our noses and ears literally froze. We even had ice droplets on our eyebrows. I believe that I'd never been so deeply frozen in my life!

We discovered the America of drugstores and Chinatowns. As well as concerts in hotels before mealtimes. Washington was where we discovered this practice that was something new for us. These one-hour concerts took place at the Mayflower, which was a very fashionable hotel. The audience principally consisted of women from the federal capital who wanted to hear a bit of music and, in particular, to discuss the artist's merits with their friends afterward over some chicken salad.

In Washington, we also played a two-piano concert at the French Embassy.

During this tour, we had the opportunity to meet here and there some of our Fontainebleau students. It was very gratifying to meet familiar people in this gigantic country where, I must confess, we were admittedly feeling a bit lost. Distances were so vast for us because, at this time, we were only accustomed to countries with more limited dimensions.

We also saw the architect Jean Labatut again; he was a professor at the Fontainebleau Schools, and he taught architecture at Princeton University. After our luncheon, he took us to visit a farm where automated milking took place. We were quite impressed by this system that hadn't crossed the Atlantic yet. The cows entered through a turnstile, milking attachments were placed upon their udders, and milking began automatically. We considered this method to be brilliant. . . . Cows in New Jersey produced smooth milk with a thick layer of cream, and, during the war, we always bought our milk from this farm. The children loved it.

Robert composed prolifically between concerts. Occasionally, he worked from nine o'clock in the morning until midnight.

Robert adored jazz, and, of course, he wanted to go to Harlem to hear it. We received a marvelous welcome from the Black musicians. They exhibited an adoration for France, which was a far less racist country than the United States.

Robert believed that jazz was one of the forms of chamber music: four or five musicians getting together to play music, for the pleasure of shared music, with each one contributing all of his heart and soul. He didn't like big band jazz as much. For him, it wasn't really pure jazz.

Robert made his first American appearances with the New York Philharmonic Orchestra. The critics were mixed. It was said, in a nutshell, that Robert was undoubtedly an extremely skilled pianist, although it was difficult to judge him in a Mozart concerto . . . that it was obvious that he was part of the *Société des Instruments anciens* for having chosen such a work. Actually, the critics had confused him with his uncles who'd visited New York several years earlier. These observations bothered us somewhat, as you can well imagine, but some of our friends explained that, in order to appeal to the public in New York, Robert possibly should've played a more brilliant work, displaying the virtuoso.

At the Sunday concert in New York—where the Philharmonic's concerts were given three times, on Thursday evenings, Friday afternoons, and on Sundays—Arturo Toscanini was in the hall, which wasn't extraordinary in any way, because he was the musical director of the Philharmonic at that time. We were told that, when the concerto ended, he'd stood up to applaud and that the entire audience imitated him. I wasn't in the hall, but people told me about it. I believe that he, Toscanini, must have appreciated a composition by Mozart, who was hardly ever heard in those days. Liszt and Tchaikovsky were the trend.

At the end of the concert, Toscanini asked to see Robert, and, after the customary courtesies, he asked Robert to come and play for him the following year. It was the highest compliment that could've been offered to Robert— because Toscanini invited very few soloists, insofar as he preferred to play pure symphonic works. Moreover, the only guests that he invited during the following year were Rudolf Serkin and Robert. Toscanini asked Robert what he wished to play, and Robert unhesitatingly responded that he'd gladly play Brahms' *2nd Concerto*. Toscanini displayed a slight hesitation, for he was undoubtedly astounded by my husband's self-assurance. After Toscanini had left the green room, I couldn't refrain from telling Robert that he could've been somewhat less affirmative and that he could've asked Toscanini what he himself would want. . . . Because he was astonished by the invitation, Robert hadn't even thought about it.

This first stay in New York took place under the best conditions. We'd met up with one of our childhood friends who was a commercial attaché at the French Consulate, and he guided us around the city, enabling us to discover even its tiniest nooks. In spite of his interest in all of these new things, Robert was slightly disappointed by this trip. He'd found that expending so much energy and coming from such a distance in order to give only ten concerts, which therefore yielded very limited financial returns, was rather frustrating. Indeed, we just managed to cover our travel and lodging expenses because we gave a commission representing twenty percent of our fees to the agent, and also because all of the expenses had been our responsibility. Nevertheless, the contracts with Columbia Artists Management, which is one of the largest concert agencies in the United States, were structured in this way. In any case, it always functioned like that, and it even appears that some soloists must contribute an even higher percentage today. Advertising for concerts was remarkably inconspicuous. Few posters were put up in the city, except for 57th Street near Carnegie Hall, where the impresarios were located, and except for the walls of the concert hall. Carnegie Hall published a monthly bulletin containing a listing of the events and that was all. Even today, in New York City, portraits of artists with concert announcements like those that are seen in France aren't displayed. Of course, there were announcements in Sunday newspaper editions, along with schedules for films, the theatre, or art exhibitions.

Upon returning to Paris, we saw Toscanini again, when he came there to conduct a concert. Subsequently, we met again in Salzburg, where Robert and I performed Mozart's *Concerto No 10 en mi bemol majeur pour deux pianos* at the Mozarteum, with Bruno Walter conducting. At this time, Bruno Walter and Arturo Toscanini jointly reigned over musical life in Salzburg.

Toscanini came to hear us. We also met with him for a luncheon. He was accompanied by his wife and their daughter Wanda, who'd just married Vladimir Horowitz. During this luncheon, Horowitz made a significant profession of faith in our presence, stating that he wasn't playing enough "serious" music . . . that he should include Fauré and Franck in his programs. We immediately understood that his father-in-law was beginning to exercise a degree of influence upon him.

Toscanini possessed an extremely strong sense of family. He always traveled with his wife and, in many instances, with his two daughters. The year came to an end with concerts for Robert, which were intersected by the courses that he was continuing to teach regularly and by long hours devoted to composition. As for me, I divided my time between my two sons and the piano. I always wanted to keep myself fully available for them.

On January 8, 1936, we embarked on the old Transatlantic vessel, the *S.S. Lafayette*, for another United States tour. We left the children in France, which was always a heartbreaking situation for me, even though I knew that Aunt Rosette would take care of them with exceptional kindness and perfect competence.

Aboard the ship, we met with the Toscaninis once again, because they were returning to New York for the winter season. At the start of the voyage, the sea was very rough, but then the sun made an appearance, so that we were able to stay on the deck for long intervals. We met Toscanini on the deck, and we engaged in long conversations with him. He adored talking about politics and music. He always discussed topics passionately. His face became animated, and sometimes it even got flushed. He'd become at least twenty years younger! He never stopped railing against Hitler and Mussolini, as well as Stalin. He considered all three of them to be wretched, and he no longer wished to set foot in Germany, or Russia, or even Italy.

He harbored a fierce hatred of communism. He'd helped a substantial number of his Jewish friends, including the Busch brothers and Bruno Walter, to leave Germany. Bruno Walter ended up residing in Paris, and he acquired French citizenship. I attended his naturalization ceremony. As you know, he emigrated to the United States afterward, and he became an American citizen.

Toscanini possessed a veritable passion for Verdi, whom he considered one of the greatest composers in the history of music. For him, Verdi was a

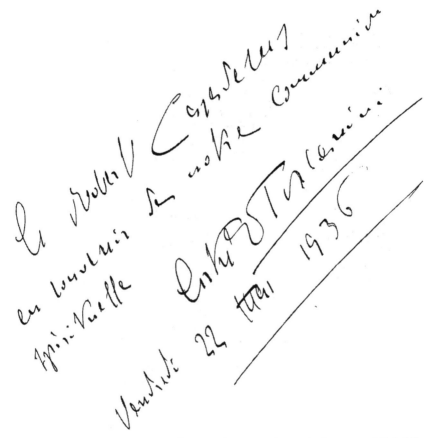

**Figure 10.1.** A note by Toscanini after a Paris concert in 1936. *Courtesy of Gabrielle Casadesus Estate.*

veritable god who incarnated the passion for liberty. It's obvious that Verdi constituted a model for him.

During this trip, he told us that, while he was completing his studies, he deprived himself of food so that he could buy scores. He also told us that, if he'd arrived where he was, it was because he'd studied *solfège* scrupulously. In his opinion, *solfège* was the keystone of a musician's profession, regardless of whether a person was a performer or a conductor. Furthermore, he conducted entirely from memory. In those days, this was not customary. One day, he nevertheless confided to us that, because he couldn't see clearly up close, he decided to give up the scores. In contrast, he could see perfectly from a distance, and this enabled him to identify each musician in an orchestra, including the percussionist situated far at the back of the stage. He had an excellent ear that was extremely keen and precise. He could hear the slightest wrong note . . . and he knew how to tune an orchestra like no one else.

We got the impression from our conversations that he couldn't stand Germanic "high" culture and that, in his opinion, instinct was worth more than culture for artists. He maintained great respect for manuscripts, but, in spite of everything, instinct was an attribute that he considered especially important, and I remember that one day, in Paris, he told us during the course of a luncheon at our home, " Imagine that I went to the Conservatory to consult the manuscript for *Don Giovanni*. It's extraordinary, but, for the overture, Mozart actually indicated a 2/2 beat. I was sure of it. I felt it!" In order to understand his excitement, it must be added that Bruno Walter conducted the overture in 4/4 beat, while Toscanini conducted in 2/2, and, because there was a certain rivalry between them, he was really pleased to have had the instinct to use a two-beat measure when the scores indicated four beats. This approach allowed stronger momentum for the crescendo that's present at the beginning of the overture. I also remember in this regard that, for one of Beethoven's overtures, although I don't recall which one anymore, Toscanini believed that there was a certain passage where a natural "*do*" instead of a "*do*" sharp was necessary, as shown in the score. One day when he had the original manuscript in his hands, he was thrilled to bits when he observed that Beethoven had indeed written a natural "*do*." His instinct had indeed inspired him once again.

During the 1930s, I must say that there were actually two different clans: the clan of Toscanini fanatics and the clan of Bruno Walter fanatics. Bruno Walter relied upon the concept of culture, whereas Toscanini relied upon instinct.

Bruno Walter was a pure product of Germanic culture: he published books, and he was interested in literature, as well as in the arts in general. For his part, Toscanini couldn't deny his Latin origins with his vivacity, his sudden outbursts of anger, an instinctive sense of things, and that flair. . . . He sparkled! Some people believed that Walter adopted tempos that were too slow and too drawn out while Toscanini, on the contrary, conducted too quickly. Personally speaking, I never found Toscanini's interpretations to be overly rushed. Rather, they were full of life. It is true that, if someone only listened to Toscanini's recordings, he could sometimes appear to be rather fast, but a completely different impression would emerge from observing him when he was conducting. His interpretations of Brahms' works were beautiful enough to bring you to tears. He filled his interpretations with a breadth and fullness that were superb.

Toscanini maintained a firm grip upon his orchestra. He was also extremely irascible, and it has been said that, in a towering rage, he'd thrown his baton at a musician one day! It's true that he had rather abrupt ways of doing things. . . . He was known to stop the orchestra and shout: "It's dreadful. You don't know how to produce a proper crescendo! In order to perform a good crescendo, you need to become red in the face. It's not enough to stroke an instrument or to blow into it. You have to put your whole heart and all you've got into it. You have to explode." He gave a lot of himself and communicated his passion and his energy to the orchestra unsparingly. He had a perfect sense of rhythm and a rare refinement in expressing himself. It's been said that conductors who direct operas always feel somewhat superior to those who only direct symphonic groups, and I don't know whether it's fair to generalize, but it's obvious that Toscanini, who'd directed at *La Scala* innumerable times, was a conductor at the very highest level. His command of the orchestra was totally incredible. Having reached the age of sixty-nine, he hoped to reduce his activities and to relinquish his baton to guest conductors on one occasion or another. This compromise wasn't accepted by the management, who believed that it wasn't desirable for the orchestra to pass from one pair of hands to another. In my opinion, they committed an error in allowing him to leave. He was immediately welcomed by the NBC Orchestra, where he was able to do as he pleased for ten years. John Barbirolli succeeded him at the helm of the New York Philharmonic.

In another more intimate vein, I must point out that Toscanini was someone who was extremely difficult to satisfy at the table. I recall that, on the *Lafayette,* he'd told us on several occasions that the cuisine wasn't acceptable, although this wasn't Robert's opinion at all. Robert, who can be regarded as a sophisticated gourmet, believed that the ship's restaurant was comparable to the best restaurants in Paris. It was also one of the attractions of the Atlantic crossing. In contrast, Toscanini turned the menu over in every direction repeatedly for ten minutes, before ultimately ordering *spaghetti alla bolognese,* which he never considered cooked right in any case! . . . He'd kept his preference for Italian cuisine.

Mme. Toscanini always traveled with her Brussels griffon that never stopped barking. . . . When Toscanini noticed his wife and her dog, he never failed to excite the dog, which inevitably responded loudly. I don't know whether Toscanini liked this dog, but he teased it incessantly.

Obviously, Toscanini and Robert discussed music, and I recall that, during this crossing, Mozart was at the center of their conversations. Toscanini adored Mozart, just as Robert did. In this period, Robert played concertos that no one would've thought of including in his programs. I can even say that Robert played certain Mozart concertos as first performances, at least for the twentieth century in the United States. So (as I said before), for their first concert together, they interpreted Brahms' *2nd Concerto*. They proceeded with a reading of the concerto and only one rehearsal on the same day as the concert itself. The result was excellent, and, for Robert, it was a great joy to arrive at a complete communion with such a prestigious conductor. You can also imagine my own joy and emotion.

I've already told you that the concert was given three times. On Friday afternoon, the concert was intended for elderly ladies who didn't wish to go out alone in the evening. Saturday was therefore a rest day, and Toscanini displayed exceptional kindness by inviting us to go on an excursion with him that day. He took us to New Jersey in his luxurious Lincoln that was driven by his chauffeur, because he wanted to show us the newly opened Holland Tunnel, which crossed the mouth of the Hudson and allowed travelers to reach the other side of the river in ten minutes. Other tunnels of this kind were built later, but, at this time, it seemed extraordinary to travel under the sea in an automobile.

Toscanini and his wife invited us to dine in an Italian restaurant. The weather was gorgeous. Everything was covered with snow. For the return trip, we crossed the George Washington Bridge and were therefore able to discover New York's network of highways.

Toscanini lived in the famous Astor Hotel in the heart of New York, where the noise was most infernal, but this hotel was owned by friends of his, and he felt at home there.

Robert and I were very moved by his kind offer to spend time with us on our day off, on the eve of a concert that would also be broadcast directly on the radio. In fact, I have a copy of the concert program! Everything was perfect: the conductor, the pianist, the orchestra.

I can assure you that, throughout our career, we didn't encounter many conductors who did this for soloists. I believe that Toscanini found us to be congenial . . . and, in addition, we were Europeans like him! That had to be significant! We spoke to him about our children. He told us that he'd lost a son, who died in South America from the croup. He advised us to be prudent when we'd travel to these countries in Latin America, and he even recommended using a few drops of Listerine in water for the slightest sore throat.

After the Sunday concert, we were invited to a cocktail party in the home of the Heifetzes, who were friends of Toscanini. We encountered many other pianists there: Josef Hoffmann, Egon Petri, and Alexander Braïlowsky.. In another regard, Toscanini adored Jascha Heifetz's very pure violin playing.

After the success of this concert, Robert gave a recital at Town Hall. It was a rather well-known hall-somewhat like the Salle Gaveau in Paris, which has ceased to exist since then. Mme. Toscanini attended, and she was delighted to hear works by Scarlatti. At this time, Scarlatti's *Sonatas* were not heard very often, especially when they were played by a pianist. I can recall that the famous harpsichordist Wanda Landowska said to Robert one day: "You play Scarlatti on the piano so well!" This was a compliment that meant a lot to Robert, as you can be sure.

At the end of the year, Robert always recorded statistics for his activities in his datebook. That's how, at the close of 1936, I was able to find out that we'd spent eighty-seven days in America, ninety-five in Paris, fifty in Russia, fifty-one at Fontainebleau, twenty-four in the south of France, fifty-six in Europe, and twenty-two . . . at sea. If you add it all up, you'll get 365 days! He'd also prepared a list of the persons whom we met in New York, along with our visits to museums: to the Metropolitan in New York and to the Hermitage in Leningrad, along with the most noteworthy or most famous paintings. Moreover, he never forgot to provide the total for the time that he spent composing and at the piano.

# Chapter 11

# 1937–1939

## *Pre-War Tours*

As we did each year, we returned to Poland via Berlin in 1937. In spite of the political situation, which was becoming quite alarming, we undertook a new tour in Russia. We could've gone to the Caucasus, but we preferred to return home on account of our children. I greatly regretted it afterward, because it would've been a privilege to visit this region that was under military control. Our tour took us to Kharkov, Kiev, and Odessa. We were able to visit the Lacra Monastery. Robert gave two recitals in Odessa, and this gave us a chance to discover the Black Sea. In Odessa, we met all of the leading violin professionals. As you know, this port, which was a popular vacation destination, was also the seedbed of the Russian violin school. David Oistrakh was from Odessa.

After our stay in southern Russia, we returned to Moscow for a series of concerts before traveling to Leningrad, where Robert was expected to give two recitals. We had sufficient time to visit the outskirts of the city and the charming Peterhof Palace, which is a sort of miniature Russian Versailles with distinctly Western features, it's situated within a magnificent forest. Inside the palace, it was possible to see photos of Czar Nicholas II and his family, mounted upon pedestal-tables within beautiful frames.

Of course, Robert insisted upon returning to the Hermitage. In just one year, the appearance of the crowd on Leningrad's streets had changed. In the prior year, it was still possible to see people in business attire that was threadbare, but they were still wearing actual suits. This time, we observed that these people were no longer there. They'd disappeared. They'd been relocated to Vladivostok, we were told. Now, we encountered people with an extremely unkempt appearance who blew their noses onto their fingers. The czars' city, which had been one of the world's most beautiful cities, belonged to them at last. . . . It saddened me greatly.

I can recall that we'd noticed that store windows were filled with children's drawings. It was explained to us that a contest had taken place and that this was a way of honoring the winners. Whatever the case, there wasn't any merchandise to be displayed in the windows. Leningrad and all of Russia seemed to lack everything.

Upon returning to Paris in May, Robert played at the Salle Pleyel with Toscanini conducting for a concert that was a tribute to Saint-Saëns on the centennial of his birth. I had to compel him to play the *Concerto No 4*. In those days, he didn't like it at all and had even been reluctant to accept Toscanini's invitation.

At the end of the concert, Toscanini didn't come out on stage to take a bow, and we were wondering why. Very simply, in the final portion, an instrumentalist hadn't played well, and the composition hadn't sounded the way that Toscanini wished. That had made him furious!

That summer, we stayed with the children in Brolles in the vicinity of Fontainebleau. The house was a charming Directoire-style dwelling. The light was stunning because the rooms were surrounded by windows that opened onto an immense garden, which was a delight for the boys. I set myself up in a small pavilion that was separate from the house, and we placed a piano there so that I could isolate myself in order to practice while the children were playing. I was teaching at Fontainebleau three times per week. Robert was much busier than I, because, in addition to his interpretation courses, he was performing administrative duties inasmuch as he needed to supervise all of the piano classes, without neglecting his personal work at the piano or composing.

At Fontainebleau, we saw Jean Labatut again. He'd returned from the United States in a Zeppelin, which was one of those dirigibles with a metal frame. Because of his enthusiasm for this aerial crossing of the Atlantic, he showed us photos that authenticated his exploit. He'd flown from New York and had traveled for three days in order to reach Paris. This adventure seemed to originate from recklessness or rashness, whichever it may have been.

After Fontainebleau, we left with the children for an actual vacation in the Basque Region. We stayed at a hotel in Vieux Boucau. We went to the beach each day on our bicycles, with the children riding on small seats behind each of us. We were three to four kilometers from the beach. We ate our lunch in a small beachside bungalow that belonged to the hotel. This beach was simple and family-friendly. It's extremely fine and wonderful sand thrilled the children. We spent a happy vacation there, swimming whenever the sea wasn't too rough, as well as playing cards, while the children, like all children, built sandcastles surrounded by trenches where the sea would come rushing in.

When we returned to Paris, Robert was hired by Concerts Siohan. This concert organization, that had acquired a sound reputation, had been founded by Robert Siohan, a musician and musicologist. Siohan, who wasn't conducting this particular concert, informed Robert that the conductor would be Charles Munch. Robert asked him: "Who's that?" and Siohan replied: "He's an excellent violinist. He's the one who was the first violin when you played Saint-Saëns' *Concerto No 4* with Toscanini at the Salle Pleyel. He believes that the first violin is the best observation point in the orchestra!" Robert recalled a certain Fritz Munch whom he'd met in Germany and who was completely in sympathy with Hitler's doctrines. There were actually two Munch brothers, but Charles didn't at all share his brother's convictions. Hence, this is how Robert became acquainted with Charles Munch, with whom he performed quite frequently thereafter. Charles Munch even premiered some of Robert's works.

Munch asked Robert to play Brahms for their first concert. He'd read the excellent critiques that appeared after the New York concert with Toscanini, and, because he adored Brahms, he made an immediate choice. Very shortly after this concert, we embarked once again for New York, aboard the famous *Normandie* this time. The boys accompanied us, and we booked a cabin for them in a lower class than ours, which infuriated them because they wouldn't be granted access to the first-class lounge! Nevertheless, we explained to them that we couldn't allow ourselves so much luxury and that it was necessary to be reasonable. We met André Maurois, who let us know about his passion for Wagner. He knew all of Wagner's operas by heart. Moreover, he had a predilection for German music. I tried to explain to him that French music also possessed strengths and that true beauty existed in Debussy's or Ravel's works. Something certainly different from Mahler's or Bruckner's music. I pursued my demonstration further by explaining to him that, at most, Mahler and Bruckner belonged to another era and that it would never be possible to say enough about the eminent role that Debussy and Ravel had played in the evolution of music. There had been a lot of discussion of Schönberg's role and of his new theories, while the role of our two French musicians was practically consigned to silence. I astonished myself by being such a jingoist or chauvinistic, as you wish!

Upon arriving in New York at the beginning of November 1936, we were dazzled by the autumn colors that were flooding Central Park. We discovered the American autumn with its flaming colors. This is undoubtedly the most beautiful period of the year. We admired Rockefeller Center, which had just been completed. Its perfect whiteness and its imposing silhouette were impressive. With a superior air, it now dominated the New York Cathedral, which seemed rather small alongside it! Fifth Avenue was undergoing a complete evolution.

The Empire State Building rose skyward with nearly a hundred floors. It was possible to ascend as far as the 35th floor by elevator all at once, and that seemed to be an extraordinary technical feat.

Before returning to France, we attended a rehearsal for one of Stravinsky's concerts where he himself conducted. We felt an enormous admiration for him, and we considered him to be on the same level as Debussy and Ravel. We knew him quite well, and I can recall that, when we'd informed him, several years earlier, that Jean was destined for a career as a pianist, Stravinsky said: "Well, he has courage, because becoming a pianist when you have a father who's a pianist like his, that means not choosing the easy way." One of his sons, Igor, was an excellent pianist, and Stravinsky knew what he was talking about. It seemed to him that pursuing this career was like putting your toe into a mousetrap.

The children had been glad to spend Christmas in New York. It was our first American Christmas. You know the importance that this holiday has in the United States. The children were dazzled by it. Unfortunately, Guy caught the whooping cough, but that didn't undermine his pleasure very much.

On January 25, 1937, we re-embarked on the *Normandie*. On this trip, we met Clark Gable, Mistinguett, and the publisher André Salabert. These ocean liners were veritable floating salons where members of what we now call the *Jet Set* rubbed elbows, although, in those times, it was just the *Ship Set*.

As soon as we'd arrived in France, Robert went on a tour again. He went to Denmark first and visited the Castle of Elsinore between two concerts. Then he went to Norway, where the Oslo orchestra revealed itself as an excellent accompanist. Subsequently, he performed in Berlin, Munich, Dresden, and Wiesbaden, with his tour ending in Vienna.

During this period, people began to notice that military aircraft flights were becoming increasingly numerous. All of it conveyed an unpleasant scent of war.

I can recall that, one time in Berlin, we were strolling calmly down a street when we suddenly saw a fire breaking out in a store. Being surprised that no one rushed to control it, we asked a passerby why the firemen hadn't arrived, and he said in a detached way: "Oh, it's nothing. That's a Jewish store!" Because incidents of this kind happened several times, we quickly realized that these fires weren't accidental and that something horrible was on its way.

During the 1936 Olympic Games, Robert was invited to give a concert at the Charlottenburg Palace, not far from Berlin. It was a marvelous site. Goering attended this recital. He sat in the first row, quite impressive in his uniform festooned with all of his decorations.

It was summertime, and the immense chandeliers, which were illuminated with candles, were all lit during the entire concert. I'd remarked to Robert that he'd be sweltering, and, moreover, that it was dangerous. Goering listened very attentively, almost prayerfully, and he discreetly wiped his forehead at various times, because it was so hot. Robert and I were furious because the French ambassador had managed to arrive late.

At the end of the concert, Goering came over to congratulate Robert, and, in excellent French, he said: "You know, I adore Paris. It's a magnificent city! I like your country very much!" When he had left, I didn't conceal my anxieties in contemplating his overly enthusiastic statements about Paris and France.

On one occasion when Robert had traveled to Germany alone, he'd told me that, upon leaving a dinner, someone had offered a toast to him in these terms: "To our future countryman!" Apparently, everyone had looked at each other rolling their eyes, and this person had continued: "Yes, indeed, you'll soon become one of our countrymen!" Robert had burst into laughter so as to express his disapproval and in order to let it be understood that this viewpoint didn't find favor with him in any way. He'd been outraged by such excessive confidence. The Germans were already annexing France. It must be said that they quite clearly envisioned themselves entering France without warfare, as in Czechoslovakia. They were counting on our weakness, which was pretty obvious to them, because, with our Maginot Line, they could easily dream of such an outcome. . . . It was sufficient to travel to the border to see cows grazing peacefully on the French side and to see smoke from the Ruhr's factories on the German side, gushing day and night. We truly exhibited a naïve trust or, rather total unawareness.

During this extensive German tour, we visited Liszt's house in Dresden, where we also saw an exceptionally beautiful retrospective for Lucas Cranach. In Wiesbaden, we also attended a performance of *Ariadne auf Naxos*. Robert greatly admired Richard Strauss' works, but, as strange as it may seem, we never had an opportunity to meet him.

It was during this period that Robert began recording regularly. In Paris, he recorded at the Gaumont Palace on the Place Clichy, which was also being used as a studio. In particular, he recorded Gabriel Fauré's *Quatuor No 1* with the Calvet Quartet, as well as compositions by Ravel, Chabrier, and Déodat de Séverac. He also recorded his own *Sonate pour flute*, with René Le Roy, which he had composed several years earlier. During this period, he also recorded with our friend Georges Truc, who was an excellent pianist. He was a *solfège* instructor at the Rue de Madrid (the Paris Conservatory) as well as being a voice coach at the Opera. He was married to the pianist Lucette Descaves, who taught at the Conservatoire Supérieur de Musique de Paris until quite recently.

On January 1, 1938, we departed for our tour of the United States, as we did each year now. I liked to hear the tugboats' horns during arrivals in the port of New York. A long journey awaited us. That year, we truly crisscrossed the United States in every direction.

In New York, Robert gave Toscanini the quartet manuscript that he'd just completed, which was dedicated to Toscanini. I can recall that, in Detroit, we played before two thousand and three hundred people for the first time in our lives. The concert took place at the Ford plant, and it was offered by its management to employees and to some of the company's clients. They'd made an enormous Lincoln available to us, and we felt lost in such a large automobile.

For the first time, Robert also participated in the *Telephone Hour* concerts. These were radio concerts offered by Bell Telephone, which covered the entire territory. Later, these concerts were televised. In consideration of the time lag from one coast to the other, the concert had to be given twice. The first performance took place at 9:00 p.m. The second performance was at midnight. The fee for this concert was substantial, and the concert was heard by millions of people which provided excellent promotion for the performers. In each city, we took the time to visit museums and libraries, which are amazingly well endowed.

In Cincinnati, Robert gave a recital, and he also played under the baton of Eugene Goossens. In Saint Louis, we again met our friend Vladimir Golschmann, with whom we stayed. That was somewhat of a change from life in hotels. . . . Subsequently, we went to Memphis, and, from there, we took a train to go to New Orleans. It was an extremely long trip: one and one-half days. Robert took advantage of it for his work. He was composing and making copies. The trains were rather comfortable, with sleeping berths that were installed on each side of a long corridor and were concealed by curtains that could be drawn shut in the evening. The trains traveled very slowly, and the cars were enormous and ponderous. Because there were no rail crossings, the train gave warnings far in advance of its passage by means of long highly characteristic whistle blasts that could be heard from quite far away.

During these interminable journeys, there was a particularly agreeable occasion, namely that of the lavish American breakfast: eggs with bacon, fruit juice, cereal, coffee, and toast. You know that, in America, only powdered sugar is served. I detested it, because the sugar was always stained with coffee, with small spoons being used both for serving sugar and for stirring the coffee. We were served by Black waiters who were quite stylish, albeit exceptionally slow.

Because the United States was a majority Protestant country, even puritanical shall we say, Sundays devoid of alcohol or movies were strictly observed at this time. When people traveled through a state where these restrictions were applied, alcohol consumption ceased aboard trains, and in towns, the cinemas were closed.

In New Orleans, as in each city where we were performing, Robert went to test the piano, and what a surprise it was to discover that the piano supplier was none other than Clemenceau's son. In New Orleans, Robert played in an auditorium with three thousand seats. This hall seemed enormous to us. Today, no one would be surprised.

We continued our tour to Baltimore, Philadelphia, and then to Chicago. To go from Philadelphia to Chicago, it took a night aboard the train. In Chicago, we visited the famous slaughterhouses. It was quite astounding to see pigs' or cattle's carcasses transported in lines. Unacceptable animals were automatically eliminated, and, within half an hour, pigs were transformed into sausages! Robert was so "upset" by Jewish ritual slaughtering, which took place in a particular section of the plant, that he couldn't dine that evening. Personally speaking, I hadn't wanted to look.

After Chicago, we went to Jacksonville and then to Atlanta before returning to New York, where Robert played for the New York Philharmonic, where John Barbirolli, who'd just replaced Toscanini at the head of this famous orchestra, was the conductor.

We went one evening to see Verdi's *Otello* at the former Metropolitan Opera which no longer exists today. Afterward, we dined at the "Lafayette," a restaurant where souvenirs from Lindbergh's crossing were displayed. All of his friends who'd helped him in his exploit had met there as witnesses to this adventure that became legendary.

A concert in Boston was followed by another in Montreal. At this time, a night aboard a train was also required to travel from Boston to Montreal. Then back again to New York, where we sailed on March 27 to return to France. Instead of landing in Le Havre, as we usually did, we were rerouted to Cherbourg on account of a strike by harbor workers. Strikes were beginning to multiply, and there was awareness of the social unrest that was developing.

At Easter, we went to Brittany with the children for a brief vacation, and we visited Benodet, La Trinité-sur-Mer, and Mont-Saint-Michel.

Robert then departed for Germany, where he played for the first time under the baton of Hans Rosbaud, who was a wonderful Mozartian conductor. You know that, after the war, Gabriel Dussurget invited him to conduct at the Aix-en-Provence Festival, where he was to leave unforgettable memories.

During this period, Robert was composing every day, even when he was touring. I believe that this was a form of relaxation for him.

In Brussels, he served on the jury of the Eugène Ysaÿe International Competition. During this visit, we gave a concert together, and the program included: Mozart's *Concerto pour deux pianos,* the *Quintette des Oiseaux* that Robert had transcribed for us, and, as a finale, the *Sonate pour deux pianos.* I believe that Robert also played the *Sonate en Fa* as a solo. Queen Elizabeth of Belgium attended the concert, and she is the person who had requested, moreover, that our concert should be devoted to Mozart. She was a great admirer of music, and the Ysaÿe Competition was given her name, which it still bears! This is one of the most important competitions on an international scale. It was during that year that the young Russian pianist, Emil Gilels, participated in the competition. Walter Gieseking, as well as Braïlowsky and Rubinstein, were jury members along with Robert. Gieseking displayed one of the most disagreeable attitudes toward Gilels. My husband had said before the session: "I'm convinced that this young man will win the prize. I heard him in Moscow. He's fantastic!" Gieseking replied, however, in an extremely scornful tone: "It's out of the question; he's a Jew!" Gieseking was one hundred percent in favor of Hitler's regime, which doesn't negate his talent as a pianist in any way. He had a reputation for being a generous man, although he was totally anti-Semitic. Quite obviously, Gilels won first prize in spite of Gieseking's opposition.

On the cusp of summer, in late May or early June, Robert and I went to pay a visit to Mademoiselle Simon, his former teacher, who'd retired to the countryside. For several years, she'd lived in Septeuil, not far from Paris. She was one of those people who refuse to decline with aging. She'd therefore preferred to leave her private dwelling in Montmartre in due time, fearing to lack the funds for its upkeep. In Septeuil, she was leading a calm and simple life. We were glad to see her again.

As we did each summer, we again took up our quarters in Fontainebleau. The reputation of the courses kept growing and it was attracting increasing numbers of young Americans, especially for piano classes.

In September, we took a short vacation in southern France, and, in early Fall, Robert completed a tour in Germany once again—Berlin, Potsdam, Dresden, and Munich—accompanied by Joseph Calvet, the violinist who was the founder of the Quartet that bore his name and who acquired an exceptional reputation before the war.

At the end of October, we traveled to Budapest for the first time, and we met Ernest von Dohnányi, the great composer who was a contemporary of Bartók and who undoubtedly influenced new generations of musicians on account of his theories that were both loyal to the past and innovative.

After leaving Hungary, Robert still had other concerts in Munich and Koenigsberg, whereupon we departed for Poland: Warsaw, Lodz, Riga, followed by a return to Germany with stopovers in Hamburg and Munster, and then to Switzerland, where he performed in Geneva, St. Gall, and Basel. This tour ended in Holland.

We arrived in Paris somewhat exhausted from these long train trips. When I think about it, I wonder how we managed to maintain such a rhythm. Not least because we'd covered more than ten thousand kilometers in the United

States that year. Very precisely, 10,300! Robert had done the computations, and he'd recorded this figure in his datebook.

On January 1, 1939, we left for the United States, where a journey essentially the same as the previous year's journey awaited us. During this visit, we tried a new means of transportation. We took a seaplane to go to Havana, where Robert was giving a concert. We'd thought of taking a boat from Miami, but this opportunity was offered to us. I must confess that we were somewhat fearful . . . one of our friends had offered us a bottle of whiskey for the trip. . . . We hadn't informed anyone about this trip, and we subsequently felt that we'd been somewhat reckless because of not having said anything to anyone when we were leaving two children behind us. When the fearfulness of the flight was behind us, we enjoyed discovering Havana and its magnificent bay. We were very well received, and we were astonished to hear French spoken. Everyone—or almost everyone—spoke French in Cuba at that time. As I recall, it was dreadfully hot, and, obviously, air conditioning for the houses wasn't available yet.

This is the period when we started playing by memory, because the American public was very appreciative of it. I don't know whether you can imagine how much work was needed to memorize our entire repertoire. I still recollect that we rehearsed a single work more than twenty hours so that we could offer a sacrifice to this new trend.

When we returned to New York, Robert gave his first recital at Carnegie Hall. Until then, he'd only played with an orchestra in other halls. That was an important landmark in his musical life in the United States. After the recital, we were invited to dine by Mr. Grainer, the manager of Steinway Pianos. At this dinner, we met Alexander Braïlowsky and Serge Rachmaninoff, who was a very distinguished and extremely simple man, with exceptional modesty. He confessed to Robert that he was incapable of playing Ravel's *Toccata*. Unfortunately, I've never had an opportunity to hear him.

In those days, people didn't receive fees for recitals at Carnegie Hall. They were paid according to the proceeds. Some people had tried to dissuade us from attempting such an experience. For my part, I was convinced that it was necessary to do it. And I was right!

Robert continued his wide-ranging tour: Detroit, Madison in Wisconsin, Nashville, and Chicago. You can imagine these train rides! Sixteen hours of train travel to go from Columbus, Ohio to Phoenix, Arizona.

Then it was the West Coast: Los Angeles, and San Diego, where we admired superb primitives and exceptionally beautiful English paintings in the museum. Oakland and San Francisco. Then we returned by the northern route: Seattle, Minneapolis, and Saint-Paul, where it was 21 degrees below zero on April 1.

We returned to France slightly dazed from this tour, and we spent a long weekend at Recloses, near Fontainebleau, in order to recuperate.

Very quickly thereafter, Robert left for Amsterdam. Jean earned his first *solfège* medal at the Conservatory on Rue de Madrid. The date was June 6, 1939. He'd be twelve years old in July. He'd enrolled in the Conservatory a year earlier, and he wanted to continue piano classes there. At that time, I believed that he could possibly become a conductor.

Upon returning from Holland, Robert was a jury member at the Paris Conservatory, and then it was the yearly relocation to Fontainebleau, where he was teaching five hours of courses per day, two days in a row. I was also teaching a small group of students.

In August, Robert practiced a lot at the piano. The rumors of war became increasingly strident. Nevertheless, we departed for Holland, where he performed at Scheveningen one more time with Schuricht conducting. I remember having played Beethoven's *1st Concerto* there on one occasion, without a chance to rehearse with the orchestra, which was hardly to my liking. Everything went very well in spite of stage fright. In Amsterdam, we had enough time to see a rather all-encompassing exhibit of Van Gogh's works.

On August 19, Robert received the insignia of the Legion of Honor from the hands of the architect Jacques Carlu, who was the Director of the Fontainebleau School of Fine Arts. Carlu is the person who, along with Boileau and Azema, had erected the Palace of Chaillot at the time when the Hill of Chaillot at the Trocadéro was undergoing renovation. We were very close friends of his.

After a quick excursion to the Verdon gorges, we returned to Fontainebleau. During the summer of 1939, we were visited by the composer Henri Rabaud,[1] who was the Director of the Paris Conservatory at that time. He had succeeded Gabriel Fauré in 1922, and he remained in his position until 1941. During a luncheon, he offered Robert an instructor's position, although he hadn't expected it at all: "We wish you'd accept. In fact, we don't want Mme. Chautemps, who has been enthusiastically recommended to us. She's the mistress of Cabinet Minister Camille Chautemps, and she isn't concealing it. (Moreover, she married him shortly thereafter.) When she shows up late, she proclaims with radiant authority, 'I've been delayed on account of the Minister.'"

The offer left Robert perplexed. He responded very quickly to Rabaud, however: "If I accept this position, I could no longer give so many concerts. I adore teaching, but I'm already at Fontainebleau for two months during the summer, and, each year, I go on a tour in the United States that keeps me there for at least two months. Therefore, I think that it's difficult, to reconcile my career with permanent teaching." It should be pointed out that, during this period, there was very little time off when someone was teaching at the Conservatory, to such an extent that it was necessary to choose between teaching and a career, but one couldn't actually do both as people do today. This was an extremely difficult period to live through. There was a terrible tension. At the end of August, we sent our young au pair girl back to Switzerland, because we didn't want her to face the risk of being detained in France. Everyone sensed that the war was imminent."

On August 31, we left Brolles, when our lease came to an end, but we didn't want to return to Paris, because we feared that the capital would be bombarded. Thus, with the children and all of our luggage, we stayed in a hotel in Recloses that belonged to a friend of my father-in-law. I can say that we were a bit lost. What to do? Where to go? We wandered between Barbizon and Grey-sur-Loing. Were we going to rent a house? An opportunity became available. Some Americans who were returning to the United States offered their house to us. They were prepared to leave their servants in our service, because they preferred having their quite beautiful home occupied rather than empty and exposed to who knew what kind of fate. Robert didn't favor this arrangement, and we continued to ponder what to do. . . . On September 3, we learned about the declaration of war. We were still in Recloses with Aunt Rosette, the children, and our luggage. Finally, on September 9, we decided to leave. Our direction: southward. School hadn't started yet. By short stages, we arrived in Vichy, where we had friends. The husband was a physician. They found us an apartment that we could rent. We set up housekeeping there with a two-month lease. We enrolled the children in a school right next to our building. This place of refuge suited us pretty well because it was located near Robert's father, who, at this time, was living in a rest home for performing artists quite close to Vichy. The poor man, who was suffering from cancer, died several months later, while we were in the United States.

I can still remember our address: 2-bis rue du Maréchal Foch. We rented an upright piano that allowed us to work so effectively that our fallback arrangement didn't turn out to be so unfavorable.

Shortly thereafter, we left Vichy, while we left the children in Aunt Rosette's care, because Robert had to go to Amsterdam, and I had to do recordings in Paris. At that time, recordings for radio were produced at the Grand Palais. I recall playing Fauré's *Nocturne No 1* with all my heart! When I was leaving the studio, the sound engineer, who was literally furious, was shouting: "You told me that it would last four minutes, but it's five and a half minutes!"

During these times, a sound recording lasted five minutes, and it was a key issue not to exceed it. I was so shocked by events that I was probably taking a bit of pleasure from sorrowful lyricism, so that I'd forgotten the real tempo for this composition.

As for Robert, he returned from Amsterdam immediately after his concert, because he'd been told that the Germans were expected to invade Holland the next day.

When he returned to Paris, Robert adopted his usual rhythm. An average of five hours of piano per day. He was a jury member for the Conservatory, and he gave a series of concerts in Zurich, Lausanne, and Geneva.

French radio broadcasting had been relocated to Rennes, and I can recall that Robert and I went there to play his *Concerto pour deux pianos.*

After his return, we prepared for our departure for the United States. Robert had obtained a mission order from the Ministry of Cultural Affairs that authorized him to leave for foreign tours. We didn't imagine that this would be a long departure and an absence from France that would last six years.

Then we learned that two French ocean liners had been torpedoed and sunk.

The entire family urged us to leave the children in France. Fortunately, we didn't listen to them. All four of us sailed on an Italian vessel that was subject to a lower risk of being torpedoed than a French vessel because the Italians were the Germans' allies.

Before arriving in Italy where we would be embarking, we went to pay a visit to friends in Nice with whom we left our car. It's pointless to tell you that we never got it back after the war. The Delberts had lent it to people who wanted to go to Italy, and, obviously, the car was never returned!

In Nice, we learned that Aunt Rosette had broken her leg, and we were profoundly upset about leaving her alone and handicapped. What else could we do, however? We were quite sad to be leaving under such circumstances. While traveling to Nice, we'd stopped near Vichy to pay a visit to my father-in-law. We found him very emaciated, and we were very worried as we left him. We also went to embrace my father, who was managing the Charities Bureau in Marseille. At that time, we couldn't imagine that we'd never see any of the three again. . . . My father died two months after my father-in-law in the spring of 1940 from an untreatable intestinal obstruction. On January 1, 1940, after a rather subdued New Year's Eve with the Delberts, we took a train to Genoa, where we were expecting to board our Italian ocean liner.

On January 2, we boarded the *S/S Rex.* On January 3, there was a stopover in Naples to take on passengers. In Gibraltar, we ran into the Francescattis, who were returning from their tour in the United States. Then, there was the prolonged Atlantic crossing. As always, life at sea continued in a very pleasant way. Robert practiced the piano. Jean participated in a ping-pong tournament, where he emerged as the winner.

The ship's captain was a very friendly man, and we chatted with him a lot. He loved music, and we felt that he enjoyed discussing it with professionals. One evening, during dinner, he announced to us with a sad look on his face: "This will be the last voyage for the *Rex.* Mussolini promised Hitler that he'd go to war. We have to get ready. We're all extremely distressed but there's nothing that we can do to counter his decision." We were appalled by this news.

## NOTE

1. Henri Rabaud (1873–1949), author of *Marouf, The Cobbler of Cairo.*

## Chapter 12

# Exile in America

Upon arriving in New York, we stayed at the Hotel Navarro near Central Park, as we'd been doing since 1936. I enrolled the children in the Lycée Français (French school) that had been established in 1935 by Count Charles de Ferry de Fontnouvelle, who was the French consul in New York at that time. Moreover, we'd given a concert at Carnegie Hall for the school's "fundraising," with Lily Pons and the flutist René Le Roy also participating.

We returned to our American ways: concerts in Washington, Houston, New Orleans, Kansas City, Davenport, Chicago, Louisville, and Toledo.

When we were in New York, we consistently went to the Steinway studios for our piano practice.

In Princeton, New Jersey, we renewed contact with our friends, the Labatuts. This university town became a veritable French and European colony. We saw Thomas Mann and André Maurois there, among others, along with Professor Albert Einstein.

I've already told you how we'd managed to transfer the Fontainebleau Conservatory to the United States for its 1940 summer session, after negotiations that became complicated on account of increasingly difficult communication with France. From that point on, things would begin to accelerate.

One day, when we were talking with friends, they put forth an extremely wise suggestion: "Since you're staying all summer, you should rent a house in Princeton, and you should look for a place in this region where you could set up your classes. For three months, it's worth it. You'll have a more peaceful situation than in New York, and it will turn out to be less expensive than living at the hotel and having your meals in restaurants, especially for four of you."

A friend of the Labatuts quickly found a small house that we leased for three months.

I must say that I wasn't dissatisfied with this solution, which was likewise favorable for the boys. I'd discovered that they were making hardly any progress in English, because they'd only been speaking French at the Lycée

Français, and I believed that living in an American environment would be beneficial for them.

When we finally received an authorization for extending our stay, we immediately contacted our students, and we were glad to observe that all of them went into action to help us to organize this session. One of them took me to Newport, Rhode Island in order to visit a private school that he'd attended, which was unoccupied during the summer. I was immediately pleased with this location, and we quickly decided to establish the Fontainebleau "branch" there, because staying in Princeton, where it was much hotter in the summer, was out of the question.

Robert didn't waste time in renting a car because it was difficult to get along without one. Fortunately, the garage owner was French-Canadian, which allowed Robert to conduct negotiations in French, because his English wasn't very fluent! Actually, he hardly dared to speak, and I was always the one who served as his interpreter. My English was far from perfect, but, at least, I could speak the language! On the other hand, Robert made do with a broad smile whenever someone spoke to him. Actually, neither he nor I learned English in school. We'd learned it phonetically. Robert constantly inquired about spellings of words, but he also said half-jokingly: "It's very good not to speak a language because that will discourage people who want to tell you their life stories!" Later, when we celebrated the twenty-fifth year of his career in the United States, I can assure you that he was fully capable of improvising a speech . . . in any event in twenty-five years, he'd made some progress!

We enrolled the children in the public school. I recall that the wife of a Belgian Cabinet minister, who'd also sought refuge in Princeton, had enrolled her children there. Her daughter offered to serve as an interpreter for Guy, but he proudly declined her help. He was only eight years old, but he didn't want in any way to show that he was in a position of inferiority.

In three months, the children made spectacular progress in English. It's true that they only played with young Americans and that this is certainly one of the best ways to learn a language.

We, therefore, moved to a charming little house that was adjacent to another small house. It had a ground floor and an upper floor. Our landlady, Mrs. Cuyler, who knew France well because of having visited there on multiple occasions, was quite the Francophile. Until the defeat was announced, she brought me a red rose from her garden every day. When we heard about the Armistice, we kindly asked her to suspend this expression of friendship and to wait until victory before resuming it.

Throughout this period, we had few ways of obtaining information about what was happening in our homeland. Our only source of information in French was Radio Canada. That's where we could glean the most information.

We also read *Time Magazine*, which was relatively well informed about the military situation, but we could never find any French newspapers, of course, and we felt a bit lost.

When we moved into the house on Edgehill Street with our trunks, we didn't know yet that the name of our neighbor a few hundred meters away was Albert Einstein.

It was the two Belgian families with whom we'd become friendly who introduced him to us. He was living with his sister, his wife's daughter, and a secretary. Both he and his sister had extremely spectacular and abundant white hair, he adored music, and, as you know, he played the violin. Later, when I proposed to him playing music with me, he was delighted, and he agreed without hesitation. I quickly observed that his technique was somewhat limited. I didn't have a lot of knowledge of my own about the violin, but I actually believe that he didn't go beyond the third position.[1] He played with sensitivity and emotion, however. With adagios, for example, he managed to obtain deep, intense, and superbly internalized sounds to such an extent that it would have been possible to perceive him as a professional. He especially liked Bach, Haydn, Mozart, and Beethoven's works from his youth. He wasn't interested in the Romantic era. A few years later, he came to play Bach's *Concerto for Two Violins* in our home with Zino Francescatti and Robert, and I recall that he played extremely well. On several occasions, I went to practice in his home. One day, he even agreed to give a concert at the charming Present Day Club hall, and he asked me to accompany him for a sonata by Mozart. The hall was overflowing. Photographers were blasting away, and I feared that the flashbulbs would make him furious. Quite the contrary, he smiled politely at each one, and he seemed gratified by the interest that was being shown in him. He spoke English with a heavy German accent that didn't always make conversation easy. With us, he scattered French words in his sentences. He was intensely francophile and wasn't very American. In fact, he felt very European, and he was passionate about what was happening on the old continent. Once, he insisted that we should participate in a benefit concert at Carnegie Hall for the Russians. Although he was totally opposed to the Communist regime, he believed that people should show solidarity with everyone who was fighting against Nazism, regardless of their political tendencies.

The news that was reaching us via Canada was depressing. We were distressed to learn that France had been cut in two by a demarcation line. What did "free zone" or "occupied zone" mean? What a monstrosity!

On May 8 or May 9—I no longer remember which it was—we received a letter announcing my father-in-law's death. The shock was terrible for all of us. At the end of the year, Robert recorded it in his datebook under the heading "Obituary," which he carefully maintained: "Papa"—without a precise date.

During these long months of anguish, Robert and I worked relentlessly, undoubtedly in order to avoid thinking too much. We'd obtained two pianos from Steinway: one was a grand piano, and the other was an upright piano. It was during this period that I started practicing Robert's *Études*.

Princeton is one hour from New York by train. I traveled there once a week in order to give lessons. I had a few pupils who studied regularly with me. I always took advantage of these days in New York in order to do a little shopping. The stores were very tempting!

In May, Robert recorded Chopin's *Sonate pour piano et violoncelle* with Gregor Piatigorsky, but the record was never released. I believe that Robert didn't get along very well with Piatigorsky. They hadn't agreed about which style to adopt for this particular work. They didn't share the same perspective. In spite of the failure of this professional encounter, we were delighted with the few hours that we spent with him. He was a great artist. He'd married a Rothschild who was also a musician.

Throughout this entire period, Robert was composing with exceptional regularity. When he wasn't working, he listened to the radio so that he could try to pick up some news.

I recall that we went to hear the Budapest Quartet, which performed the entirety of Beethoven's *Quartets*. Robert, who adored these quartets, had been delighted to hear them performed by this excellent ensemble, where each member was a superbly talented soloist. They were perpetuating the great European tradition of chamber music in the United States.

In June, Robert performed at Carnegie Hall with Ernest Schelling conducting. This concert took place within the context of the series intended for children that had been initiated by the New York Philharmonic Orchestra. Later, Leonard Bernstein would continue this venture, and, with the orchestra, he would produce the famous television series titled "Young People's Concerts."

Schelling was a handsome wild man . . . he owned a collection of portraits of musicians on slides that he'd gladly project when people visited him. When he went to Europe, he often stayed in Switzerland, in a house that the pianist Ignace Paderewski would lend to him.

I don't know whether you remember that, in 1919, Paderewski became the Chairman of the Cabinet and Minister of Foreign Affairs in Poland. He'd been an extremely renowned pianist, and everyone was awaiting his arrival in the United States. Unfortunately, he didn't encounter the expected success because some of his concerts were disappointing. Did he develop stage fright as he grew older? In any instance, he was no longer at the level of his reputation. He died in New York in 1941, without ever returning to his country.

After General Philippe Pétain's speech, whose impact reached us and deeply saddened us, as you can imagine, our children were treated as collaborators and Nazis by their American peers. To tell the truth, Jean was somewhat mischievous, and, for example, he didn't hesitate to tie one of his playmates to a tree and to shout at him so as to scare him: "I'm going to kill you!" which led to his being regarded as a "Nazi." Jean was very shocked, because he was intensely proud of being French and never failed to let that be known.

Miss Sender, the secretary who'd worked for us at Fontainebleau, joined us in Princeton in order to launch the first American session. The school that was chosen wasn't located in the elegant portion of Newport, where the *nouveaux riches* at the end of the nineteenth century had commissioned construction of imitations of the Loire châteaux, with each of them being uglier and more ridiculous than the others . . . whereas the school was on a hill with a view of the ocean. Like every American private school, it included a vast athletic field.

Throughout this period, Robert scrupulously recorded in his datebook each of the events reported by Canadian Radio: June 16—the Maginot Line was broken, he wrote. June 18—General De Gaulle's Appeal from London. June 19—Capture of Rennes by the Germans. June 20—Lyon fell to the Germans. June 22—Signing of the Armistice. . . . Thus, it was amid the echoes of this faraway catastrophe that I set up Fontainebleau in Newport. Fortunately, we were able to keep the school's cook throughout the session, and that saved me from worries about meal service.

Jean was assiduously practicing the piano, and, from time to time, Robert gave him some advice or repertoire lists. Robert never actually made him work, however. I was even astonished to observe that Robert didn't express annoyance when he heard him make mistakes. As for me, I was completely the opposite! I made comments such as: "Count your beats!" We worked together on the repertoire that his father established, and he was always very responsive to my comments. Jean displayed extraordinary obedience. Was it because he knew that we could only give him wise advice? He was a marvelous student for me. Subsequently, I attempted to get Guy started with the violin, although without notable success. Because I wasn't a violinist, he believed that I didn't have any competence! Jean was practicing the piano for three-quarters of an hour every morning before leaving for school. In the evening, when he came home, he studied again for two hours. He dreamed of becoming a pianist like his father. He also adored sports. He played baseball, and I can recall one occasion in Newport when I seriously scolded him because he'd gone out to play before a class. I was so afraid that he'd injure his hands. I thought that tennis, soccer, or swimming were more appropriate sports for a pianist.

Mme. Pillois, who'd taught French at Fontainebleau in the summer and at Bryn Mawr College during the winter, also joined us. She was a charming and straightforward woman who understood American attitudes perfectly, which was extremely helpful for us. She always came to the School accompanied by her large dog, to the overwhelming joy of the students, who adored her.

Robert worked enormously throughout the summer. I always wondered whether this wasn't to some extent a way of distracting himself and forgetting about events in France. He gave as many as six hours of courses per day, and his master classes and permanent personal work should be added to that figure.

In July, he gave a concert in Lewisohn Stadium (a stadium belonging to the City College of New York). These outdoor concerts were extremely popular, and they attracted huge audiences. They were prohibited as soon as air traffic over New York intensified.

On July 25, my father died, but we didn't find out until much later, and it was awful to receive in September a letter from him that was written just before his death, where he complained of having some intestinal upsets, but nothing serious. What a shock it was for me to see his handwriting when I knew that he was no longer alive! I learned subsequently that my sister had unfortunately arrived too late, and it was horrible for us to experience this misfortune when we were so far apart.

We were also very worried about Aunt Rosette, who'd found refuge among friends in southern France. She was hoping that Marius could join us. We'd done everything to obtain the necessary papers for his arrival, but it began to be very difficult to enter the United States. Too many people were seeking visas, and the Americans proceeded to put limits on this exodus. Unfortunately, in spite of our connections, we didn't succeed in enabling him to come. We were more successful in our efforts on behalf of Daniel Guilevitch, the Calvet Quartet's second violin. With René Le Roy, we managed to arrange a fictitious hiring by the Radio City orchestra, where the theatre pianist, Oscar Lifshey, who was one of my father-in-law's friends, was working. Daniel Guilevitch, who was Jewish, had fled to Algeria, but he couldn't manage to leave. When he finally arrived in the United States, he changed his surname to Guilet. We'd paid his travel expenses before his departure, as if they'd been included in the contract. He was an excellent violinist. He didn't encounter any difficulties in finding work. He became a solo violinist for Toscanini on NBC, and he founded the Guilet Quartet, which subsequently became the Beaux Arts Trio that's familiar to all music lovers.

This period was truly exceedingly difficult.

In mid-September, when we returned to Princeton, we had a feeling that the Fontainebleau School had accomplished its mission in Newport as effectively as at the Château.

On November 10, Roosevelt was re-elected to the presidency of the United States, and he did everything in his power to help a Europe that had been dragged into a war that seemed destined to last. He sent vessels with food supplies to Spain and to England. He was very eager to help oppressed people who had to battle invaders.

During the Fall, we went to attend a recital given by Béla Bartók at Rutgers University, which is located in New Brunswick, New Jersey, not far from New York, and we were extremely saddened when we observed that there were only about fifty people in the hall. We knew that Bartók was having severe financial problems and that he was living in semi-poverty. I believe that he'd made a mistake by intending to teach piano instead of composition, and also by giving recitals that only included his own work. To be sure, this fulfilled the curiosity of some dedicated music-lovers, but the general audience, which knew nothing of his works, felt somewhat at a loss. Robert and I appreciated his innovative genius, and we spoke with him extensively about his work. He truly possessed a talent that was far from ordinary. We spoke French with him. You know that he became ill and died in New York in 1945. He was only sixty years old.

I've always believed that the precarious situation that Bartók was facing led to a decline in his health. Without any doubt, Serge Koussevitsky is one of the few people who helped him in the United States. You know that he's the person who commissioned Bartók's *Concerto for Orchestra*, which gained immediate success.

We never failed to listen to rebroadcasting of Toscanini's concerts on NBC. Even today, I can still recall a profoundly moving Verdi *Requiem*.

In December, Robert gave a recital at Carnegie Hall, and then we traveled to Canada in order to regularize our status as residents in the United States. It was out of the question for us to return to France in the immediate future, but we never thought of acquiring American citizenship. We kept our "residents" status until 1970.

During the year 1940, we experienced the trials and tribulations of repeated changes of residence. When we returned from Newport on September 15, we moved into 341 Nassau Street. The house was beautiful and spacious, and the owner had divided the house into two areas. On the ground floor, there was a living room with an upright piano, a dining room, and a kitchen. The three bedrooms were on the upper floor. We were sharing the house with an attorney. We weren't far from the Country Day School, where the boys were going to school. We were able to practice the piano until ten o'clock in the evening without disturbing anyone. This house had a lot of charm with its porch that faced a magnificent garden. Unfortunately, our landlady became ill, and she died. The house was sold, and we needed to look for another place to live. Although we didn't have any furniture to move, because we'd leased the house with its furniture, I was very upset by having to move when we'd barely arrived.

Then we moved into 41 Harrison Street, a house that was unfortunately smaller. . . . In June, we returned to Newport for the Fontainebleau School's second American session.

At the end of August, we traveled to Mexico, where Robert performed Ravel's *Concerto pour la main gauche* with Carlos Chávez, the well-known composer and orchestra conductor. It was an immense success for Robert. And Chávez had the orchestra play a piece that's usually played after a bull-fight in order to celebrate the matador's victory! This tribute amused Robert considerably.

In order to go to Mexico, we took a boat from Newport to New York, and then we took a train to Mexico. The trip lasted four days! We suffocated in spite of a rather ingenious cooling system that consisted of slabs of ice that were replaced at each station. The cars were outfitted with superimposed berths and a bathroom in each compartment. A lounge-smoking area was available for passengers. It was sort of a Trans-Siberian railway in a more elegant form.

In 1941, the train was the only mode of transportation for traveling to Mexico. One of our friends told us that he'd spent more time going from Texas to Mexico by automobile than we'd spent traveling from New York by train!

I can recall that, in Mexico, it had been a great pleasure to visit the store known as the "Palacio de Hierro" that was managed by Frenchmen. It was possible to find clothing that came from France, and I can confess that I was unable to withstand temptation! I was so attached to French fashion, and I was missing it.

At the end of the year, Robert was still working on his *Quatrième symphonie*, and he attended a premiere of his *Deuxième symphonie* in Cincinnati. He was highly pleased with Eugene Goossens' performance. It's always a magical but rather agonizing moment for a composer to listen to live sounds emanating from his inner listening.

Robert gave a series of concerts in Boston, Cleveland, Rochester, and Detroit. I joined him in Chicago, where we went to hear a recital by Horowitz. During the first portion, Horowitz had played a sonata by Beethoven, and I can recall that, during the intermission, everyone was discussing his interpretation. Some people said, "It's a bit lifeless," and others said: "That wasn't perfect." As for us, we considered his Beethoven to be quite good. I believe that these discussions reflected the fact that, during this period, Horowitz didn't have the reputation of being a Beethovenian pianist. You know how reputations can depend upon so few things! A few social conversations, a somewhat harsh review, and then the audience takes everything *en bloc* and regards these opinions as definitive. At the end of his recital, he played his arrangement of *Carmen,* which unleashed the audience's enthusiasm. We went to greet him in his dressing room, and he said to Robert: "I hope that you're going to play my arrangement for *Carmen* too." I must confess that Robert was never very keen on adding it to his programs. It was felt pretty obviously then that Horowitz was subject to the influence of his father-in-law Toscanini.

As I've already said, he (Horowitz) wanted to commit himself to practicing the classics: Bach and Beethoven, whom he'd never played until then. We also sensed that the audience would only express approval when he showed off his fantastic technique.

In December, Robert and I gave a two piano recital in Miami. I was six months pregnant. . . . I can recall that a cricket had nested in one of the green plants that was decorating the stage and that it didn't stop chirping during the entire Mozart *Sonata.* That annoyed me, and I always wondered whether the audience had heard the cricket as much as we did.!

The great event at the end of 1941, however, was undoubtedly the announcement of the Americans' entry into the war, after the attack on Pearl Harbor by the Japanese on December 7. We were waiting impatiently for the Americans to come to the aid of occupied Europe. From that point on, Roosevelt became totally committed to the conflict.

In 1942, we moved again. This time, the house was quite beautiful in terms of its external appearance, but its interior was rather mournful. It had an advantage that the other houses lacked. It had a porch and a cooler bedroom, and this was rather pleasant during Princeton's torrid summers. In April, the bedroom was where we accommodated our daughter Thérèse, who'd just been born.

Jean had phoned me while we were in Miami in order to tell me that a large house would be available. The owner was departing for the war, and his wife didn't want to be alone. I told him to apply for it without hesitation, and that's how we moved into a house that I hadn't even seen.

Upon our arrival, our landlady informed us that we'd possibly have trouble sleeping on account of the squirrels making a racket in the attic nearly every night. This perspective hardly gladdened us! We were also told a story about a ghost in the house. . . . A soldier from the Revolutionary War who appeared on Christmas Eve. . . . He'd been murdered near the chimney one Christmas Eve, in the darkest portion of the living room. . . . It should be pointed out that the house dated from 1750.

The first night, we slept very poorly, and we believed that we could hear footsteps! Actually, it was the squirrels who were frolicking. One day, shortly after our arrival, we were overwhelmed by a pestilential odor. After very thorough investigations, we found a dead squirrel between the wooden slats of the façade. We sprayed the wood with eau de Cologne, and, in spite of this deluxe disinfection, it was extremely difficult to eliminate this intolerable odor.

Another time, we experienced a terrible fright because a conflagration originating from a chimney fire was detected in the house next door. Its roof was shingled, and sparks had set the roof on fire. We feared that the wind would carry the fire to our house. Fortunately, the wind wasn't very strong, and the worst was avoided.

I'd alerted the firemen, who arrived rather quickly and then discovered the owners of the other house calmly sitting by the fireplace! They hadn't been aware of anything.

## NOTE

1. There are five different hand positions upon a violin's strings, from bottom to top.

## Chapter 13

# United States, Continued

## *A Daughter Is Born*

Thérèse was born on April 12, 1942, at 7:00 a.m. Robert was touring at the other end of the country, and he learned of his daughter's arrival by means of a telegram that I'd sent to him aboard the train taking him from Seattle to Portland. I won't tell you about the difficulties that I experienced with getting to the hospital in the middle of the night, because Jean, from the pinnacle of his fourteen and a half years, wasn't able to help me very much at three o'clock in the morning when Thérèse announced her arrival! I hadn't orga- nized anything because I was convinced that I'd be giving birth when Robert returned. Robert wasn't able to become acquainted with Thérèse until April 19. I'd described her to him on the telephone, and I'd even told him that she looked somewhat like a Mexican child which had worried him slightly. It must be said that her skin had an altogether coppery tint and that she had a flat nose when I first saw her, because I'd been sedated as soon as I arrived at the hospital. At that time, this was frequently done in American hospitals. In fact, I was also quite surprised to see her in her crib a few hours after the delivery, which I can't remember at all. Robert was quickly reassured when he saw her eight days later, because eight days make a difference for a baby. This was a gorgeous spring. In the United States, nature bursts forth all of a sudden. Robert, who was overcome with joy at the birth of a daughter, devoted a lot of time to composition as soon as he returned. He even dedicated a piece to her that he titled *Pour la naissance d'une dauphine*.

That year, we were obliged to give up Newport for strategic reasons. The Americans, who possessed an exceptionally important naval base there, had taken over the entire coast, and they'd declared the region to be prohibited to civilians. It was therefore necessary to begin searching for a new place to continue the Fontainebleau School. After some searching, we decided upon a location in Great Barrington, Massachusetts.

Great Barrington is located fifteen kilometers from Tanglewood, which was already known as an excellent music school. Courses were given throughout the summer by the greatest musicians of that era. We'd discovered a splendid imitation Renaissance chateau! A search for pianos immediately became a necessity for us because Steinway's trucks were no longer authorized to complete deliveries outside New York as a result of fuel restriction issues. I was obliged to knock on the doors of each home in this small town in order to find pianos. Private citizens were sympathetic, and they agreed to lease me their instruments without too much reluctance. You can imagine the problem that this was for me! Very quickly, I became aware that this location was less congenial than the school in Newport. And it was far less practical. The rooms were enormous, which isn't at all surprising for a chateau that hadn't been designed to accommodate pianos and, in particular, large numbers of students.

We needed to accommodate the students with several sharing each bedroom, which was less comfortable. We also converted one of the garages into a studio. Ultimately, that wasn't ideal! Furthermore, Miss Sender had disappeared, and we had to find someone to perform secretarial functions. One of the students, Emma Pizzuto, efficiently took on this responsibility. In exchange, she didn't have to pay any tuition. Two other young ladies had agreed to help in the refectory. A cook was responsible for meals.

That year, approximately forty students had enrolled. That was a large number, especially because Robert and I were obliged to bear responsibility for all of the courses alone. I taught the less prepared students, and Robert taught more advanced students.

We rented a house in a nearby location for ourselves and the children, and we were accompanied by our steadfast Black servant, Edna, who was deeply attached to Thérèse. Her presence was enormously helpful for taking care of the baby during my courses.

Not far from Great Barrington, there's a lake, and the Francescattis had moved into a house on the shore. The French community got together whenever it was possible. We'd also met up with the Guilets. Zino Francescatti visited us very regularly in order to play music with Robert, and it can be said that this is where their duo originated . . . at first for enjoyment . . . and then as a professional "team."

Robert, that year, composed his *Deuxième sonate* for violin and piano, and dedicated it to Zino. In spite of his being extremely busy with his classes and masterclasses, he always found time to compose.

The flutist, René Le Roy, also lived quite close to us. His home was where we met Mme. de Saint-Exupéry, an absolutely charming and very unpretentious lady. One day, René came to pay us a visit, and we decided to go for a drive. Our two cars were following one another, and the second car attempted to pass the first. A few moments later, we were halted by the highway police for speeding. In the United States, speed isn't a laughing matter. We explained to the policemen that we were in a hurry because I needed to nurse my baby who'd remained at our house. That was completely untrue. . . . The police didn't want to listen, and we were obliged to pay a fine. Shortly thereafter, on July 14 (how could a date of this kind be forgotten?), we were summoned to court, where we were told: "In commemoration of the spirit of liberty that your country inaugurated on this date, the fine that we'd applied to you on the date of your offense will be revoked, but we're obligated to suspend your drivers' licenses for a three-month period!" We asked ourselves which was harsher: the fine or suspension of our drivers' licenses?

After Thérèse's birth, I quickly resumed my activities. In November, I played a two-piano concert with Robert for the "French Relief" and a sonata with René Le Roy and Marcel Hubert, a French cellist who'd been living in the United States for many years. He belonged to the New York Philharmonic Orchestra.

We were frequently criticized for these concerts that were intended to provide aid for French children who were subject to food restrictions. I was told that the packages of food that we were sending as a result of money collected at concerts definitely wouldn't reach their intended recipients and that we were actually feeding the Germans. People who sent packages directly to prisoners had told us that packages for children were being intercepted. I believe, however, that packages actually arrived, because, after our return to France, people told me about it. For my part, I also sent packages to our family and to our friends. It became a ritual. In the evening, when I was at home, I prepared my packages. I had to ensure that each package didn't exceed three kilograms, that everything was well packed, and that items couldn't move around inside the package. I sent lentils, rice, and coffee. Unfortunately, the coffee hadn't been roasted according to French preferences. I learned about it later. Some people who were cleverer than others roasted it again . . . and they discovered that it was better than not having coffee at all! On one occasion, I even sent a child's overcoat cut in two. When Robert wasn't touring, he stayed beside me while I prepared my packages as we listened to rebroadcasts of concerts on the radio.

The Princeton University library was extremely high-level, and we visited it regularly. The museum possessed paintings of exceptional quality. I remember a superb painting by Hieronymus Bosch: a Christ being beaten by armed men with clubs during his ascent of Calvary. Together with Robert, we wondered whether Americans had bought this painting because the clubs resembled baseball bats?

During this time, we were often in contact with the Belgian art connoisseur Charles Leyrens, as well as the French Cabinet member Jacques Stern, who sought refuge in the United States as we'd done. Princeton had also welcomed supporters of the Spanish Republic, who formed a rather large community. We hosted dinners for one another, and that's how we became acquainted with Mme. Schiaparelli, the famous dress designer, who also left France when the war began. She'd bought a very quirky house not far from ours, and we saw each other quite often. I remember that once she said to me: "A well-dressed woman should live with two tailored suits: a black one and a white one. That way, you can be sure to be elegant at all times. Fabrics must be of truly fine quality, they should provide a perfect fit, and, in a word, they should be stylish. That's how you can be perfect under any circumstances in the winter or the summer. You can accessorize with jewelry or a pretty blouse, and you'll be perfect!" I recognized a tasteful and classy lady. After the war, we saw one another again in France, and we met rather regularly. This distinctly Parisian type of conversation uplifted me during this sad period.

During his train trips, Robert always read a lot, and he occasionally recorded his impressions in his datebook. In rereading his datebook for 1942, I observed that, in terms of François Mauriac's *Chemins de la mer*, he'd written: "Admirable!" At Princeton, we frequently saw André Maurois, who also dedicated a certain number of his novels to us.

On November 7, 1942, we learned of the Americans' landing in North Africa. We were in Chicago visiting one of our friends, a cultural attaché at the Consulate, who announced this news to us. Thus, the Americans were truly becoming involved in the old continent's war. Just before Christmas, we learned about the assassination of Admiral Darlan in Algiers, as well as De Gaulle's arrival in Algeria.

We followed all of these events passionately, and we talked about them among ourselves. The French community in Princeton gathered frequently to discuss the news. This is how we regularly saw André Maurois and Maurice Coindreau, who was the French translator for a large number of American writers and who'd taught at Princeton University before the war, although he didn't return to France. We became friends. At one point or another, Jean de Lacretelle, a friend of Coindreau's and an "adopted citizen" of Princeton, also joined us.

As he did each year, Robert reviewed the year at the end of 1942 and diligently included notes in his datebook: 145 hours of composing (He'd completed his *Concerto pour flûte*), 621 hours at the piano, 126 hours of teaching, 160 hours of copying, and 653 hours aboard trains, including thirty-five at night.

From this time forward, Robert began recording music more frequently. He prepared his recording sessions with Goddard Lieberson, the artistic director for Columbia Records, which became CBS Records during the

1960's. Goddard very quickly became a friend of ours. You know, because you knew him, what a charming man he was. He was very American and, at the same time, very much a gentleman. He made enormous contributions to disseminating music by means of records. One can cite his recordings of the entirety of Stravinsky's work; contemporary music under Robert Craft's guidance: Alban Berg, Anton Webern, and Arnold Schönberg, as well as the first recordings of Edgard Varèse. He was a pioneer in his own way. He'd obtained contracts with the New York Philharmonic Orchestra, the Philadelphia Orchestra, Bruno Walter, Eugene Ormandy, Rudolf Serkin, Isaac Stern, the Budapest Quartet, and, subsequently, the Cleveland Orchestra, and George Szell. Dmitri Mitropoulos belonged to his team. There's a long list. . . . This was a man with a fantastic flair, somewhat like Walter Legge at EMI. Adequate tribute can never be given to these promoters of music, men with culture, taste, and initiative at the same time, and who were capable of putting their trust in artists so that music could always be better served.

In New York, we met Léon Barzin, a French conductor who'd married a very wealthy American and was living in the United States. He'd created an orchestra for young people that he was teaching about the profession. His orchestra had been chosen by Leopold Stokowski for an entire series of New York concerts that were immensely successful. He would've liked to become John Barbirolli's successor at the head of the New York Philharmonic, but that didn't happen. He was a good conductor, but he lacked the stature of a Mitropoulos, a Szell, or a Rodzinski, however. After the war, he became the conductor of the Juilliard School's orchestra.

At the beginning of 1943, Robert left for his extensive winter tour. He played for the first time under the baton of George Szell in Boston. This became the beginning of an artistic collaboration and a friendship that would only end when they died.

Apart from his own career, Robert and I regularly gave two piano recitals, but it's true that I traveled increasingly less often with him because I preferred to stay with the children. Thérèse was still just a baby, and the boys needed my continuous presence.

Furthermore, I had to stay in Princeton because I was rather seriously ill. Since Thérèse's birth, I'd experienced frequent urinary tract infections that were enormously debilitating. Robert was very worried, and he telephoned me every day, even when he was on the other side of the United States.

That year, he'd traveled the entire West Coast, including Winnipeg, Portland, and San Francisco, where he played with Pierre Monteux as a conductor. He wrote in his datebook that he'd dined with Leonard Bernstein and Darius Milhaud, who were likewise there. Denver, Colorado Springs, and Dallas. Cities and concerts became interwoven according to the rhythm of his long train trips. Sometimes, a single trip would last twenty-two hours.

In March, my health problems subsided, and I was able to give a concert for two pianos with Robert in Rochester, New York. During this evening, when José Iturbi was conducting, we were present for the premiere of Robert's *Troisième Suite sur le nom de Rameau*.

In Saint Louis, Missouri, my husband performed under the baton of our dear friend Vladimir Golschmann, who conducted the city's orchestra. We also gave a concert for two pianos at the University of Indiana, at Bloomington. Then Robert traveled alone to Oxford, Mississippi. The river there is magnificent and peaceful. Paddle wheelers proceed downstream slowly and majestically. Completely like what can be seen in old engravings from the previous century: large white colonial houses whose porches have colonnades that can be seen from the river, behind the clusters of trees; luxuriant vegetation, where Spanish moss dangles from the trees and connects them to one another. On one occasion, we descended the river as far as Baton Rouge. Thus, in real life, I was able to experience the descriptions that so many American writers had made us dream of through their novels.

I listened rather frequently to the New York radio station WQXR. I recall that, in 1943, with the cellist Yves Chardon, I'd given a premiere there of the *Sonate pour piano et violoncello* that Robert had composed in 1936. I greatly enjoyed these radio concerts. At that time, radio possessed enormous impact.

On April 12, we celebrated Thérèse's first birthday. She was a delightful little girl who brought joy to all of us. Her brothers worshipped her, and Robert equally!

On May 7, we learned of the victory at Bizerte, and, just as he did whenever an important event in the war became known to us, Robert recorded it in his datebook. This was also the beginning of the campaign by Leclerc, who, after having left Chad with four soldiers, increased his forces as he proceeded across Africa. We knew an American woman who'd joined the 2nd Armored Division and for whom Leclerc was a deity.

Although it wasn't comparable with what happened in Europe, we also experienced rationing. First of all, there were fuel restrictions. We weren't allowed the necessary amount for making a round trip between our home and the railway station. For us, it was five kilometers going there and five kilometers to return. We'd compute the number of trips for a week, and we'd receive our rationed amount.

Milk and butter were also rationed. I made my own butter with cream from the two liters of milk that were delivered to our door every morning. This milk contained cream that was twenty centimeters thick! This rationing had nothing to do with what people experienced in France. . . . We didn't have any right to complain. And, what's more, we were free.

It was during this period that Robert finished his *Sarabande pour deux pianos*. We immediately started practicing it for hours at a time. It was included in his collection titled *Danses méditerranéennes*. In May, René Le Roy gave a premiere of the *Concerto pour flûte* that Robert had composed for him. In July, we returned to Great Barrington for the fourth American summer session of the Fontainebleau School. We rented a home four kilometers from the "château," in South Egremont. The Francescattis were our neighbors, and this allowed Zino and Robert to go on long bicycle excursions after working. The countryside was beautiful, and the heat was completely bearable in this region.

On July 23, we learned about the taking of Palermo by the Americans. We were assiduously listening to the radio, waiting for news.

Although Robert's schedule was overloaded, he did find enough time to create his own cadenza for Haydn's *Concerto*. Indeed, I hardly helped him at all that summer because I'd undergone an operation in June that debilitated me considerably. Therefore, Robert was obligated to teach his courses, to give master classes, and to oversee management of the school.

In addition, we'd planned to organize an end of session concert with the seventy students who'd converged on the school in Great Barrington, and the atmosphere was buzzing with excitement. Every floor of the imitation Renaissance chateau was a-twitter. On the cook's day off, we organized picnics in our house's garden. Everyone helped me prepare sandwiches. We were barbecuing hamburgers and sausages. The atmosphere was casual and fun-loving, and it was the "American way of life." The students had rented a horse-drawn cart to go from the chateau to the house. I can still see this vehicle going back and forth bringing its joyful and exuberant passengers. Bicycles weren't as fashionable during that period. Therefore, Robert and Zino created a spectacle when they traveled throughout the countryside on their two-wheelers. Today, in Central Park, certain paths are closed to automobiles so that New Yorkers can be allowed to ride their bicycles. It's the latest fashionable sport.

We also feverishly kept up with the news on the radio, and, on August 17, we heard about the liberation of Sicily. That renewed our hopes.

Robert continued to record all of these events in his datebook although he never included the titles of works that he was playing or the names of conductors whom he was working with! Yet he never failed to record on his scores the dates, times, orchestras, and conductors for each performance.

On September 8, he wrote: Italy out. On August 30, he'd mentioned an event with greater relevance to the family: Thérèse is walking.

At the same period, we listened on the radio to a pianist who was said to have the potential for a wonderful future. His name was Claudio Arrau. Later, we happened to meet, but I can't say that we really knew one another, even though we're from the same generation.

In the Fall, Jean entered Lawrenceville, a secondary school for boys. Because I wanted him to practice the piano for three hours every day, I asked the headmaster to release him from attending the religious services that took place before classes each morning. In this way, he was able to practice for an hour after breakfast. I obtained permission without too much difficulty because the headmaster knew that Jean was practicing the piano in a serious way. Usually, I drove him to the school, which was ten kilometers from our home. When I couldn't go with him, he took a bus.

I greatly admired the American school system with its daily hour of athletic activity. Jean adored it. He played soccer, but not American football! Although he was at an age where a youngster absorbs local customs quite quickly and where it's extremely easy to imitate one's peers, Jean remained very French in terms of his tastes. He was completely bilingual, and he completed a year of university education before definitively choosing his career as a pianist. Because he was filled with the spirit of camaraderie, he was well-liked and extremely popular. When I lost him thirty years later, I received poignant letters from his former classmates.

In fact, we were living in a refugee community. We often saw the Oppenheims, who left Germany in order to escape from Nazism. They'd lived through a horrible drama. Mr. Oppenheim's parents hadn't wanted to leave Germany with their son, because they believed that they were too old to start a new life. In order to escape from antisemitism, they committed suicide. . . . They were a family that deeply loved music. They'd known Brahms, and they possessed Schubert manuscripts that Mr. Oppenheim had brought with him, and he'd entrusted them to the library at Princeton University. One day, he very kindly offered a copy of the manuscript for the *Impromptus* to Robert, who was delighted to possess this document that allowed him to see certain details written in Schubert's own hand.

Einstein was, of course, one of the most prominent figures in this uprooted German community. He'd kept his German ways, although he was profoundly anti-Nazi. He lived amid German furnishings. At home, he spoke German with his sister and stepdaughter. He was a man of extraordinary simplicity. He always traveled on foot to the Institute that was located outside the town. This Institute was his life.

He adored children, and he'd adopted Thérèse immediately. I can recall a charming scene. Once when we'd gone to visit him, he'd taken Thérèse in his arms. She was probably about three years old. She stroked his completely white hair, and he'd allowed her to do this! After he placed her on the floor, and after we sat down, Thérèse approached his feet so that she could stroke his furry moccasins. At home, Einstein wore fur-lined moccasins that he'd wear without socks! You know how much children love fur, and, indeed, Einstein let Thérèse enjoy this childlike pleasure! He even seemed delighted.

One day during the Fall, in the same year of 1943, Robert was giving a recital in Saint Louis, Missouri when he experienced a somewhat annoying incident: one of the pedals on his piano broke . . . and he had to play an entire Mozart sonata without pedals. Before continuing with his recital, he requested replacement of his piano. There happened to be a piano on the stage, and it was being used for rehearsals. In order for everything to go more quickly, he'd tried to help the stagehands push the piano to the center of the stage. A catastrophe! . . . one of the piano's legs broke! The press seized upon this incident, and, shortly thereafter, we were to read in *Time Magazine:* "Robert Casadesus, the pianist who breaks pianos, etc." "What fine publicity," his manager said to him.

In regard to pianos, Robert always said that what would be fantastic for a pianist would be to have several pianos available that he or she could choose from according to the work that was to be played. For Mozart, he'd play on a Pleyel or an Érard instead of a Steinway, which is superb for Brahms or Schumann, although it lacks the lightness and clearness that's necessary for Mozart. . . . In Russia, Robert had been delighted to be able to play Liszt and Chopin on a Bechstein, which sounds quite well for music of that type.

Robert was perfectly capable of adapting to a new piano. Moreover, he used to say with a smile that it was the same problem as with conductors! He could also adapt very well to conductors who liked him considerably because he was able to follow them. On one occasion, with Saint-Saëns' *Concerto No 4*, a conductor completely omitted a measure, and Robert skipped it with him, thereby avoiding a catastrophe! There's a golden rule for musicians, as there is for actors, too: namely never stopping, regardless of what happens. Always. That's the least of catastrophes. Better a hitch than a total blackout.

At the end of November, Robert played in Pittsburgh with Fritz Reiner conducting. In the orchestra, among the first violins, there was a young thirteen or fourteen year old violinist who became a famous conductor: Lorin Maazel. He must have been only about fifteen years old when he began conducting. You know that he was a child prodigy. This was the first time that Robert had met him. During the rehearsal, he played with his legs crossed, which isn't the conventional position for violinists! Reiner also told him in a stern but also kindly tone: "You'll see when you're a conductor how enjoyable it is to see musicians sitting any way they wish or looking somewhere else instead of doing what they need to be doing!" I think that Maazel didn't appreciate this public reproach, but he must have understood it later. Robert liked to remind him of this distant recollection. . . . They always enjoyed being together. We knew his parents, who were living in Paris when he was born. His father was a singer, and his mother was a talented musician. In spite of his returning to the United States, Maazel always continued speaking French. I knew his first wife, who was an Englishwoman, and their two children. His second wife, Israïl, was an excellent pianist. They also had two delightful children. I recently met his third wife, who is young and charming. They had a son. I like Maazel very much, and I know both his strengths and his shortcomings! Maazel was trained by Reiner's assistant, Vladimir Bakaleinikoff. This Russian, who'd emigrated to the United States a long time ago, was enormously talented. He'd obtained a special authorization so that Lorin could conduct the orchestra when he was still quite young.

# Chapter 14

# Introducing Jean Casadesus, the Family's Third Pianist

The end of the year 1943 was marked by a major event in our lives as parents: Jean gave his first concert. Indeed, it was his first public recital. This baptism by fire took place in Princeton, at the Present Day Club. Anyone can imagine our feelings! The audience gave him a veritable ovation, to such an extent that our anxiety gave way to a certain pride that was quite legitimate for us as his parents! Now the family had one more pianist.

Robert and Zino Francescatti practiced together with increasing frequency. They'd manage to put together as many as ten different sonatas in a single day. They centered their repertoire upon piano-violin duos by Beethoven, Debussy, and Fauré. Later, they recorded Beethoven's ten *Sonatas*, which continue to be a standard for interpreting these chamber music masterpieces.

For my part, I gladly devoted myself to Robert's works that I was glad to include in my programs on a regular basis. During this period, I frequently played the *Deuxième sonate pour violon et piano* with our friend Guilet as my partner. I also played Robert's *Études*.

In June 1944, we learned that events were accelerating in Europe. In his datebook, Robert recorded all the news that he was hearing on the radio on a daily basis. June 3: Capturing of Rome; June 6: Landing at Le Havre. Later, we learned that it hadn't occurred specifically at Le Havre, and we understood that most Americans were unfamiliar with the coast of Normandy in a detailed way. Le Havre had been cited as a reference, because everyone could identify the terminus of the New York/France line. You can't imagine how important these days were to us. . . . We spent nearly all our time with our ears glued to the radio.

In New York, we met the painter André Girard, a member of the Resistance from the very start, who'd been sent on a mission to the United States. Through him, we learned details about the Resistance movement that were wholly unknown to us, as you can realize. After his mission, André Girard stayed in the United States. He often told us about what was happening in the clandestine milieux, and we were able to measure the danger that faced those who'd joined this undercover struggle. He himself was directly affected because his wife, who was also a Resistance member, had been deported, and he obviously hadn't received any news about her. He lived in anguish because he knew the fate that the Gestapo reserved for those who fell into its hands. A few years afterward, he became Jean's father-in-law when Jean married his daughter Evie, who is none other than Danièle Delorme's sister. Jean had met both at the Conservatory, where they were enrolled in the same *solfège* class just before the war.

During a luncheon one day, Leopold Stokowski suggested to Robert that he'd gladly conduct his *Deuxième concerto pour piano* that he'd had an opportunity to hear and whose style he admired. You can imagine Robert's joy at playing one of his own works under Stokowski's conductorship! As a prodigious musician who was passionate about all types of music, Stokowski was fascinated by recorded sound. He oversaw the quality of his recordings with scrupulous attention and required high level reproduction. He no longer needed to reinforce his reputation among sound engineers! I think that, with his having been an organist in his youth, he'd retained a preoccupation with defining sound colors. He was an extremely important figure in music, but he was very down to earth despite his star status. He was the principal sponsor of Varèse, Ives, Stravinsky, and Berg, as well as Prokofiev, for whom he conducted premieres of a sizeable number of his works in the United States. He was a remarkable interpreter of Mahler, Shostakovich, or Sibelius. His extremely long life—he died at the age of ninety-five—allowed him to conduct music from both the twentieth century and the nineteenth century. At this time, there were rumors about his relationship with Greta Garbo and his subsequent marriage to Cornelia Vanderbilt, who was forty years younger than Stokowski.

During this period, our professional concerns somewhat took the back seat. Of course, we kept on working, but our attention gravitated mostly toward the other side of the Atlantic. Despite this excitement, which was reinforced by the distance, we needed to prepare for the summer courses in Great Barrington. The main problem was still that of renting pianos. How to obtain approximately fifteen pianos became a real brainteaser . . . and, once again, I had to involve myself in the trials and tribulations of knocking on doors.

After this canvassing that was exhausting for me, we took a vacation on Nantucket, as we did every year. Thérèse, who'd just turned two years old, wanted at all costs to swim like her brothers. She plunged into the sea without any trepidation, and she took much delight in splashing everyone.

At the end of August, we learned about the liberation of Paris. I can't describe our joy to you! Moreover, we immediately celebrated this event with our students. I absolutely wanted to offer them something typically French---and I only found some Dubonnet---which flowed in abundance.

Amid this jubilation, Robert found the time to create a composition inspired by the liberation of Paris.

Robert and Zino gave a concert in the small auditorium that we'd set up in the chateau (at Great Barrington). This was one of their first public concerts! Indeed, their first truly professional concert took place at the Bohemian Club in New York, after Great Barrington had closed.

At the end of August, a telegram informed us of Aunt Rosette's death.

She died in Paris in July, and this time lag made the shock even more painful. We learned afterward that she'd left southern France to begin living in our apartment, so that it wouldn't undergo requisitioning. Throughout the war, Marius had avoided requisitioning by lending the apartment to friends. Among them, there were Simone Signoret and Yves Allegret. . . . Losing Aunt Rosette was a cruel blow for my husband. He suffered profoundly from having been unable to be with his father and his aunt in their final moments.

In October, Robert left for his long yearly tour across the United States.

In San Francisco, he saw Pierre Monteux, with whom he was in complete communion. I haven't spoken to you yet about his wife! She was an American. Because she was extremely proud of her husband, she criticized all the other conductors very openly and without exceptions. That's how she said to me: "My husband's much better than Toscanini. Of course, Arturo conducts by heart, but he isn't the only one. Pierre also conducts without a score, and the only difference is that Pierre has a far more extensive repertoire than Toscanini, who settles for always playing the same 'stuff' . . . the great classics, the Romantics. And that's all! Whereas Pierre also conducts contemporary music." What she was saying was true enough, but she showed such a strong bias.

We ended the year with a concert for two pianos and recording sessions for works by Chabrier, Satie, Milhaud, Debussy, Ravel, and Casadesus with one or two pianos.

A short interval for the New Year's Eve celebration, in Princeton. During that period, we'd listened to the radio premiere of Bela Bartók's *Concerto for Orchestra* by the Boston Symphony Orchestra, with Koussevitzky conducting. We were immediately fascinated by this work's richness of sound, and it became a twentieth-century classic.

In July, we informed the approximately fifty students who were coming to Great Barrington that we'd undoubtedly be returning to Fontainebleau in the following year.

That was a demonstration of optimism! In fact, we naively believed that, with the end of the war, life would soon renew its course, as it had done before. We didn't imagine the impact created by five years of occupation, and we'd have to wait until 1946 to return to France.

In 1945, when we left Great Barrington, we turned the property over to Serge Koussevitzky, who converted the chateau into an extension of Tanglewood. Arthur Honegger and Bohuslav Martinu would be teaching composition there.

We'd met Martinu in Paris before the war because he always attended premieres of his works at the Société Nationale de Musique. We subsequently saw him again in New York, where he'd taken refuge. He regularly came to Princeton University to teach composition, and he began living in our house when we returned to France.

One day when he'd been visiting us in Great Barrington, he was the victim of a senseless accident. He was chatting on the terrace, and as he was talking, he unfortunately stepped backward without realizing that he was standing on the edge of the steps of the main stairway! He experienced a serious fall because he fractured his skull.

Robert greatly admired Martinu's music. He also liked him as a person, as a figure with exceptional human qualities, who didn't disdain good food and good wine. He had only one flaw: he was terribly absent-minded. His wife had told us that, on one occasion where it was expected that one of his quartets would be performed for a premiere, and when it was impossible to locate the score, he had to rewrite it during the night! He'd composed a new quartet. . . . He wrote a lullaby for Thérèse. After returning to Europe, he chose to reside in Switzerland with assistance from the conductor Paul Sacher. That's where he died in 1959 after a long illness. It was only after his death that Czechoslovakia honored him properly.

In February, our landlady informed us that her husband was returning from the war and that we'd need to find another home. I can tell you that I hardly had the time to undertake a search for another house, especially because it was becoming exceedingly difficult to find one with all the soldiers who were coming home, while their wives were reclaiming the apartments that they'd been renting during their husbands' absence. I was distraught and devastated! How were we going to get along? Robert was extremely busy with his concerts, we needed to keep practicing the piano, and now there were three pianists in the house. Faced by the failure of my searches, we had to move into a hotel while we were waiting to find something. The hotel had a charming name—the Peacock Inn, but it cost us a fortune!

We began practicing in a friend's home. All this was hardly easy. Personally speaking, I was panic-stricken by this arrangement. Robert, on the other hand, seemed quite happy, and he spent hours composing or orchestrating. When we needed to practice with two pianos, we went to the home of our friends the Harpers, who were fortunate to own two pianos. Although this situation was helpful to us, they were compelled to put up with our hours of rehearsals stoically. When Robert had lessons, the Labatuts lent him their home. Luckily, this nomadism only lasted for a month. That amount of time had already seemed unduly long to me.

During this period, Robert recorded Saint-Saëns' *Concerto No 4 pour piano* with Artur Rodzinski as his conductor. It was also at this point that he had Charles Rosen and Grant Johannesen as pupils. These two pianists pursued careers that you're familiar with, and neither one forgot his stay in Great Barrington. Charles Rosen studied at Princeton University, and he contacted Robert to practice French music, for which he had a true passion, as he did for everything that was French.

It was also in 1945 that we attended Grant Johannesen's first recital in New York, at the Town Hall, which is the hall where recitals took place. He included Robert's *Sonate No 2 pour piano*, which, incidentally, was dedicated to him, in his program.

Robert's *Cello Concerto* was also performed that year in Minneapolis. The French cellist Yves Chardon, who'd lived in the United States for a long time, was the soloist, with Mitropoulos conducting.

Musical life in Princeton was extremely active. The most renowned musicians gave concerts there. We regularly heard the Busches, Fritz, Adolf, and Hermann, and the harpsichordist Wanda Landowska. She'd introduced combined recitals—half piano and half harpsichord. It seemed as if she was using the piano as a foil for demonstrating that the harpsichord was far more interesting! She was very whimsical and would sometimes make people wait three-quarters of an hour before coming onto the stage. In the hall, there were rumors that it was because someone had forgotten to send roses to her hotel. It was also said that she'd only sleep on black sheets. She herself said that she slept well only on dark-colored sheets. All this gossip was of no importance since, above all, she was a marvelous artist. Because she performed in extremely large halls, she'd promoted production of harpsichords with sound ranges that were far more powerful than those of harpsichords from the seventeenth and eighteenth centuries. She had her devotees, and she had a superb career. Today there are people who blame her for having brought attention to the harpsichord. . . . That's how it is with fads.

Robert and I also gave several concerts on behalf of the Red Cross, which was working quite actively to come to the aid of people who'd suffered from the war.

On April 12, which was Thérèse's birthday, we learned of Roosevelt's death. On May 7, we learned that the Germans had signed an unconditional surrender at General Eisenhower's headquarters. When this news was announced, a crowd filled New York's streets. General jubilation broke out. A concert was organized in the morning in Central Park, and we participated in it. We played the piece for two pianos that Robert had composed for the liberation of Paris. On the same evening, we played it again in an improvised concert in Carnegie Hall.

Shortly thereafter, our friend André Girard had organized a visit to the famous Barnes Collection for us. Barnes had a reputation for being ill-tempered and for rarely opening his door to guests. It was said that he'd refused to welcome Le Corbusier and had uttered a dreadfully coarse word to cancel his visit. Barnes greeted us very amicably. He was wearing a Breton fisherman's outfit made of a red-brick fabric, along with a navy-blue beret, undoubtedly to appear more French! He was resplendent! He was a perfect guide with vast erudition, and he was completely familiar with the smallest details in the history of each of his paintings. One of his paintings was precisely a Seurat that portrayed nude women. It had come from a storage area at the Louvre, which didn't want to display the painting on account of the subjects' nudity. When it was placed on sale, Barnes bought it. . . . He invited us to stay for dinner and told us that he'd arranged preparation for a meal *à la française* with excellent wines. His invitation placed us in a quandary because Jean was playing Beethoven's *5th Concerto* that evening with the Princeton University orchestra, and missing his concert was out of the question for us. Therefore, we declined his invitation. Shortly thereafter, Girard and the art dealer who'd accompanied him told us that not only had we missed a delicious meal but also that the wines were sublime.

The concert took place in Alexander Hall. Jean had just graduated from the Lawrenceville School, and he was eager to attend Princeton University. I'd been greatly impressed by the ceremony for awarding diplomas, which, as you know, possesses an extremely formal quality in American schools. It was difficult for me to believe that I already had such a mature son, and all of a sudden, I felt myself aging.

Our life continued at its usual pace. When we were in Princeton, we ate regularly with our little French clan. All of us were much more relaxed after the liberation of Paris. During this time, we often saw the American Composer Roger Sessions, who taught composition at the University. He was three years older than Robert, and he died in 1985. We often traveled on the train together when we were going to New York, and we had long conversations about music. He greatly admired Hector Berlioz.

Before Great Barrington reopened, we took our traditional vacation on Nantucket, which always delighted Guy and Thérèse.

On August 6, the Hiroshima bomb was dropped, and on the 11th, the Japanese surrendered.

The "French Relief" concerts continued, and the one that took place at the Metropolitan Opera in the Fall took on the character of an exceptional occurrence. Anne Morgan from the Morgan Bank, who was the sponsor, was intensely Francophile. She let her joy burst forth, and she expressed her love for our country that had finally been delivered. Indeed, long months of struggling remained for truly restoring freedom, but, from the vantage point of New York, everything seemed to have been completed. This concert brought together all the French celebrities who were living in the United States. I'd recognized among the spectators Charles Boyer, Lily Pons, and Rachel Meyer, who were joined by friends of France: the composer Gian Carlo Menotti and the critic Virgil Thompson, a devoted friend of France, where he'd made long visits before the war and afterward. Now he lives in New York.

That year Robert began orchestrating the finale of Saint-Saëns' *Concerto No 5*. This project had been close to his heart for a long time. He'd often discussed it with Ravel. Both believed that the finale wasn't at the level of other movements and that this was a shame. Ravel had even used the adjective "pathetic" to characterize it. On the other hand, Saint-Saëns had written a toccata that he'd titled *Toccata pour le concerto No 5*, which was superb. Robert therefore came up with the idea of orchestrating the toccata and replacing the existing finale with it. Durand, the publisher of the concerto, agreed with the concept, and that encouraged Robert to start working. A few years later, with the New York Philharmonic conducted by Mitropoulos, Jean performed *Concerto No 5* with the toccata arranged by his father. Moreover, he always played it that way. Unfortunately, none of his colleagues adopted this finale. They undoubtedly preferred to keep the initial finale that can indeed be deemed less inspiring, without offering surprises for listeners who are accustomed to it.

In December, we went to hear Grace Moore when she was singing Gustave Charpentier's *Louise*. She died shortly afterward in an airplane accident. We were incredibly sad because we liked her so much. She was a striking and extremely charming woman.

In 1946, we began taking airplanes to travel within the United States or to travel to Canada. You can't imagine what this meant for us because it's so commonplace to take a plane today. Robert didn't fail to record this significant first experience in his datebook: "La Guardia Airport: airplane delayed for five hours." He was traveling to Canada, where he'd be playing with the Montreal Orchestra, whose conductor at this time was Dufour, and Robert was furious about this delay. Nevertheless, we still waited a few years before plunging into an Atlantic crossing. I greatly enjoyed boat trips that allowed us to have a few days of vacationing under idyllic conditions . . . especially when the weather was good.

We bought Jean an old Ford for his birthday. It was high on its wheels, and it cost us the royal sum of fifty dollars! As you can imagine, he was delighted, and he even drove his brother to school. He drove somewhat recklessly as every boy his age does, just to show off in front of others. I constantly gave him recommendations about being careful as every mother does. . . . Like all young people, he went out on Saturday nights, of course, and I lived in anguish until he returned. Our house was in the woods, and I could hear gears shifting whenever cars approached the bottom of the hill. From midnight on, I listened for the slightest automobile noises. . . . I couldn't breathe anymore! Incidentally, for the first time, Robert wrote in his datebook: "Jean's return: 3:00 a.m." The following morning, he told us, when we'd expressed our objections to him, that he'd had a breakdown as he approached the hill.

The year 1946 was truly an important year in our life. First, it was the year of our return to France, after an absence of six years, but it's also the year of Jean's entry into the profession. In 1946, he won the first prize in the Young People's Concerts competition, where the award was a concert with the Philadelphia Orchestra conducted by Eugene Ormandy. So much emotion for us! The program included Ravel's *Concerto en sol majeur*. Robert and I arrived after the morning rehearsal. Jean left the stage telling us that he didn't feel very well, that he must have caught a cold. In the evening on the preceding day, he'd gone out with a friend and had gone to bed late, which isn't recommended before a concert. He was coughing constantly, and he had a fever of at least 102 degrees. I immediately telephoned the Orchestra's management to explain that Jean wasn't well and that there was a risk of jeopardizing the concert. The manager didn't want to believe me, however, and he replied: "But Mrs. Casadesus, you're nervous. Jean played very well this morning. You shouldn't have any worries. Everything will go very well!" He believed that Jean was having stage fright that was completely ordinary and that, as his mother, I was trying to protect him. Without knowing which saint I should invoke for making the manager understand that Jean was truly ill, I telephoned some friends in order to ask their advice, and none of them wanted to believe my account about his being ill. They all thought that I too had stage fright, and they all advised me to relax! "Take it easy, dear!" they were all saying unanimously. I went back to see Jean in his bedroom, and I explained to him that nobody wanted to believe that he had the flu. Then, I deployed all the remedies that I knew to get rid of his sore throat, which was becoming increasingly painful, including application of hot compresses to his throat. I'd already used this folk remedy, which was infallible for preventing a constant dry cough. Jean's cough subsided, but he played nevertheless with a 102-degree fever. Very honestly, I must acknowledge that he interpreted this extremely well-known concerto very well. The next day, however, we drove him to the hospital in a dreadful state. Jean never forgot his initial appearance with the Philadelphia Orchestra. . . . As for us, we started the new year with a concert in Washington, at Constitution Hall. This round hall wasn't ideal for listening to music. Furthermore, I think that it's more annoying for musicians, who can't hear what they're playing, than it is for audiences, because sound travels in a circle.

Shortly thereafter, we went to Chicago, where Robert would perform with the Minneapolis Orchestra, with Mitropolous conducting. The critics weren't highly laudatory because they believed that the orchestra was out of tune. In other words, this meant that the orchestra had played sour notes. This wasn't wholly accurate, however. A few days later, I gave a recital at the Arts Club. Mitropolous came to listen to me, and I found this quite touching.

In February, we received a visit from Danièle Girard, who wasn't using the name Danièle Delorme yet . . . she'd come to see her father. Her mother hadn't returned from deportation yet, and both were extremely concerned because all the camps had been liberated. Somewhat later, we finally learned about her return.

Danièle was so pleased to have been able to leave France. The war had been difficult for her and her sisters. She'd begun to do theatre and films, but she also had to take on small jobs to earn a living. She'd announced to us that she was expecting a baby and that its father was a young actor, like her. His name was Daniel Gélin. She seemed extremely preoccupied with acquiring a house soon, and she dreamed of moving into it.

It was also the beginning of 1946 when Robert and Zino completed their first record for Columbia. Robert was also spending long hours composing.

Our return to France was approaching. On June 6, we went to say farewell to Professor Einstein, and, on June 7, we sailed on the *S.S. John Ericson.* During the entire crossing, Robert didn't stop working on copies. I felt that he needed to have an activity that would neutralize the anxiousness that was overwhelming both of us. . . . At last, on June 17, at 10:00 a.m., we docked in Le Havre, at Pier Number 10.

How can I describe our feelings to you? It's impossible to tell you. . . . We had lumps in our throats, but, at the same time, we were happy to be returning to our country after such a long absence, and we were so sad that our first view was the view of Le Havre in ruins. That was a horrible shock. In fact, we spent these hours in a daze. We were literally floating. We were in some kind of otherworldly state, and we felt a form of paralysis invading our bodies. We felt weak as if we were anesthetized yet with our eyes still open. We'd waited for this moment such a long time . . . the moment had arrived, and we felt we were experiencing it so poorly.

We quickly boarded the train that was intended to take us to the Gare Saint-Lazare. A five-hour trip that seemed like an eternity to us. With profound sadness, we discovered our wounded country.

Upon arriving in Paris, we went to a hotel that wasn't far from our apartment, because there was no possibility of staying there in the immediate future. The boiler and the water heater had burst . . . the furniture had been moved . . . in short, the apartment was unrecognizable! I must say that this homecoming wasn't what we'd dreamed about for so long.

There was joy, nonetheless. The joy of seeing the entire family again: my sister, the Casadesus family . . . finally, everyone.

Two days after our arrival, Robert went to the Salle Pleyel to practice the piano.

We had to relearn how to live here.

We went to the cemetery, to the tombs of Robert Senior and Aunt Rosette.

Thérèse didn't understand why we'd praised beautiful France so much. She discovered a country in ruins and found that the food wasn't good.

On June 25, Robert gave a recital at the Salle Pleyel. After the concert, Mme. Schiaparelli gave a dinner in our honor. Life was taking shape again.

# Chapter 15

# Da Capo

Reopening Fontainebleau was accomplished very quickly by July 4, which, as you know, is Independence Day for Americans. Jean joined us, and he was accompanied by seventeen students. That was quite a small number in comparison with the previous year in Great Barrington! It must be said that many parents were hesitant about sending their children to France, where food rationing was still going on. The former American ambassador, Dean Jay, gave us a very official welcome on July 6. Jean-Paul Alaux, the President of the Écoles d'Art, was present, as well as Mr. Dommange, the British consul, along with the Mayor and the Prefect. It felt somewhat like the return of the Prodigal Son!

We started with our work. Classes were formed, and the faculty members took up their positions. Paul Bazelaire was teaching cello, and André Asselin taught violin. Robert was appointed as the administrative director, and this didn't release him from his courses. We organized concerts again in the Jeu de Paume Hall, and faculty members participated in them. At the beginning of August, we gave a party for the students. I remember the date quite well. It was August 9, the date of my birthday. The students had found out, and they literally covered me with flowers. Robert and I played works by the Spanish composer Manuel Infante, who'd joined us for the Fontainebleau School's reopening.

Between his courses and his administrative work, Robert found the time to put on a session of sonatas with Marius—they were so glad to be reunited!

During our free time, we rode our bicycles in the area, thereby returning to our pre-war habits.

One evening, we went to dinner in the home of the Salabert family, who'd kept their house in Grey-sur-Loing. André Salabert was in excellent form, and he informed us about his plans. He wanted to establish a branch of his music publishing company in New York, and he was passionately looking toward the future. He was full of ideas. He wanted to open his activities to the New

World and to new music. He possessed an extraordinary flair. Unfortunately, he died in an airplane accident before being able to fulfill his plans.

Concerts took place throughout the summer at Fontainebleau. Robert resumed his duos with Marius. I accompanied Pierre Bernac in an art song cycle. In spite of its somewhat limited staff, the School reached its second wind, and we were already preparing for the coming year during a Board meeting whose members included Francis Casadesus and Mr. Dommange. Everyone was full of energy, plans were being made, and the issue of renting pianos, which had arisen here as it did in America, was being resolved.

Touring resumed very quickly.

Robert and I departed for Belgium and Holland: Brussels, the Hague, Amsterdam, and Utrecht, where I played on a radio broadcast. We were glad to observe that, after a long absence and after events that were so difficult for Europe, the world of music hadn't lost its vitality. We hadn't been forgotten . . . and that warmed our hearts. Our return to France didn't cause us to forego our American commitments; quite to the contrary, we sailed on the *S.S. America* at the end of November. We arrived in New York on November 30, and, as of December 3, Robert resumed his customary winter tour. We decided to buy a house in Princeton that would be our home base during our stays in the United States.

After having earned his diploma from the Princeton Country Day School, Guy decided to return to France in order to prepare for his studies in Political Science in Paris. As for Thérèse, she accompanied us because it was impossible to leave her alone in France for six months. Robert gave his yearly recital at Carnegie Hall, and we played together in Philadelphia.

In May, in New York, we met Mitropoulos again, when he'd just become the director of the New York Philharmonic Orchestra. He'd allowed himself to be persuaded to come to New York, but he confessed to us that he'd regretted leaving his orchestra in Minneapolis that he'd molded and that he got along with so well.

Initially, as is always true with the New York Philharmonic, he gained enormous success. Everyone was hailing him as a genius! That's true because he was a remarkable musician and an excellent pianist. He had fantastic brio. As an extraordinarily open-minded musician, he was a proponent of varied programs that allowed people to listen to repertory works and to new works. In addition, he frequently conducted Robert's works, he said, and many others said it after him, that this was the only way of accustoming people to hear sounds that could seem unusual or aggressive to ears that were familiar with Bach, Beethoven, and Tchaikovsky. At this time, this concept was highly innovative.

He conducted with expansive gestures, activating his shoulders! He had an athletic side . . . in contrast to Fritz Reiner, for example, who conducted by means of his fingertips or just his hands. One had sweeping gestures, and the other kept them in check. Strangely enough, this divergence offered almost the same outcome. An excellent outcome! Mitropoulos possessed an incredible memory, and he conducted not only concerts but rehearsals without using scores. He was also a perfect opera conductor. As a confirmed bachelor, he once asked Robert how he managed to reconcile his family life and his career, and he stated that, for his part, he didn't have the time to manage both. Much later, the pianist Jorge Bolet, whom I met at the Curtis Institute, told me the same thing. I can assure you that Robert was perfectly capable of reconciling both!

We had a genuine affection for Mitropoulos, beyond the pleasure of working together. He was a person with exceptional kindness and profound humility, which is a quality that isn't always extremely widespread among conductors.

Robert was once again crisscrossing the United States in every direction, and he took advantage of his long train trips for composing, writing orchestration or copying out. During this period, he finished his *Cinquième symphonie.*

Throughout his touring, he met students from Great Barrington, and these friendships were among the greatest joys of his life.

One day—when I'd stayed in Princeton with Thérèse—I received a telephone call from Robert, who announced that he'd broken three ribs by accidentally falling in the bathtub. I was distraught and I advised him to cancel his concerts because it's impossible to breathe normally with three broken ribs. Although it may surprise you, breathing is actually essential for a pianist as it likewise is for any instrumentalist. Without hesitation, I told him that I'd board the first airplane, and do you know what he shouted from the other end of the United States? "Absolutely not! I forbid you to take a plane; there could be an accident!" There you have an example of my husband's optimistic nature! In order to avoid challenging him, I took a train, but what a trip! Three days to go, and three days to return.

Quite obviously, he refused to cancel his commitments, and he played while he was completely bandaged. Among other works, he played Brahms' *2nd Concerto,* and that was truly torture for him. He therefore replaced it with a concerto by Mozart that didn't require such intense breathing and so much muscle strength. Then he continued his tour, saying that he felt better on stage. He had to think about what he was playing there, and he could forget his pain.

It was impossible for him to undress alone or to put his shoes on. It's true that he could have stopped and relied upon his insurance, but he didn't want to. One day, he recounted the incident to Pierre Monteux, who said with a burst of amused laughter, "You've played with three broken ribs. As for me, I conducted once with six cracked ribs." Monteux loved to "crack a joke."

He always had a paternally affectionate attitude toward Robert, whom he'd known since he was quite young, and whom he regarded somewhat as his son. There was a difference of twenty-four years between them.

It wasn't Robert's style to cancel his commitments because of illness or even for something more serious. I've seen him play with a fever of 102 degrees F. For him, commitments were sacred.

That year, we experienced the joy of meeting Mme. Girard, who joined her husband in Princeton after her release. It was quite difficult to find housing, and I helped her with her searches. Finally, they found a house, and André Girard was so delighted with it that he painted Parisian scenes on the dining room walls! At the beginning of 1947, Robert didn't stop working. He was rehearsing with Zino, and he was recording for Columbia. He wasn't an enthusiast as far as recording goes! He yielded to technical requirements without too much reluctance, but he detested listening to recordings in a booth! Usually, he raced off once the last note was played, while letting the technicians and the artistic director take responsibility for judging his work.

In May, we returned to France on a freighter that was actually sailing to Antwerp. It was extremely difficult to cross the Atlantic at this time because regular lines hadn't resumed their voyages. The *S.S. Oufaliz* carried nearly a dozen passengers, along with mostly freight. Our crossing lasted ten days, which I didn't find unpleasant.

As always, Robert took advantage of these long stretches of quiet time by composing.

We gradually returned to our *à la française* habits, but we were incredibly surprised by the atmosphere that prevailed in France. We observed a genuine enmity between those who'd been active Resistance members and those who'd been, shall we say, "sympathizers" and whom people didn't hesitate to brand as collaborators. These divisions could exist within the same family, and, because we hadn't experienced the war period directly "on the ground," they surprised us.

Of course, we were happily reunited with all of our friends. At a dinner given by Mme. Salabert, we saw Arthur Honegger, whom we hadn't seen for years. Our absence had cut us off from so many of our old friendships.

Honegger was a very amusing man with an unanticipated exhibitionistic and clownish side. He adored putting on costumes, and no one imagined that a man with such a serious appearance, could be capable of lifting up his shirt in the middle of a salon in order to display his belly adorned with designs that he himself had created!

At this time, he was living with Andrée Vaurabourg, whom he married later when they had a daughter. He'd fathered a son with the singer Claire Croiza many years earlier.

Before the Fontainebleau session, we rented an automobile, and we traveled to southern France for a few days of rest. We were shocked as we discovered our country in ruins. Cities still bore the scars of bombing and battles for their liberation. It was truly a desolate spectacle. We hadn't imagined that France would've been mutilated to such an extent.

In Nice, we met Emmanuel Chabrier's daughter-in-law, who owned some of her father-in-law's scores, including some that were unfinished. She asked Robert whether he'd want to finish a few of them. When we returned to Paris, Robert discussed the idea with Francis Poulenc, who adored Chabrier's music, and, after reading these drafts, they both decided that it was difficult to make use of this material that was often quite scanty.

Robert accepted a few pupils again, and during this period, he regularly supervised Claude Helffer and Jean-Claude Ambrosini as they practiced. Ambrosini died several years ago when he was still young.

In July, during the annual session in Fontainebleau, Robert departed for several days in order to give recitals or concerts here and there. Taking advantage of his trip to Interlaken, he traveled to the Olsteig Cemetery to visit the tombs of Schumann's two daughters. This was undoubtedly his way of offering homage to this composer whom he adored. Furthermore, he believed that Schumann's works didn't have the prominence that they deserved in concert programs, whereas they are sublime. As for Robert, he played Schumann frequently.

At Fontainebleau, there was always the same ritual: courses, masterclasses, as well as students' and instructors' concerts, which received favorable responses within our community. Nadia Boulanger played four hand duets with the composer Jean Françaix, while Francis Poulenc and Pierre Bernac gave indescribable art songs recitals!

At this time, Jean joined the team. He didn't teach courses yet, but he participated in concerts as a soloist. In addition, during the same year, which was 1947, he took part in the Geneva competition, where he successfully completed the initial examinations. Robert was a member of the examining jury, but, in compliance with the rules, he abstained from voting for his son! Jean obtained a first-place award. He'd just turned twenty.

As for Guy, we were certain by now that music wouldn't be his career, notwithstanding genuine gifts for the piano and the violin. He'd just entered the Lycée Carnot because, in spite of the difficulties that he could encounter, he'd decided upon pursuing a French curriculum after highly successful schooling that was entirely American. He was hoping that, from France, he could pursue a career in international affairs.

Through our friend André Girard, we became acquainted with Georges Rouault at this time. We'd seen some of his paintings in the United States and had even bought reproductions of his works on post cards. In Pittsburgh, we'd admired his *King David*. When we visited him at the quite opulent apartment where he lived near the Gare de Lyon, we showed him the post card with *King David*, and he seemed completely astonished that this painting should be in the United States.

Shortly thereafter, I got the idea of giving Robert a lithograph by Rouault for his birthday and of having it dedicated to him by the artist. Robert had been deeply moved by Rouault's *Stations of the Cross*, and I was therefore looking for a subject associated with this religious theme. On the Rue des Saints Pères, I found an exceptionally fine Christ, and I requested a meeting with Rouault, so that he could dedicate it. I was greeted by one of his daughters, and I gave her the lithograph. A certain amount of time went by without my receiving any word. Finally, she called me and asked me to come and see the lithograph, without giving me any other details. At that point, I wondered whether the lithograph was a forgery, because of her having been so mysterious. That wasn't the case, but, when she opened the door for me, she immediately asked me not to show her father this lithograph, because he'd be furious upon seeing that it wasn't consistent with the original painting. Then she walked over to a piece of furniture where she opened a drawer and removed a Christ with a dark background, although the one that I'd bought had a light background. She instructed me to choose the one that I liked: "Above all, don't show my father the one you bought. He's likely to tear it up because he won't tolerate lithographs that aren't consistent with the originals. Another time when the background had been lightened, that drove him into a towering rage." Robert was delighted with my gift, which he appreciated even more because it had received Rouault's approval.

Once again, we sailed to the United States, where we spent a white Christmas in Princeton, much to Thérèse's delight.

The traditional touring began, and Robert was pleased to perform in Saint Louis with our friend Vladimir Goldschmann as the conductor. We met Ernest Ansermet at NBC, and we had an opportunity to hear Nathan Milstein in Philadelphia.

A two piano French music concert at New York's Metropolitan Museum of Art. The program included: Milhaud's *Bal Martiniquais,* Chabrier, Satie's *Trois pièces en forme de poire*, and Robert's *Trois Danses méditerranéennes.*

Robert recorded Saint-Saëns' *4th Concerto*, and we both recorded Satie's *Trois Morceaux en forme de poire*, which amused us considerably because we wondered what each composer's response would've been if he'd known that, one day, they'd end up back-to-back on a black vinyl disk! As I'd done on each of our trips to the United States, I recorded for *Polydor* or *Vox*. That year, I recorded Mendelssohn's *Romances sans paroles* and Mozart's *Concerto Jeune Homme* (Piano Concerto No 9) with Paul Paray conducting. On the reverse side of the Mozart recording, I was accompanied by Jacques Thibaud.

We went to hear a concert by Lotte Lehmann. She possessed perfect diction, and she mastered phrasing with a stunning expansiveness that was at once so human and so unreal.

Jean's career had truly been launched, and this delighted us. Robert made him practice for his concerts whenever it was possible.

In April, after four months in the United States, we sailed on an American freighter, the *S.S. Wisconsin*, and we reached Le Havre. Upon our arrival in Paris, Robert returned to composing because his first recital wouldn't be given until the month of May, at the Théâtre des Champs Elysées.

We took advantage of evenings when there were no professional obligations to go to the theatre. We went to the Comédie Française to see Gisèle Casadesus because Robert never failed to attend his cousin's new roles. We also went to the Théâtre du Gymnase to applaud Daniel Gélin, who'd become Danièle Delorme's husband. We likewise enjoyed quiet evenings at home, which was something that only occurred very rarely.

Shortly after our return, Thérèse, who was nearly six years old, caught scarlet fever. Although she'd never been unwell, she was exhausted by this illness. Because I needed to be away to attend a First Communion in the provinces, Robert became a nurse, and he availed himself of this interlude for composing under calm conditions. At this time, he was orchestrating his *Opus 43*. It was also during this period that he completed his *Nonetto pour piano, quatuor à cordes et quatuor à vent*.

Thérèse had to remain in bed for thirty days, and I stayed with her. Robert left for a tour, and he mentioned in his datebook that he had the opportunity to see *Don Giovanni* and *Così fan tutte*, which are two of Mozart's operas that he knew by heart and adored.

When he returned, Thérèse was feeling much better, and that allowed us to leave home and to attend an exhibition of works by Dunoyer de Segonzac, a painter whom both of us admired enormously.

Then we departed for the Strasbourg Festival, where Robert performed with Roger Desormière conducting and where we gave a two pianos and four hands concert. We saw Henri Sauguet, Francis Poulenc, and Daniel Lesur there. The Strasbourg Festival was one of those ideal venues for music after the war. There was one incident that amused Robert greatly:

Mme. Jolivet slapped a critic who'd dared to speak unfavorably about her husband's music . . . which induced Robert to remark that the occupation of being a critic was a dangerous job!

Upon returning from Strasbourg, we took Thérèse to spend a few days in Brittany, which totally reinvigorated her.

On July 7 at Fontainebleau, we celebrated Jean's twenty-first birthday. Then courses started again.

During this session, I gave a radio premiere of Robert's *Klavierstücke* with Jean Clergue. For me, this work remained linked to the Fontainebleau School's history and to the tragedy that befell us that year and overturned all of our lives. Our beautiful little girl was stricken with polio-at that time a poliomyelitis vaccine did not yet exist.

Robert was desperate, but, for several months, he retained hopes for a cure.

From the outset, people advised us to encourage her to ride a tricycle. We took her to the Boulevard des Invalides so that she could take long rides on this toy that became a rehabilitation tool. This form of exercise was excellent for her legs. In Princeton, even when there was cold weather, she'd ride her tricycle on the porch of our house. She adored it, and it gave her a lot of enjoyment.

When we embarked for the United States, she was riding her tricycle on the decks of the *De Grasse*.

A few doctors aboard the ship told us that she was wearing suitable shoes that supported her feet perfectly. Any encouragement was welcome to us.

As of January 1949, Thérèse returned to school in Princeton. Providing a normal school life for her was one of our needs, and everyone treated her so well. She was very funny because she already spoke English quite well with her schoolmates at Miss Fine's School or with our Black maid. At home, we always spoke French, but the boys often spoke English to one another, so that we couldn't understand what they were saying!

Thérèse pronounced her name the French way or the American way interchangeably! She liked to joke around and kept up her good spirits in spite of her misfortunes.

Robert was always hopeful. As for me, I was more clear-sighted, and I realized that Thérèse would never regain her original ability to walk.

Our work actually saved Robert and me to some extent. . . . For my part, I decreased my activities, and I sought to devote my time to Thérèse.

For years, we proceeded from one treatment to another—to Rotterdam, to Affoltern in Switzerland, near Zurich, where people stricken with polio were being treated, and to Brittany . . . constantly trying new treatments and new movements to allow her to achieve some improvement, because a complete cure couldn't be envisioned.

For years, I went to swimming pools with her, performing exercises simultaneously in order to give her courage. You can imagine what that represents in terms of courage and tenacity in a child!

Our friends were a great source of comfort for us.

For a certain period of time, Robert stopped composing. The only thing that he wrote during this period is a sonata dedicated to Thérèse, which is an authentic description of the tragedy that she was experiencing: the first movement is light-hearted, playful, happy, and serene. The second, which is an adagio, is infinitely sad, and it will bring you to tears when you know about Thérèse's circumstances. The finale, in turn, evokes a march that is certainly somewhat irregular, but it's joyful nonetheless.

In Switzerland, at Affoltern, which had been recommended to us as a perfect location for treating polio, we hardly observed any progress. We therefore decided to let Thérèse stay there for a long-term treatment, with the hope that time would allow improvement. We entrusted her to the hospital, where she received treatment in a regular and continuous manner. We obtained accommodations in a hotel near the hospital for our dear friend Rosine Cazenave, who was helping me with Thérèse then, so that she could be a companion for Thérèse beyond the intended treatment hours.

It was quite difficult for a seven-year-old girl to find herself alone in a hospital where people only spoke *Schweizerdeutsch*. Some of the nurses who knew a little French and a little English could indicate movements in both languages, but there was no question of their speaking to her about other things. We found this situation to be very cruel.

During the summer, we'd leased a chalet so that we could take over for Rosine, who certainly deserved some vacation time. This chalet belonged to our friend, the conductor Volkmar Andreae, and it had a piano, which allowed us to practice when we weren't with our daughter.

Robert continued his summer tours. When he returned, he went back to composing. Sometimes, he worked as much as five hours per day. He finished his *Opus 45* that year.

That summer was very distressing for us, because, whenever we left Thérèse at the end of the day, she burst into tears. It was heartbreaking for us.

As he did every year after our return, Robert took part in the Lucerne Festival. One evening when he wasn't performing, we listened to Haydn's *Creation* conducted by Wilhelm Furtwangler. We'd been able to attend one of the rehearsals, and we'd been fascinated by his way of conducting. His entrances were surprising and disturbing. There was a sort of extended hesitation with his two long arms, and then his gestures suddenly became precise, and they all began playing as if they were electrified. The effect was extraordinary!

Subsequently, I accompanied Robert to Milan, where he played with Rafael Kubelik conducting. We were expecting to hear about Toscanini. Not a word about him. He'd left the country and La Scala, and his countrymen appeared to have forgotten him. . . . I've always wondered whether there wasn't a bit of jealousy that accounted for this lockout. The success that he'd achieved in the United States may not have pleased everyone. Later, this banishment ended, and he once again became somewhat of a musical deity in his native land.

After Robert's concerts, we returned to being with Thérèse, and we heard Clara Haskil in Zurich one evening. We liked her considerably. We'd heard her debut in Paris. She was a reserved woman. She had an unprepossessing appearance that was quickly forgotten as audiences only took delight in her sumptuous musicality. At the beginning of her career, she'd become extremely disillusioned because Cortot, whose pupil she'd been, hardly helped her at all. Audiences, however, were capable of validating her, and her recordings still offer priceless testimony to how great a musician she was.

In October, we returned to Paris with Thérèse. Jean was returning to the United States. Guy earned his baccalaureate with Honors for the second session. Robert recorded Franck's *Symphonic Variations.*

Then a new treatment being applied in Rotterdam was recommended to us. We didn't hesitate an instant about taking Thérèse there. At this point, Rotterdam was still entirely destroyed. Only the hospital had escaped the bombings. The city was a disaster area, but we didn't pay any attention to it. Only one thing mattered to us: helping our daughter. Robert decided at this moment that she could abandon her tricycle in order to graduate to a bicycle. It was very touching to see him running after his daughter in order to teach her how to balance herself on two wheels. He spent hours in a park with her, giving lessons with unlimited patience.

In November, we left for the United States, and, this time, we sailed on the magnificent *Ile-de-France.* Upon our arrival in New York, we learned that the ship was restricted to the docks for twenty-four hours. Robert was in a frenzy because he needed to be in Philadelphia for a rehearsal two days later. No exemption was given to him. Finally, disembarkation took place at 4:00 a.m. . . . and Robert only had enough time to jump into a taxi and to be driven to Philadelphia. It was 6:00 a.m., and the rehearsal would be taking place at 10:00 a.m.! Fortunately, everything ended well, however. It was possible for the rehearsal to begin at the appointed time.

We returned to our habits in Princeton. Thérèse went back to school. A teacher supervised her work so closely that the lag was quickly overcome. She was very diligent. I accompanied her regularly to the swimming pool, which, unfortunately, was located outside Princeton, and this didn't make things easy.

In turn, Robert adopted his usual itinerary, and he crisscrossed the United States. He was reunited with his loyal companions and with Zino Francescatti to perform as a duo. They recorded for Columbia, and they played at the Library of Congress in Washington. From time to time, I joined Robert for joint concerts, but I avoided leaving Thérèse too long. Robert encouraged me to pursue my personal work and our four hands and two piano work.

During one of our trips, we had an opportunity to meet Margaret Truman, President Truman's daughter, who was a singer. She was very friendly, but it must be admitted that she didn't possess extraordinary musical talent. The red carpet was literally rolled out for her wherever she appeared. She displayed notable elegance. Her father spoke about her enthusiastically and proudly. She was very much an object of media attention, as we'd say today. She received very mixed reviews to quite a large extent, and people didn't refrain from letting it be known that, if she hadn't been the president's daughter, etc.

Before returning to France, we paid a visit to Professor Einstein, and we had a long conversation with him about politics, which he adored! He had a lucidity and a vision of things that were fantastic. He foresaw events with an extraordinary acuity and flair.

Upon our arrival, Robert departed immediately for his tour in Europe. We took Thérèse to Rotterdam so that she could continue her treatment under Rosine Cazenave's monitoring. It was considered excellent, and you can't imagine our joy when we saw her making progress.

"May in Bordeaux" festival for Robert, where we dined with Jacques Chaban-Delmas. He spoke about the Resistance in a fascinating way, and he enabled us to discover a vast amount about the history of the Second World War.

An extensive circuit in Italy. A concert in Rome, where we dined with Jacques Ibert, who administered the Villa Medici. In Turin, Robert performed under the conductorship of Antal Dorati, who introduced me to *Campari Soda*.

Then we went to Naples and Sicily: Palermo, Siragusa, and Taormina, where we joyfully went swimming as it was so hot. I can recall that the sand was burning so much that we couldn't walk on it barefooted! Then we went to Catania, which neither Robert nor I liked.

It was a sad and dark city, so different from the rest of the island. This stay in Sicily was extremely pleasant because it allowed us to combine work and tourism. Both of us had a strong need to find periods of escape in order to alleviate our great sadness and our constant concerns about Thérèse.

Just after returning to Paris, we went to pick her up in Rotterdam, and we took her to Brittany, to Kersaint, where we settled for the summer. This place is very cold, and it's therefore very invigorating.

We listened to a lot of music on the radio, and we were glad that, one evening, we could hear Dinu Lipati again. When he was ill, he'd been forced to suspend his activities for a while. You know that this wonderful pianist was stricken with leukemia and that he died at the age of thirty-three . . . far too young! He'd gone to Lourdes, and he said that he felt better. There was a remission in the course of his illness. He'd been so kind as to write to us because he was aware of Thérèse's condition. Unfortunately, I didn't keep a copy of his letter, but I can remember its content that was so touching: "I'm not a believer," he wrote, "but water from Lourdes did me a lot of good. I'm sending some of it to you, so that you can rub your daughter's legs with it. I'm sure that this will help her." We followed his advice, but we didn't observe any improvement. For a quite long time, I kept this bottle. I'd been so moved by the kindness of a man who'd taken the time to think of others, even though he himself was quite ill. This act exemplified the generous person whom he was. His generosity could be seen in each of his performances. After his death, we saw his wife again in Geneva.

That year, Robert participated in the Edinburgh Festival. After the concert, we dined in the home of the cultural attaché, Marc-André Bera, who'd married the pianist Nadia Tagrine. We continued to London, where Robert appeared on the BBC and at the famous Proms at the Royal Albert Hall. We took advantage of being there in order to sample sole at Prunier. Do you know that sole from this side of the English Channel is far better than what's caught in France? Between two concerts, we visited the Wallace Collection and the Tate Gallery. We even went as far as Cambridge, to which we'd never traveled previously.

After returning to Paris, Robert recorded some of de Falla's art songs with his cousin Jacqueline Pianavia de Courville, who was his uncle Henri's daughter and who was an excellent singer. He'd also recorded the piano portion that she used to rehearse in the small theatre that she owned, and this allowed her to dispense with an accompanist. She was delighted to be able to have Robert as her permanent accompanist in this way! This method of recording accompaniments separately expanded subsequently, and many soloists or singers are using it to practice their repertoires.

*Chapter 16*

# The First Family of the Piano

From this period on, we were playing more often three pianos with Jean in both Europe and the United States. It was Dimitri Mitropoulos who placed our feet in the stirrups. After having conducted for one of Jean's concerts where he recognized Jean's talent, Mitropoulos proposed that Bach's concerto for three keyboards should be played on three pianos at a New York Philharmonic concert that had been planned for the bicentennial of the Cantor's death. On the following day, we recorded it, along with one of the two keyboard concerti that Robert and I also played during this commemorative concert. I recall that recording of the concerto for three pianos was taking place marvelously without any unanticipated problems when the sound engineer halted us at the next to last measure. Surprised by this unjustified interruption, we heard him give instructions over the microphone: "The session is over." It was out of the question that the orchestra's musicians should go beyond the schedule, even for a single measure. . . . You can imagine how easy it is to repeat two measures separately twenty-four hours later in order to finish a concerto. This incident made us furious! It demonstrated the omnipotence of "Unions" in the United States.

For nearly twenty years, beginning in the 1950s, our musical life and our family life acquired a regular unchanging rhythm, or, I'd even say, a certain serenity. Apart from our constant hope of finding a miracle cure for helping Thérèse, we'd spend six months in Europe and six months in the United States. Thérèse attended school in the United States for three months and in France for six months.

Princeton continued to be our home port on the other side of the Atlantic, while the Rue Vaneau was our European base.

Robert's career was characterized by a stability that went hand in hand with consistency. He revisited the same cities and the same conductors, who were hiring him from one year to the next.

Loyalty and cooperation of this kind were a pleasure for Robert. For instance, when he'd see Pierre Monteux in San Francisco again, he never grew tired of working under Monteux's calm authority. Personally speaking, I savored the rehearsals that I attended. Monteux displayed an extraordinary equanimity.

Monteux, who was restrained with his gestures, never raised his voice to make a comment to a musician. He almost spoke *sotto voce*. Therefore, rehearsals took place in a peaceful atmosphere. Robert experienced this same atmosphere with Carlo Maria Giulini. Monteux and Giulini belonged to a breed of aristocrats. This serene calm was occasionally interrupted by Mme. Monteux, who always attended her husband's rehearsals. All of a sudden, she'd be heard shouting "Pierre! Pierre!" and she'd inform him of a thought that was passing through her head. . . . Monteux conducted differently from Toscanini. When he wished to indicate a crescendo, he didn't say that becoming red in the face was necessary, as Toscanini did! Quite the contrary! He explained very gently that, in order to create a crescendo, it was necessary to begin calmly and then to intensify the notes, and he specified that crescendos should be carefully controlled by each musician. That was his particular way of suggesting music. A certain wisdom flowed from him. He was a charming man who was very unpretentious and very modest, and he never talked about himself. He possessed exceptional discretion. Almost too much! He liked Robert enormously. He often sent pupils to Robert, and, whenever he discovered someone interesting, Monteux would ask Robert to listen so as to obtain his opinion.

Monteux, who'd originally been a viola player, loved to recount this anecdote that Robert would repeat in turn: One day, when he was being interviewed, a journalist asked him: "Why did you choose the viola, Maestro?" and Monteux replied, "Because it's easier than playing the violin." And the journalist continued: "And why did you become a conductor?" "But because it's easier than playing an instrument. . . . But being a critic is even easier!" He loved to tell this story, even to critics.

Whenever we could, we went to listen to music created by others, and that's how, in 1951, we attended the French premiere of Menotti's *The Consul*, at the Théâtre des Champs Elysées. We'd already had an opportunity to meet Menotti in Milan. One day, the publisher Schirmer had said to us: "Menotti, he's the new Verdi!" We liked his opera tremendously. Menotti was a marvelous musician. He wrote good music, even though some persons believe that it doesn't open new horizons. The subject had interested us even more after the period that we'd just lived through. This story of invasive bureaucracy and the struggle for freedom acquired an exceptional dimension. It's a poignant work that impresses every audience. Menotti, like Wagner, wrote the libretto himself.

The opera was conducted by Thomas Schippers, a young and extremely gifted American conductor who was a very handsome fellow—which didn't detract from anything. He became a pillar of the Festival of Two Worlds that Menotti created in Spoleto in 1958. Unfortunately, he died of cancer in 1977. He was only forty-seven years old.

On the evening of The Consul's premiere, we were truly sad to observe that there were only about fifty people in the hall. Fortunately, The Consul subsequently achieved success that can't be denied.

During this period, we also heard the pianist Edwin Fischer, who gave a recital at the Salle Gaveau. He was sixty-five years old. He played Bach admirably, and he had a prodigious memory. We heard him quite often in Switzerland. I believe that I can recall that he performed Chopin's *24 Préludes* and *24 Études* that particular evening. It was a colossal program. At the end of the concert, we went to congratulate him backstage, and he said: "I must stop playing the *Études*. At my age, I'll have to remove them from my repertoire. I have rheumatism in my fingers, and they don't respond the way that I want." I was deeply moved by his straightforwardness. He'd recognized that he wasn't at his prior level for the *Études*, and he didn't hesitate to acknowledge it. This comment also influenced Robert, who was playing the *Études* frequently. As he approached his sixtieth year, he stopped including them in his programs, thereby considering the observation offered by the outstanding master that Edwin Fischer was.

Beginning in the 1950s, Robert participated in the Aix-en-Provence festival every year. Of course, he played under the baton of Hans Rosbaud, this exceptional Mozart conductor, who'd been the Festival's leading conductor since its creation by Gabriel Dussurget in 1947. He also performed there with Zino Francescatti. For these sonata concert, people sometimes went to the Thoronet Abbey, an extremely beautiful Romanesque complex at the foot of Mount Sainte-Victoire. For the most part, however, concerts were given in the Archbishops' Hall.

In the summer, Robert would tackle composing anew. During one of those summers, he composed *Variations* on a theme that Manuel de Falla had composed for guitar in memory of Debussy.

From this time on, Robert became a regular attendee at European festivals, which continued to be his essential activity during the summer, along with vacations and composing. Since its creation in 1950, he was invited to the Menton Festival, where he returned each year until his death. That's where we heard Jacques Thibaud shortly before his airplane accident.

You may recall that he died in 1953, when he was traveling to Japan for a series of concerts. He was seventy-three years old. I remember that he'd played one of Mozart's four violin concertos. We'd observed that he took certain liberties because there was evidence of this, but he never descended into vulgarity. He knew how to stop at the right time . . . and how to convey superb emotion.

At this point, Jean was taking charge of the course of his career. Whenever it was possible, his father made him practice. We were regularly invited to play at the Library of Congress in Washington, where primarily chamber music concerts are given. The Library possesses an extremely beautiful collection of Stradivariuses that it lends to musicians who come there to perform. As the name indicates, it's a library, somewhat like the Bibliothèque Nationale in Paris. At the request of Mrs. Coolidge, the founder of the Music Department, Robert donated the manuscript for his *Troisième Symphonie* to it, and the last time that I played there, not so long ago, they'd shown the laudable gesture of exhibiting the manuscript in the hall's lobby.

I played there in 1976, with the Juilliard Quartet that's affiliated with the Library. Hence, the regulations require that members of the quartet must play on instruments from the collection.

Moreover, these Stradivariuses are superb. The Quartet's members performed Fauré's *Quatuor* with me, and I also played Robert's *Sonate pour violon et piano* with the second violin. We rehearsed in New York, and, as soon as we arrived in Washington, he said: "Too bad for the Library's Strad! I play my own violin because it's too dangerous to adjust my playing for a violin that I only play very infrequently and that I'm therefore unfamiliar with." And he contravened the Library's regulations.

The Library's administrators were very protective about their collection, and I remember having heard a violinist be sharply reprimanded for having simply set down the precious instrument on a chair before coming on stage. Another year, I also played Robert's *Sextuor* with the Philadelphia Winds Quintet, which demonstrates that the programs don't disdain twentieth-century music. The Library also created a sound archive where it keeps radio recordings. I found that it contained several concertos that Robert had played with the New York Philharmonic.

From then on, we saw the Szells again each year in Cleveland or elsewhere during the tours and appearances that George and Robert obtained together. They were bound by a true friendship, and their recordings of Mozart's concertos are a perfect testimony to their close collaboration.

When we were in Cleveland, they often played four hands after supper. Just for pleasure. George was an excellent pianist, and, like Robert, he was an excellent sight reader. Schubert was often their preference. Their relationship only ended with George's death in 1970.

As a conductor with exceptional precision, he displayed a constant concern with maintaining the general line of a work and of retaining its rhythmic pulsation from one end to another. Some persons believed that he beat time excessively! It's true that he'd even have beaten time during a cadence, where a soloist plays alone! He was quite strict with his orchestra and was equally demanding of himself. During recording sessions, he listened to each take multiple times. He was a perfectionist. I recorded Mozart's *K448* with him in New York, as well as the two-piano concerto, and I've kept a marvelous recollection of these work sessions.

When Pierre Bernac and Françis Poulenc came to give recitals in the United States, they never failed to pay us a visit in Princeton. One year, Bernac was expected to record Schumann's *Dichterliebe*. At the last moment, Francis felt that he lacked the technical ability to play this work for a recording session, and he asked Robert to replace him. Robert and Bernac succeeded in forming a team without any difficulties. Bernac described the recording session to me: "We rehearsed once, just before recording . . . and we only made one take! We placed ourselves under concert conditions, and it worked!"

We liked Poulenc a lot. He was so funny, with a sense of humor that can only be characterized as extremely Gallic. He had the same passion for Chabrier as Robert did.

He adored food shopping at Les Halles when the market was still in the heart of Paris. Because he knew that I liked doing this too and that Robert was not inclined to accompany me, he proposed taking me along. One morning, at 7:00 a.m., I went to pick him up by car at his home at 5 Rue Médicis. He came out impeccably dressed, with a pleasant scent of eau de Cologne, and we departed for our expedition to the market. He stopped at every stall! This was during October, and he bought mushrooms, fish that were still breathing, and flowers. Poulenc very gallantly carried my baskets.

Poulenc enjoyed life and fine cuisine. He was also a very mystical person. His *Stabat Mater* is a composition that's marked by intense belief. I enjoyed it when he played "in the manner of Stravinsky or Chabrier." He possessed enormous talent. Moreover, he admitted that he practiced the piano rather infrequently. He was gifted and he possessed a unique personality. His art songs are true marvels. The duo that he formed with Bernac was peerless. Bernac didn't have a great voice, but he possessed such perfect diction and such a sense of phrasing. He was truly made to sing art songs.

Later, in the 1970s, when we were reunited, with both of us teaching at the Académie Maurice Ravel in Saint-Jean-de-Luz, I took great pleasure in attending Bernac's courses. He'd told me, "Robert, Poulenc, and I were a good vintage, 1899." He'd just turned eighty.

During this period, Robert often gave recitals at Hunter College in New York, which offered a highly advanced musical curriculum. This college, which was located on Park Avenue, possesses a hall with excellent acoustics. It's somewhat like Bloomington, in Indiana. These are institutions where music is taught better than in our conservatories, I'd say. . . . In addition to practicing an instrument, students learn how to appear on stage, how to perform on television, and how to record. Their studies, which are at an extremely high level, train true professionals. After my husband's death, I was asked to teach six months each year in Bloomington. I didn't accept because I believe that I couldn't have put up with living alone for such a long time, far from everything and everyone. Was I possibly wrong? I believe, however, that a person shouldn't pursue this type of experience beyond a certain age. It's best to be young.

Robert began to reduce his teaching activities. He was still giving some masterclasses at Fontainebleau, but he'd kept very few private students. I think that the last ones included François-Joël Thiollier and Bernard Ringeissen. On the other hand, he participated quite regularly in juries: at the Geneva Competition, at the Paris Conservatory, and at the Queen Elizabeth Competition in Brussels. Indeed, he insisted upon increasingly setting time aside for himself and his family. During the summer, he no longer accepted commitments, except for festivals. Thus, we met Herbert von Karajan for the first time in 1952. It was at the Lucerne Festival. Robert subsequently gave a concert with him. We saw him again in Vienna, where he was staying in the same family *pension* as we were: the Opening Pension. We went to hear him at the Vienna Philharmonic, where he was conducting Clara Haskil. When we were in Vienna, we never missed performances of operas by either Mozart or Strauss. I've told you how much Robert liked Richard Strauss: *Elektra* and *Salomé* were masterpieces in his opinion. He knew all of the scores by heart. Once in Vienna, we dined with Wieland Wagner at the French Embassy. Von Karajan's former wife, who was German, also attended this dinner. During the conversation, she approached the son of the New York publisher Schirmer and told him how pleased she'd be if her husband were to be hired in New York. She added that she didn't exclude the possibility that he'd be unfavorably received on account of his career during the war, but, according to her viewpoint, he needed to perform in the United States. Similarly, she believed that he should do recordings. . . . Her wishes were fulfilled.

In Switzerland, Robert performed regularly under Hermann Scherchen as a conductor, and he was always pleased to see his friend Ansermet again. Robert always admired Ansermet's combative spirit. He'd struggled so much to popularize the music of his era. In the same way as Scherchen, moreover. Robert was very compatible with them, although their personalities were quite different. Both of them were conductors who served music with total self-sacrifice.

You know how important conductors are for soloists. Each must adapt to the other. . . . Encounters are short, and they have an extremely brief time interval to win over an audience that has come to listen to one or the other, or simply to a work by a favorite composer. Hence, they must, above all, do service to a work jointly. This means that one must sometimes make concessions, but the essential aspect is that, to the greatest possible extent, they must approach –together—that which a composer has written.

During the last twenty years of his life, Robert was fortunate to play with the greatest conductors. The list is long, and I'm certainly going to forget some . . . Sargent, Barbirolli, Giulini, Kletsky, Kubelik, Horenstein, Szell, Bernstein, Paray, Mitropoulos, Toscanini, Munch, Karajan, Cluytens, Martinon, Boulez and more. In a word, all of the great ones, without including the loyal ones: Monteux, Schuricht, Krips, Ansermet, Scherchen. It's impossible to provide a list. It would risk resembling the catalogue of Don Giovanni's conquests: One thousand and three!

On each occasion, there was the joy of getting together again and jointly communicating their love of a given work. I believe that Robert never played a work that he disliked.

There was true loyalty in relation to his fellow musicians and colleagues and great deference toward the older ones. I can recall that, for Florent Schmitt's eightieth birthday in 1952, we played his *Trois rhapsodies pour deux pianos*, and the emotion that could be seen on the face of this elderly man whom we hadn't seen for years was our most beautiful reward.

It's always been said that people never see their children grow up. This is a hackneyed comment but, like all parents, we didn't escape from the formula, or I'd even say, the rule, which is one of these rules in life that's part of the cycle.

Then there's a day when your oldest son announces that he's going to be married. Then you rejoice, and you realize how time has passed. On May 27, 1953, Jean married Evie Girard, the daughter of our friends, the Girards. Their marriage solidified our friendship somewhat more.

Guy earned his Political Science diploma, and he left for the United States in order to prepare for a master's degree at Columbia University. Parallel to his studies, he'd used his piano talents and his excellent sense of improvisation by participating actively in founding and training a jazz orchestra with students from Political Science and the Law School. For Thérèse, who'd just turned ten, it was still a period for rehabilitation that she pursued with astonishing courage. She loved music and was practicing *solfège* with her father. She showed an inclination toward everything that was musical, and later, she'd study singing.

Jean's career was becoming firmly grounded. Like us, he was dividing his time between the United States and Europe. Our trio of pianists achieved genuine success, and for the Americans, we were "the First Family of the Piano," which was the title of a significant televised broadcast that was devoted to us at a later time (1967).

Robert always played for the *Telephone Hour*. Beginning in 1960, these programs were televised, and this created an even greater impact for his concerts.

Robert always reserved his free periods for visiting art exhibitions or for revisiting museums. He never ceased to be enthusiastic about painting. Throughout his life, he kept up with the development of twentieth-century trends. When he was in Paris, he never failed to stop by the Galerie Maeght. He even brought his friend George Szell there when Szell was in Paris.

Robert was an exemplary husband and father. He was deeply attached to his family, and I recall that, in 1955, when he was performing in Boston with Charles Munch conducting, he'd taken Munch to visit the collection of early instruments that belonged to his uncle Henri, the founder of the famous Société des Instruments Anciens. This collection had been purchased by Koussevitsky in 1932 for the Boston Symphony Orchestra's collection. Among the instruments, there was the small drum that he'd played as a child, and he wasn't able to conceal his feelings when he saw it again.

At this time, he was working regularly with Paul Paray, who was the head of the Detroit Orchestra. We'd seen him frequently before the war when he was the director of the *Concerts Colonne*. During the war, he'd taken refuge in Monte-Carlo, in order to avoid collaborating with the Germans. He was an extremely impetuous man. He'd been expected to become Toscanini's successor as the head of the New York Philharmonic, but that didn't happen. He'd requested the same compensation as Toscanini, and it was denied. It should be stated that, even though he was a particularly good conductor, he wasn't Toscanini! He didn't have any sense of diplomacy . . . but musicians liked him devotedly. Robert was on extremely good terms with him.

In the same year, 1955, I experienced the sorrow of losing my sister, Robert didn't want me to take a plane to travel to attend her funeral. We'd never crossed the Atlantic on a plane yet. He undoubtedly may have feared that an accident would befall me. Nevertheless, we abandoned our beloved crossings by boat shortly thereafter, we were definitively converted to the airplane. Twelve hours of flying during this period, with two layovers, quickly became familiar to us. In Europe, we used the train as well as our car. We always took our car when we could enjoy tourism between concerts!

That's how we took a tour of Spain with the Francescattis. The weather was splendid. The concert in Córdoba had even taken place outdoors. Robert and Zino had been marvelously inspired by the atmosphere. It was a clear and mild night, without being too hot. A reception followed the concert in Manuel de Falla's home. It was divine with the scents of flowers that pervaded the gardens. Robert insisted upon going to mourn at de Falla's tomb in Cádiz. We'd kept a marvelous recollection of him. Robert adored his music and always remembered the valuable advice on interpretation that de Falla imparted to him many years before.

In September, a tour in Switzerland. In Basel, we dined with Paul Sacher, who had quite recently established his foundation. We always took pleasure in meeting this fine musician who was so cultivated and whose generosity was unbounded.

The following year, Robert performed in Berlin with Lorin Maazel conducting, for whom that was his first concert in that city. The orchestra was the radio orchestra that Maazel was later to conduct for several years.

Meeting again was full of warmth, and they had a lot of pleasure performing together. This was far from the time when the young violinist had been chastised for his poor manners. Reiner's predictions had been fulfilled: Maazel, in turn, was occupying the conductor's podium!

Then Robert decided to reduce his time in the United States. Now airplanes allowed us to only spend the necessary time for honoring our commitments.

In October 1956, in New York, he celebrated the 2,000th concert of his career. At the same time, he was recording Mozart's *K466* and *K456* concertos with George Szell.

On the final page of the 1956 datebook, a new assessment. Among the deceased, there was a person who was dear to him: his colleague Yves Nat. Robert esteemed the artist as much as the man. In 1957, Robert was playing for the first time under the baton of Karl Boehm, in Amsterdam, at the Concertgebouw. He was an impressive conductor, standing as straight as an "I" at his podium. He was sparing with his gestures, but what a musician and what an efficacious person! A piercing look filled with silent and implacable authority.

Guy was completing his military service in Algeria. The war was intensifying there. The losses were numerous. I lived in permanent anxiety.

In Vienna, Von Karajan and his very young French wife, Eliette, came to congratulate Robert at the end of one of his recitals. They'd played together in Salzburg, sometime earlier. It had gone very well. They never had other occasions to perform together, but Robert kept an excellent memory of this giant of conducting. Robert's *Quatrième symphonie* was performed as a premiere on the radio.

While we were at the Aix-en-Provence festival, Guy came there on leave (from the Algerian War). I accompanied him alone to Marseille, where he'd be re-embarking. I was falling apart, but I didn't want to let Robert see it under any circumstances.

Autumn in the United States, Christmas in Paris.

In May 1958, Robert was hired for a series of concerts in Prague and Budapest. We hadn't traveled east of the Iron Curtain yet, except to go from West Berlin to East Berlin to visit the Pergamon Museum. Thérèse accompanied us, because we didn't want to leave her alone in Paris during this period of political uncertainty. In Prague, Robert played the *K491* Mozart *Concerto*. You can be sure that we visited Mozart's house. Neither my husband nor I were fanatical about making pilgrimages, but there's always something moving about being at a site that was familiar to an exceptional person. There's a feeling of knowing them better and understanding them better, as if their presence were still alive.

The French ambassador offered a dinner in our honor. Throughout this trip, it would have been difficult for us to pursue any deviations or to speak to former friends without compromising them, because we never took a step alone. The concerts were given for the fortieth anniversary of Debussy's death. Robert and I played the extremely beautiful *En blanc et noir* suite that we liked so much, and Robert played two books from *Images*. In Budapest, we stayed at the Embassy, which had sustained some damage during the arrival of Russian tanks. Robert played Ravel's *Concerto pour la main gauche* because he'd been asked to play French music.

The French ambassador's wife very kindly took me to a market so that I could observe daily life in Hungary somewhat more closely. I was surprised to find only a few products that peasants from areas around the capital city had come there to sell. It was truly scarcity. In Budapest, we visited Bartók's house, although not without a certain emotion. We also listened to a superbly interpreted mass by Mozart in the Cathedral.

The Danube's beauty in this location is astonishing. The city was a vast construction site. Damage caused by combat in 1956 was being repaired. Life there was harsh. We'd been invited to a luncheon by the concert organizers. They'd butchered two chickens especially for us. That seemed to be an exceptional event, and it was a gala meal for them. We also had the pleasure of a luncheon with Zoltan Kodaly and Karl Richter. We brought Thérèse, who was sixteen years old then, because we believed that it would be interesting for her to meet these two personalities. Kodaly was accompanied by his extremely young wife, who must have been fifty years younger than he was . . . and, after the meal, Thérèse's comments didn't have anything to do with the presence of two eminent musicians at our table. Instead, she asked us how a woman who was so young could marry a man who was so much older, and this amused us considerably.

After this trip to Eastern Europe, which was a learning experience, we returned to our routine in the West: a recital at the Champs-Élysées for Robert, a concert in London with Jascha Horenstein conducting. Aix-en-Provence, where we met Nathan Milstein, then vacationing in Cavalière, the Menton Festival with Monteux, a tour in Switzerland with Ansermet, and the Geneva Competition, followed by our departing for New York by airplane.

Robert played in Buffalo with Josef Krips as the conductor. They hadn't yet had an opportunity to meet one another. As a noted Mozartian, Krips was endowed with extreme sensitivity. Very straightforward. He had great authority, with a preoccupation for nuances, accurately discussing *forte* and *piano* notations. Robert was perfectly in agreement with him. They both had the same concept of Mozart and the same perception of his music: simple, pure, and true. Furthermore, they performed together quite frequently from then on, whether it was in Europe or in the United States.

A return to Paris for Christmas. As we did nearly every year, we spent the threshold of the new year with our friends the Benevenutis, who owned a mansion in Louveciennes. Joseph Benevenuti was a pianist whom we'd met at the Conservatory in Diémer's class. He was slightly older than Robert. He'd been a very talented young man, but he was compelled to earn a living at a very early age in nightclubs, to such an extent that he was unable to practice the piano sufficiently to become a soloist. Hence, he didn't pursue a career as a virtuoso, but he did become an instructor for the class for chamber music ensembles at the Conservatory. He also founded a remarkable trio with the cellist André Navarra and with René Benedetti, a violin instructor at the Conservatory.

He married Diane de Rothschild, who'd been his pupil and who'd previously worked with me. They had no children, but Diane had several daughters from a prior marriage whom Joseph regarded as his own children. They were marvelous. The Benevenutis were very dear friends, and we saw them frequently when we were in France. Joseph had great affection for Jean, whom he'd known when he was very small. Moreover, he made Jean rehearse when he was in Paris.

## Chapter 17

# A Tragic Ending

The years continued to pass, and yet we didn't tire of our traveling life at all. To the contrary, I had the impression that Robert was increasingly uplifted by everything that he saw during his tours. He returned to visit museums and monuments that he'd already seen. He was happily reunited with his colleagues, his conductors, and orchestra members who were also his friends. He never failed to go back to good restaurants that he'd previously discovered and whose addresses he'd carefully kept. The random nature of touring led us to encounter other musicians who were leading an itinerant life, just as we were.

In Stockholm, we met Elisabeth Schwarzkopf once. We heard her in Salzburg in the *Rosenkavalier*, which was one of her supremely important roles, as you know. We also heard her in *Così fan tutte*, with Karl Boehm conducting. What an unforgettable evening!

On stage, she was a veritable goddess. She had a such a presence and such class, apart from her extraordinary voice and her perfect professionalism, of course. We later saw her in the hall of the hotel when she was dressed in an ordinary way, and we wouldn't have recognized her if we hadn't looked up at her exquisite face illuminated by clear blue eyes.

With unobtrusiveness off-stage, she seemed to want to go unnoticed, which isn't always the case for singers.

In 1959, Robert received the gold medal awarded by the city of Paris. On this occasion and for the very first time, we saw the City Hall's sumptuous salons with gilded paneling. Robert wasn't pursuing honors. He'd already been named an officer of the Légion d'Honneur, but that hadn't gone to his head at all. He was also a commander of the Order of Leopold and the Order of the House of Orange that had been awarded to him by Queen Wilhelmina of the Netherlands before she abdicated in favor of her daughter Juliana.

At this time, Robert was involved in establishing the Couperin Society. Robert often played Couperin's works in recitals, and he believed that Couperin was one of our great musicians. He was scandalized that we weren't paying homage to this eminent composer while the Germans or the Austrians glorify Bach, Beethoven, Mozart, and Wagner . . . apart from all the others . . . who are perhaps less famous . . . with commemorative plaques along their streets, as well as museums.

The Église Saint-Gervais and the Couperin family's house, which were destroyed during the war, had just been rebuilt, while the organ had miraculously been spared during bombing. Thus, Robert asked the City of Paris for an authorization to place a plaque upon the house that had sheltered the Couperin dynasty. The City gave its authorization without frowning, but it officially informed us that it couldn't pay for the plaque. It's pointless to tell you that the plaque didn't cost a fortune and that our association didn't hesitate to bear the expense. We were scandalized by the City's attitude! The plaque was officially installed. Robert gave a brief and quite moving speech where he explained Couperin's role in the history of French music. The organist played a few of François Couperin's works. It was a simple but touching ceremony, marked by a fervent tone. Unfortunately, we couldn't maintain the association very long. . . . In fact, no one was interested.

Robert increasingly became fond of blending French music into his concerts: Couperin, Rameau, and Ravel, of course, Franck, d'Indy, Debussy, Fauré, Saint-Saëns, Satie, Milhaud, Roussel, Schmitt, and Poulenc were well represented, alongside Bach, Mozart, Beethoven, Schumann, or Chopin.

During the 1960s, we became acquainted with the painter Marcel Gromaire, a very down-to-earth man who was excessively reserved. Perhaps too reserved, in terms    of the great artist that he was. We immediately got along famously, just as we did with Miró or Rouault. Robert had a sort of affinity with painters. I never knew how it originated . . . they understood one another tacitly. They were in communion.

In September 1960, it was Guy's turn to marry. In Cherchell, Algeria, he'd served under the command of Colonel Nicol, who had four daughters. When Guy went to pay his respects before returning to France, the youngest daughter, Joëlle, who was sixteen years old, was present, and Guy said to her: "You'll see me again when you're twenty." And he kept his word! A few months before his marriage, he visited us in order to introduce his fiancée. It was Joëlle Nicol!

We took advantage of Jean's presence on July 7, which was his birthday, for a family reunion. Robert and I were celebrating thirty-nine years of marriage, and our two sons had established households. Jean and Evie had a little girl, Agnès, who was delightful. We saw her whenever we went to the United States, where Jean was living for six months each year. During the other six months, he lived in an apartment on Boulevard de Clichy, where we also liked to see one another again. Robert was enchanted with his role as a grandfather.

In 1960, we saw our friend Mitropoulos for the last time. Robert and I were playing at the Salzburg Festival, two pianos as well as four hands. We'd included *Ma mère l'Oye* in the program, in its original version for four hands. Mitropoulos came to hear us. He'd never heard the original version of this work that Ravel had composed for the children of his friends, the Godebskis. He appreciated the work's delicacy in this form, without any effects. Its intimate quality, its accessibility to children, enchanted him, a man who'd conducted the orchestral version so many times.

In 1961, we completed a tour in Israel with Jean. We'd played one, two, and three piano repertoires with Paul Kletzki conducting. This was a very pleasant stay. We went swimming between two concerts. Then we visited Tel Aviv and Jerusalem. Jean went to perform at the *kibbutzim*, and he came back fascinated with what he'd seen in terms of reclaiming of arid land and the way of life in these pioneer communities. The country had changed so much since our first trip in 1934.

During this visit, we met a marvelously talented young conductor who'd been mentioned to us in Vienna, where he'd been completing his education. His name was Zubin Mehta. Afterward, we saw him again on many occasions.

In this same year, Robert performed in New York for the first time with Leonard Bernstein conducting. At this time, Bernstein was the composer who'd transformed musical comedies with *West Side Story*, and he was the New York Philharmonic orchestra's conductor. Lenny, as his friends call him, was an exceptional person who was gifted down to his fingertips. He's cultivated, friendly, and multilingual. He's capable of giving a lecture in five languages with the same ease, the same charm, and the same humor. Bernstein on a podium—it's music palpitating. It's impossible to resist the Bernstein effect. Some persons criticize him for doing too much. . . . However, not everyone can be a Bernstein! He very quickly became the sensation of New York. Robert admired him enormously, and their work together brought him authentic enrichment. Together, they recorded Fauré's *Ballade* and Saint-Saëns' *Concerto No 4* after having played them in concerts.

It's no secret to anyone that Bernstein loved France. He was quite familiar with Fontainebleau and Nadia Boulanger, for whom he maintained great affection. When I'd see him, it was always as if we'd seen each other the previous day.

French critics didn't always welcome him with open arms, and, when his first recordings began appearing in France, claims that his style was Hollywoodish, appropriate for Broadway, etc., appeared in many reviews. This type of *a priori* assertions always irritated me. Fortunately, that changed, and he was able to gain acceptance.

I can recall that, during the same year, we went to hear Jascha Heifetz, who was giving Beethoven's *Violin Concerto* in Paris. On the following day, in the columns of Le Figaro, we were able to read a column signed "Beethoven" that more or less stated the following: "I admired your sound quality and your technique. Your sensitivity was wonderful, but there's only one thing that bothered me somewhat. I didn't recognize my own work!" Hiding behind "Beethoven," there was "Clarendon," also known as Bernard Gavoty, whose assaults with the pen could be fierce and acerbic. After this sarcastic welcome, Heifetz never wished to set foot in Paris again. Robert and I'd considered his interpretation superb. Why didn't Gavoty like it? It's the entire mystery of the effect of an interpretation upon the audience.

The 1960s were filled with astounding activity and abundance for the three of us. Airplane trips shortened distances, and we had the impression that our life was accelerating. Nevertheless, we always maintained open periods for our private trips and our family vacations.

That accounts for our having taken Thérèse to Mexico for her twentieth birthday. We wanted to let her become acquainted with the country where we'd recognized the earliest moments of her life.

Obviously, we went to Yucatán, and we climbed up the Mayan pyramids, as well as discovering the temples. Thérèse, who'd achieved enormous progress, was dazzled by this journey that ended in the Colorado canyons.

At that point, her life changed, too.

We returned to Princeton, where she was taking courses at Princeton University, and fate led to her meeting her future husband. She'd gone to listen to a lecture that was being given in French. In the hall, a young man noticed her . . . love at first sight! Shortly before Christmas, when we left Princeton to return to Paris, this young man accompanied her to the railway station and promised that he'd come to see her in France . . . The promise was kept! A few days later, on January 1, 1963, David Rawson showed up at the Rue Vaneau. He'd talked his grandmother into funding his trip.

Robert and I quickly resumed our activities, and we were quite excited in particular by the preparations for our first "Expedition" to Japan. I've referred to an "expedition," because, in 1963, the trip resembled an expedition! People traveled by means of the polar route, with a layover in Anchorage. For us, it was a miracle to fly over these vast zones of ice, ocean, and snow, to arrive at our hotel in Tokyo, and to travel to Osaka by helicopter. To some extent we'd had some misgivings about this journey to the other end of the world, but we were thrilled very quickly. We'd encountered many of our colleagues, and we were amused by this concentration of European artists on Japanese soil. One evening, we went to listen to Georg Solti, or, on other evenings, it was Jean Martinon or Antal Dorati. Today, that wouldn't astonish anyone anymore. There was a total change of scenery, and our stay was marvelously organized because work and tourism were in harmonious alternation. Our only disappointment was the Noh Theatre that people had talked about so much. Whereas the show seemed tedious to us, the Japanese audience, which was deeply moved, wept profusely. We undoubtedly lacked the prerequisites for appreciating it.

We feasted on fish, with every variety being more exquisite than the preceding one. The ceremonies that governed cooking in restaurants fascinated us. I'll always remember the seafood attendant. He was wearing a green silk kimono and was a veritable Buddha enthroned at the middle of a table filled with shining, almost luminous fish that were often phosphorescent, as he made his selections with a serene concentration that was so distant from our Western practices. Upon leaving the restaurant and because it was raining, we were escorted to our automobiles by geishas who were carrying umbrellas that were gorgeous, lavishly decorated parasols made of wood and oiled paper, which they delicately held over our heads.

We would've very easily let ourselves be absorbed by this refined world that was so different from ours, but we still needed to bear in mind the primary reason for our presence in Japan: the Osaka Festival. Robert was expected to interpret Beethoven's *Opus 58* and Ravel's *Concerto pour la main gauche*, while Kletzki would be conducting. Kletzki was regarded as an excellent Beethoven conductor, and Robert was always pleased to see him again. They had such a strong habit of working together that rehearsals took place without difficulties, and their concerts proceeded perfectly. Robert had played before a full house for his recital.

Everything was painstakingly organized: meetings with the press, as well as visits to the temples in Kyoto and Nagoya. I was amazed by an exhibition of ancient attire where the kimonos vied with one another in terms of beauty, although the gardens were what fascinated me the most. So much refinement in simplicity! But so much subtlety too! The colors were soft. Everything was harmonious. I can recall the tea-colored azalea bushes that were completely unreal. The way that stones were arranged among the flowerbeds. . . . It was splendid.

Obviously, we were invited to Japanese dinners where a person must sit on the floor, which was hardly pleasing to Robert. We discovered meat cooked in thin slices on stones that were white-hot.

One evening, we were dining with Jean Martinon and Jane Isnard, an excellent French violinist who was living in Japan and who played a decisive role in dissemination of French violin technique in a country that was still regarded as quite remote in that time.

Our first trip to Japan wouldn't have been complete without an earthquake. One evening, when Robert was giving a recital in Tokyo, I was sitting in the concert hall when I suddenly felt a vibration beneath my chair. Then I saw all of the audience members raising their heads toward the ceiling questioningly, and also undoubtedly in order to see whether the chandelier was moving. A second tremor occurred a few seconds later. . . . My blood ran cold. I got up, and I went backstage very quickly, telling myself that, if the shocks intensified, I'd be closer to Robert. . . . Truly, I think that this was the only time that I ever left a hall during a recital! When I arrived at the stage, we'd already felt the third tremor. The lights went out, and, to my great surprise, Robert kept playing in the dark. . . . The audience didn't move; it was unconcerned. I'll let you imagine the ovation that he received at the end of the recital. Everyone came forward to congratulate him for his courage and his calmness. I'll confess that I myself was speechless.

Japanese audiences are among the most attentive that I know of. In contrast to Russian audiences, they don't beat time with their heads, and they don't mark crescendos. They don't cough between movements either, like French audiences that always create the impression that the concert hall is filled only with consumptive patients. In Japan, audiences are attentive. They don't move. They don't cough. They sit and they listen, in a state of concentration that borders on meditation. It seems that, for them, this is a vision of paradise.

At the end, a Japanese audience never holds back its gratitude or its joy, and it applauds vigorously. Charming little girls, smiling and dressed in kimonos, always bring flowers to the performers. It's very touching.

We returned to Paris via Hong Kong, where we didn't miss going to dine on one of the many junks with graceful shapes and colorful sails, moored in tight rows within the port.

As soon as we arrived in Paris, we only had enough time to consign our memories to the deepest regions of our brains. We were immediately caught up in an enormous project. We recorded Bartók's Sonata for *Two Pianos and Percussion* with Jean-Pierre Drouet and with our cousin, Jean-Claude Casadesus playing percussion. You know that he was a percussionist with the Colonne Orchestra before becoming a brilliant conductor. He's also a marvelous instrumentalist, like his brother Dominique Probst, who's a talented composer too. Both adore jazz. It's quite fascinating to see tendencies and their reappearance among cousins. Robert adored jazz too, not to mention Jean, who couldn't understand partitioning among musical tastes.

In Aix-en-Provence that year, we met the painter André Masson, who, after returning from the United States, where he too had sought refuge during the war, had moved into a house with an unrestricted view of Mount Sainte-Victoire. He completed a lot of work for the Aix-en Provence festival as a decorator. He told us that his two sons, Diego—the conductor—and Luis, had forgotten their French when they returned from the United States. That greatly surprised us.

After the construction of a building across from our apartment on Rue Vaneau, where our superb view of Paris was totally blocked, we decided to buy a house. We had intentions of building a house in Apremont-sur-Seine, but then we ultimately chose a rather old house, or, indeed, two houses with a magnificent granary in Recloses, which is approximately ten kilometers from Fontainebleau, on the edge of the forest, just next to the location where we heard the declaration of war in 1939. Here, we once again had the trees that we'd lost in Paris! That's where I always spend my weekends and a portion of my vacations.

At the end of 1963, Robert recorded the deceased in his datebook, as always. . . . Among them, there was our dear friend Poulenc and two orchestra leaders who were also our friends and with whom so many memories were linked: Fritz Reiner and Hans Rosbaud. On January 1, 1964, we hosted Thérèse's future in-laws in Princeton. The date was set for their wedding, which took place in Paris on June 29. Thérèse and David were married in our parish, Saint-François Xavier, just like us. At the end of August, they left for the United States, where Thérèse still resides, near Philadelphia. After earning a master's degree in English in Paris, she decided to complete a doctorate in French in the United States, in order to be able to teach our language, which seemed more satisfying to her, inasmuch as she was going to live there.

She participates very actively in Philadelphia's highly developed music scene, as well as in French cultural events. Moreover, she continues teaching, giving courses in Philosophy, Literature, Music History, and French Diction for musicians at the Curtis Institute in Philadelphia. She's a soprano and is so musically talented that, in spite of starting late, she's currently making her professional debut in oratorios and chamber music, while focusing on the Baroque era and naturally on the French repertoire, as would be expected.

Thérèse has two boys: Carty, who was born in July 1969 and whom Robert adored. Robert composed a lullaby for him (Carter) when he was born . . . but Robert never knew Thérèse's second son, who was born in June 1974, two years after Robert's death. Thérèse's children are very American, and they speak French with an American accent!

Guy, in turn, has three children. Hélène is twenty-eight years old now. Robert loved her very much. He told her stories when she was young because she was visually impaired and couldn't read. Two years later, there was Philippe, the little smart aleck who has grown up now! Then there was Antoine, who is twenty-three years old and of whom my husband said: "He's one of the kindest children I've ever known." I see them more often now, because they're living in France, in the South, at Cavalière, where we'd spent so many of our family vacations and where Guy decided to reside with his family quite a while ago when he became the General Manager of a company that's a subsidiary of Sonatrach in Algeria. After this grandmother's digression, I'm going to continue with my story.

At the end of the year, Ambassador Hervé Alphand presented a Commander of the Légion d'Honneur's insignia to Robert at the French Embassy in Washington. This was a simple and friendly ceremony, as Robert preferred.

Our frequent flights to the United States let us see Jean and Thérèse regularly. Jean was an artist in residence at SUNY Binghamton (about 100 miles from New York City). He rented a charming home where Agnès grew up in a half American, half French way. We always planned to spend our New Year's celebrations with our children and grandchildren in the United States, or in France, where we visited Guy and Joëlle. It was highly important for us to maintain contact with all of them, even though each one was pursuing his or her own life at this point.

We saw Jean frequently because we worked together regularly. Our professional cooperation was perfect happiness for us. Our three pianos appeared together at Carnegie Hall, as well as in Rome, Brussels, Chicago, Philadelphia, and Zurich.

In Paris, at the Maison de la Mutualité, we recorded Robert's *Concerto for Three Pianos* with Pierre Dervaux conducting. That was in 1967. The following year, we played three pianos at the Osaka Festival. I can say with complete modesty that our trio was appreciated wherever we appeared. We breathed so well together . . . and simultaneously.

Jean was pursuing his own career, and he'd join us with a quick flight whenever a performance awaited us.

What a pleasure to perform with him! We understood one another in shorthand, and we were so well-practiced that it was enough to adapt ourselves to the orchestra and the conductor in our rehearsals. Beyond that, everything functioned completely on its own! Robert was still the leader for defining our style, but he always consulted Jean and me. He wasn't dictatorial at all. Between concerts, we enjoyed being tourists. It was wonderful to be together that way.

Once in Hamburg, we went to see a Toulouse-Lautrec retrospective. At the same time, there was an exhibition of paintings by Albert Marquet, who'd painted the port so well. He'd been just as fascinated by this port as by the banks of the Seine, which he adored to the point of having also depicted them upon the wall tiles in his bathroom. On the day that I visited Mme. Marquet, she showed them to me with considerable pride and amusement, saying: "My husband, who wasn't satisfied with painting the Seine on his canvases, found a way of putting it in our bathroom!" When Jean was in Europe, he spent his free time in the small house that we'd set aside for him, which he'd happily renovated. It was just across from our house, in our garden in Recloses. The three of us took long bicycle rides in the forest of Fontainebleau.

Jean came to teach at Fontainebleau every summer after 1952. Evie and Agnès also stayed in Recloses during the summer. Everyone kept his or her independence, and, in this way, we had wonderful times.

In October 1967, Robert celebrated his 200th concert with the New York Philharmonic Orchestra, whose conductor was William Steinberg. The program included Brahms' *2nd Concerto* in commemoration of his first concert with them. The New York audience gave him a prolonged ovation that was quite touching.

We spent January 1, 1968 in the Caribbean with Thérèse and her husband before returning to Paris.

We experienced the events of May 1968 in Bordeaux, where the traditional *Mai Musical* was taking place. Robert was scheduled to play with a Polish orchestra, the Szymanowski Orchestra, which bore the name of the wonderful Polish composer whom we knew well, although he's so poorly known among French music lovers! . . . The rehearsal was completed normally. We'd just returned to our hotel when I realized that I'd forgotten my umbrella in the concert hall. I returned to the theatre and was astounded to see black flags floating from the windows of the Grand Théâtre, where a group of men standing in front of the door barred my entry. . . . In a panic, I went back to the hotel and described the incident to Robert. I informed him of my fears that the concert would be canceled on account of the demonstrators' having occupied the theatre.

The concert was indeed canceled, and we subsequently learned that the orchestra's musicians had been shut inside the theatre, that the conductor hadn't been able to leave his dressing room, that people had tossed cigarette butts into the piano, and that the plants decorating the stage had been destroyed. The Polish conductor subsequently said to us: "If that had happened in our country, they would've gone rat-a-tat-tat"—as he mimicked the movement of a machine gun spraying bullets at a crowd—and order would've been completely restored."

We remained shut inside our hotel with Rudolf Nureyev, who was also in Bordeaux. We were nonetheless able to return to Paris with our car, thanks to Jacques Chaban-Delmas, who obtained gasoline for us. . . .

Our schedule, like every French person's schedule, was modified somewhat. . . . Robert, who was supposed to give a 3rd Cycle course at Rue de Madrid, was asked to stay at home. The Paris Conservatory didn't escape the student uprising.

In August 1969, Robert took part in Cleveland's Blossom Festival for the first time. Although George Szell knew that Robert preferred to spend his vacations in France, he insisted that Robert should change his habits and that he should come to perform at this extensive cultural center that had been created a hundred kilometers outside Cleveland for the summer season. This wonderful site was a sort of a sort of Grecian amphitheater located within a hollow at the foot of a hill. It was a superb site. The terraced steps could accommodate 1,500 persons and the acoustics are particularly exceptional. On the evening when Robert performed, not only the theatre's steps but also the entire site around it had been filled. It was a gentle evening, a true summer evening. Robert played Mozart, and he didn't regret that he'd let himself be persuaded.

In October, he celebrated his seventieth birthday with the New York Philharmonic Orchestra and George Szell. They interpreted a Mozart concerto, and George conducted Robert's *Deuxième suite pour orchestre*.

In 1970, we decided to sell our house in Princeton, in order to be closer to Thérèse. We found a beautiful but smaller house in Berwyn, in the Philadelphia suburbs, a few minutes from her house. In 1971, Guy, Joëlle, and their children joined us there for Christmas. That was our last Christmas as a family.

In July, we celebrated our golden wedding anniversary in Recloses, surrounded by our children and our grandchildren. A simple gathering, just for ourselves with our very dear friends, the Lemaigres.

The year 1971 was a good and great year for us. On February 23, we had the pleasure of giving a concert in Brussels that wasn't entirely like the others. In fact, the royal family wanted to honor our family of musicians. The Queen wanted to give Robert the insignia of Commander of the Order of Leopold.

Our cousin Jean-Claude conducted the orchestra, and the four of us were pleased with this concert and with being honored with so much kindness by Queen Fabiola. We played two Bach concertos for three pianos, along with Mozart and Robert's three piano concertos.

The Casadesus family was being honored and recognized. Even if we don't let ourselves be dazzled by honors, this is something that always warms the heart.

In July, apart from our fifty years of marriage, we celebrated the fiftieth anniversary of the Fontainebleau School. . . . All of this meant a lot to us. For Robert and me, it was our entire life and its success.

And then, perhaps because everything was too perfect, everything plunged into a tragedy that was the most horrible, the most unforeseeable, the most painful, and the most unfair.

Robert and I were getting ready to return to France after our Christmas in Berwyn. At the beginning of 1972, my husband had performed with Zino Francescatti in Philadelphia. He'd also played in Washington with Dorati conducting and with me in Texas.

An extensive tour was awaiting us in Europe.

On January 22, just before our departure, Jean was expected to come for dinner at our house on a Saturday evening, after a concert at Deep River, in

Canada. He'd telephoned me on Wednesday, in order to tell me that there was an enormous snowstorm, that, in addition, there was an air transportation strike at the border, and that he didn't know how he could get to his concert. He was probably going to rent an automobile with one of the engineers from the company where he'd just given a concert. I didn't dare to dissuade him too openly, but I nevertheless said that it was possibly better to cancel.

On Thursday evening, we were having a calm dinner at Thérèse's house. At 9:30 p.m., the telephone rang. Thérèse answered it, and we heard her utter a horrible scream. She hung up and told us: "Jean had an accident!" It was as if we'd received a blow to the head. In a fraction of a second, everything stopped, and everything fell apart. It wasn't possible to accept reality. I prayed to heaven that he hadn't suffered.

We found out later on that the engineer was driving, that he'd collided with an approaching car, and that the passengers had been killed immediately. The engineer survived for eight days.

We imagined everything and supposed everything. Had he taken chances passing another vehicle? It was learned from the police report that the accident occurred at 4:00 p.m. and that visibility hadn't been good. . . . It was wintertime, and night had already fallen. There was snow on the road. . . . Jean had struck the windshield. . . . He'd been in the most dangerous seat. . . . Evie was alone with Agnès in Binghamton. She'd been notified by the police. For her too, life stopped on that road.

Thérèse didn't want us to go home to sleep at our house. We spent the night at her house.

Jean's body was brought to Binghamton. I lacked the courage to see him like that. Jean was buried on January 24, in a small cemetery with thirty crosses. Robert was unrecognizable that day. He seemed to have become ten years older because his entire being was affected so much by his pain.

Later, I decided that Jean should be brought back to France and that he should be buried in Recloses with his father.

Guy joined us. Thérèse telephoned him as soon as we were certain about the news, because we didn't want to believe it. . . . He'd boarded the earliest plane, while Joëlle had to stay with the children.

Those days were unbearable. Thérèse wanted us to stay with her until our departure. Robert was silent; he was devastated.

We arrived in France on February 5. Robert canceled all of his concerts. He wasn't playing the piano anymore. Even for himself. Guy and Joëlle wanted us to have somewhat of a change of scenery, and, practically by force, they took us to Majorca, where we saw Miró again. We spent a week there.

I don't have any memories of that trip. Nothing interested us anymore.

At that point, Robert began to complain of stomach pains. When we returned to Paris, X-rays were taken. They didn't detect anything in particular.

He lost weight and didn't have an appetite anymore. That was attributed to the horrible shock that he'd just experienced and to the immense sorrow that had invaded him.

He nonetheless returned to the piano. An hour here, an hour there. I compelled him to play, and I told him that just the effort could do him good.

He agreed not to cancel the concerts that were scheduled for Rotterdam and Amsterdam in March. He played *Concerto K 595*, which, as you know, was the last concerto that Mozart composed in 1791, during the last year of his life. This would be the last work that Robert would play with an orchestra. It's the last work that Jean had played with an orchestra. A strange sign of fate.

On April 7, the date of Robert's birthday, we left for the United States. We went to the cemetery near Jean's tomb. A thaw had occurred, and the ground left the coffin exposed, along with the wilted flowers, because it hadn't been possible to dig deeply at the time of Jean's burial. This was a horrible vision, and I believed that Robert was going to faint. I'll never forget it.

In New York, Robert nonetheless attended a reading of his *Septième Symphonie* with its chorus "To the glory of Israel," which was to be performed as a premiere by Frederic Waldman in the Fall.

On April 25, we returned to Paris. I forced Robert to work. He wasn't feeling very well. Nevertheless, we went to Brescia and Bergamo, where he had two recitals. He returned to composing a bit.

In June, Thérèse came to France with Carty. She was present with her father for placement of a plaque upon Francis' house in Montmartre. I wasn't able to go there because we didn't have anyone to take care of Carty, and we didn't want to bring such a young boy to this type of ceremony.

Then we left for Cavalière with Thérèse. Robert played *Concerto K595* again in Aix-en-Provence with George Solti, in the Saint-Louis Cloister. I can recall that the *mistral* was blowing and that the scores were flying away notwithstanding the clothespins that secured them on the music stands. Robert was disheveled and he had a drawn face that was already difficult to recognize.

At the end of July, after Robert's concert at the Palace in Monte Carlo, we went to give a recital in Prades, in the Pyrenees. That was to be our last four hand performance.

Robert endured a horrible night after the concert. We returned to Paris as fast as possible. Robert spent a few days at home. He knew that he was extremely ill. He'd also become shockingly thinner. He was very clear-thinking. On August 25, he was admitted to Professor Escoffier's department at the Hôpital Broussais. He underwent arteriography, and he had a bleeding episode. It was known then that he had cancer. It was definitely too late for him to be cured.

Surgery was performed. In the Intensive Care Unit, he asked for his date-book, where he recorded everything with his usual precision:

He wrote: "Intensive Care Unit." The canceled concerts were crossed out. For the date of September 17, he wrote: "Television: Tribute to Jean." On the page for September 19, he'd written: "Reserve *Air France* seats for trip to the U.S."

On September 19, Robert didn't go to pick up our airplane tickets. To put it quite simply, he joined Jean . . .

Both of them are resting at Recloses now.

## Chapter 18

# Life After Robert

## *Continuing the Legacy*

Words are too flimsy to express the void that arises within me. I've been overwhelmed. My sorrow is inexpressible and immeasurable. Losing a son and a husband within an interval of only a few months is a completely inhumane misfortune that's dreadful to bear.

Among the messages that were sent to me, one of them is an extraordinary source of encouragement for me. It's the one from Jacques Duhamel, who was the Minister of Cultural Affairs at that time. I'll let you read it:

> Everyone for whom music is a source of joy and hope is saddened today. Robert Casadesus' death is a blow to each of them personally. An artist with such a stature and such genius was, for millions of people who didn't know him, a source of reconciliation with themselves, someone who helped them with shedding their own selves so as to arrive more deeply at participation in universality. Those who knew the man himself and who therefore loved Robert Casadesus are going to remain inconsolable. They shall henceforth share the eternally expanding joy of his music with those whom he didn't know. They shall know, however, that his hands have ceased to be vibrant, and their sorrow shall mingle with their joy when they hear his soul sing again.
>
> Jacques Duhamel
> Minister of Cultural Affairs
> September 19, 1972

One thing, just one thing, and I'm sure of it, will therefore allow me not to sink: action. Only work and music can save me. Robert and Jean cannot totally vanish in this way. Memory is our ally in these terrible moments. It's a comfort. Survival of the soul exists, whether a person is a believer or not. It's enough to be responsible for it and to care about it.

Robert and Jean exist through their recordings. Robert is present in his compositions. It's been decided: I'll make this testimony come alive.

Robert's death was mourned. Robert was honored. The press echoed it. Radio and television too. Martinon dedicated one of his concerts to him at the Théâtre des Champs Elysées.

Later, on April 6, 1976, a commemorative plaque was placed at *54 rue Vaneau,* confirming that Robert had lived there from 1924 to 1972.

The premiere of his *Septième symphonie* took place in New York, on November 8. I was there.

On October 30, I flew to New York. As soon as I arrived, I pursued multiple meetings. First, there was Goddard Lieberson at CBS. It was essential for Robert's records to continue being distributed as if he were still alive. Critics unanimously hailed his talent, and his work is the priceless memorial to his entire life.

On November 8, at Tully Hall in New York, Frédéric Waldmann conducted the *Septième symphonie—Israël,* which was dedicated to the memory of George Szell. The orchestra and the choirs displayed exceptional fervor. That evening, New York was unfortunately experiencing a terrible snowstorm, one of its secret hallmarks. The snow came in advance of winter itself. New York's critics didn't bother to come. The concert took place but was completely ignored. There was never another performance. At that point, I thought that the symphony would be performed in Israel, but the project didn't come to pass.

You know, there are things like this that don't work.

As soon as I arrived, I saw my family again. That was comforting to me. All of them encouraged me to pursue action.

Robert's concerts that were scheduled in the United States were canceled. He was supposed to play Mozart's two piano quartets with the *Quatuor Guarneri.* I telephoned the Guarneris to cancel the concert. "Impossible," they said to me, "you'll play with us." "Me playing these two Mozart quartets? But I've never played them in my life! I'm familiar with them, to be sure, but that's all." Everyone close to me advised me to accept. The members of the quartet also insisted so strongly that I started practicing, because I was convinced that Robert would've told me to do it.

On December 14 and 15, I was with the Guarneris at the Metropolitan Museum. Robert's concerts did take place. I think that this is what completely saved me.

I didn't have the strength to return to living in our house in Berwyn. How could I envision being alone in that house? I can't make this effort on top of everything else. Thérèse welcomed me in her house. I always go to her house when I'm in the United States.

I sold our house.

Upon returning to France, I resumed my personal endeavors. I gave the recitals that had already been planned for my own schedule. Robert was due to give a recital in Brussels. The sponsors suggested that I should do it. I didn't feel energetic enough to give a recital, and the event was transformed into a concert where I played Fauré's *Quintette No. 2* with the *Quatuor de l'ORTF.* Then I played Robert's *Sonate pour violon et piano* with Jacques Dumont, who was a member of the *Quatuor.* I finished by playing Debussy's *Pour le piano.* Everyone was extremely kind to me. Fontainebleau asked me to take on Robert's teaching position. I agreed, without too much hesitation. Philippe Entremont asked me to join the Académie Maurice Ravel's team of instructors in Saint-Jean-de Luz. I taught there every summer for nine years.

One of the things that I took to heart the most was having Robert's music played. Ensuring that publishing of his music would continue. It was an enormous effort, but it has borne fruit. His music is being disseminated. All of his hours of composing won't go unechoed. The man who always wrote "Composer" across from the word "Occupation" on information forms for his identity documents is now a full-fledged composer.

I've been asked more and more often to take my husband's place on juries. I've never refused, and that's why I've been a jury member at the Paris Conservatory and for the Queen Elisabeth competition in Brussels.

Life, namely my life without Robert, has been taking shape. It must be done. I'm regularly hired by American universities where I've given recitals, as well as lectures. My programs are primarily made up of French music and, of course, Robert's own works.

In 1978, I received the *Légion d'Honneur* for my efforts on behalf of disseminating French music abroad. Raymond Loucheur, a composer, and a former director of the Conservatoire National Supérieur de Musique de Paris, was the person who pinned the red ribbon on me.

I meet musicians, and I recommend Robert's music to them. The Juilliard Quartet is among the quartets that have agreed to play his chamber music works for three and four instrumentalists.

French quartets have also included Robert in their programs. Gabriel Tacchino was the soloist for his *Concerto pour piano* in Nice. I recorded his *Quatrième sonate* and his *Huit Études* for CBS. Briefly speaking, it's snowballing . . . and I'm so glad!

One must be organized, however, in order to prevent this interest in my husband's music from declining. Therefore, we decided, along with my second son Guy, to establish the Association Robert Casadesus, whose purpose shall be to publicize Robert's music and records. We received the distinguished patronage of Queen Fabiola of Belgium and of Prince Rainier of Monaco. All of our friends who were musicians agreed to become members. In the Netherlands, where Robert left such a vivid memory, we have a branch led by Robert Haslinghuis. Another branch was established in the United States at the initiative of Dr. Alfred G. Brooks, who was a friend of Jean's. Each year, the Association produces records or cassettes for its members containing recordings by Robert.

Then the idea of a piano competition that would bear Robert's name sprouted within our minds. Thus, the Association would turn toward young musicians, and its activities would be consistent with the perspective that Robert had always upheld: allowing young pianists to advance within the profession as a result of competitions. I spoke about it to Marcel Landowski, who was serving in Jacques Duhamel's cabinet at that time. The idea appealed to him, but there was a change of ministers, and this left things in flux. . . . That was in 1974. Robert had died two years earlier, and, in my opinion, it was essential not to wait too long to launch such an endeavor. When people die, they're forgotten so quickly.

In November, I left for the United States. In fact, Rudolf Serkin asked me to give a series of courses on French music, at the Curtis Institute in Philadelphia. He'd told me during a prior trip that there wasn't anyone who truly knew Fauré, Ravel, Debussy, or Poulenc very well. Therefore, I gladly accepted his offer.

During my stay, I had an opportunity to meet with our friend Grant Johannesen, who'd just been appointed as the director of the Cleveland Institute of Music. You know how deeply loyal he was to the Fontainebleau School, and he was one of its supporting pillars in Great Barrington. Robert was very fond of him. I can say that he was one of Robert's favorite pupils. I spoke to him about my project. I'd wanted it to see the light of day in 1975, for Ravel's centennial. It would be, in my opinion, a twofold tribute: one to our great composer, and the other to his interpreter.

Johannesen immediately endorsed the idea, and he said to me: "It has to be done in Cleveland! Robert was strongly attached to the Orchestra and to George Szell, and he left exceptional memories here. This is where the competition should be established!" I should specify that the city of Cleveland is a place with a significantly active cultural life. The Cleveland Institute of Music was practically founded by Mr. and Mrs. Victor Babin, who formed a famous duo: the Vronsky-Babin duo.

Vitya Vronsky, who was born in Russia, pursued a career as a soloist in Europe, notably in France and in the United States, before forming a duo with her husband.

As quickly as possible, Grant arranged a meeting for me with Martha Joseph, who'd been the Chairwoman of the Cleveland Institute of Music's Board of Directors for six years, and also with her husband, the President of the Cleveland Orchestra. I also met Odette Valabrègue-Wurzburger, a

Frenchwoman who was an international attorney and whose husband had been the French consul in Cleveland for many years.

We'd always see one another again when we were in Cleveland.

Both women, in turn, were enthusiastic about the idea of a Robert Casadesus piano competition in Cleveland.

They immediately started doing everything they could so that organizing and management of the competition could begin without delays.

It was December 1974 then and the first competition took place in August 1975. It was dedicated to George Szell in honor of our friendship.

It was decided that this competition would take place every two years.

I could never be sufficiently grateful to Martha Joseph and to Odette Valabrègue-Wurzburger, who did everything so the competition could exist and continue.

You're familiar with American efficiency and professionalism.

Everything is always organized perfectly!

The young pianist-candidates are housed and fed at no cost.

The jury members eat lunch together, and, instead of eating hamburgers, we enjoy gourmet cuisine.

There's always superb floral decoration, and promotion of the competition is marvelously accomplished, from brochures that are sent throughout the world for obtaining applications to newspaper announcements. American radio covers the competition. I've also arranged for *Radio France* to send a representative to Cleveland, so that she could send echoes of the competition's proceedings back to France.

I don't think that we could've received a better welcome anywhere else.

It can be said that the competition receives international recognition today. Since 1981, we've also been members of the World Federation of International Music Competitions.

Its purpose is obviously to help young musicians become known.

In the programs, French music occupies a suitable position, as you can guess, Messiaen, Dutilleux, and Ravel obviously, along with Fauré, Debussy, one of Robert's sonatas, and, for the finale, a Mozart concerto.

An American, John Owings, was the first person to win a First Prize in the initial competition. His style was so close to my husband's style that, when he played *Scarbo* from *Gaspard de la Nuit*, I had tears in my eyes. He must have listened to Robert's records for being so close to Robert's interpretation, although, of course, he never met him.

It was Henri Dutilleux who was the head of the first jury. I also asked José Iturbi to belong to the first jury. His response was: "I'll be there for my friend Robert!" In 1977, it was the French pianist Nathalie Bera-Tagrine, the pianist Nadia Tagrine's daughter, who won First Prize. In 1979, an American won once again: Edward Newman. In 1981, Philippe Bianconi, a young man from

Nice, who was twenty-four years old, was the winner. Ah! I don't want to forget to tell you that, in 1979, the second prize was won by another Frenchman, Jean-Yves Thibaudet. In 1983, the first prize was received by a Korean who'd studied in Paris with Lucette Descaves. Unfortunately, her name is somewhat difficult for us to remember: Youngshin An. In 1985, another Korean: Daejin Kim; and, in 1987, a Frenchman: Thierry Huillet.

Grant and I select the programs for the examinations. Apart from a sum of $10,000 that's offered by the Robert Casadesus Association, the winner is hired by the Cleveland Orchestra and by different concert organizations in France and in the United States, with a New York recital to cap it all. As a whole, there are seven awards per competition, so that the finalists aren't overlooked.

Apart from the competitions, I'm working on editing the publication of Ravel's works for Schirmer in the United States. I'm introducing Robert's fingerings as well as his indications for the pedals. I'm also overseeing and correcting Robert's works, that were recently published by the International Music Company. They've just printed his *Sextuor pour piano et instruments à vent*, as well as his *Hommage à Chausson*, the *Quintette pour harpe, flute et cordes*, and the *Sonate d'alto* (viola sonata).

For several years, I've been reducing my activities as a pianist, but I still maintain my teaching activities in France and also in the United States. In the United States, I've adopted the formula of offering a course followed by a concert. I greatly enjoy this formula that combines teaching and personal interpretation.

After ten years at the Académie Ravel in Saint-Jean-de-Luz from 1973 to 1983, I've also relinquished my summer courses at the Mozarteum in Salzburg, where I've been teaching for three years. Teaching absorbs an enormous amount of energy, and, unfortunately, this energy also abandons you a bit more every year. I've met young musicians there who are full of potential. It's a shame to be working with them for only three weeks. It's such a short period for achieving something durable.

In France, I'm preparing young people for competitions, and I make them practice for their recitals.

I've continued to be a member of the administrative board for the American Conservatory in Fontainebleau. Teaching is also a pleasant way of staying active. I must say, however, that I'm focusing all of my energy on the Association in Europe and the United States, along with the Cleveland Competition, with help from my children. In addition, I don't forget working on publicizing Robert's work. That's my own way of continuing along our journey together, all the way to the end.

# Appendix

## *Genealogy*

### GABY

**Table A.1. Gaby**

| *Grandparents* | |
|---|---|
| *Father's Side* | *Mother's Side* |
| Nicholas L'Hôte (1834–1889) | Jean Reynaud (1840–1905) |
| Gabrielle Luigi (1847–1923) | Octavie Bérard (1946–1911) |
| **Parents** | |
| Jules L'Hôte (1872–1940) | Thérèse Reynaud (1866–1917) |
| Two Daughters: | |
| Jeanne (1895–1960) | |
| Gabrielle (1901–1999) | |

*Created by* Thérèse Casadesus Rawson.

### ROBERT

**Table A.2. Robert**

| *Casadesus family as referenced in My Musical Notes* | |
|---|---|
| **Grandparents** | |
| *Father's Side* | *Mother's Side* |
| Luis Casadesus (1850–1919) | Frédéric Louis Antoine Varnet (1849–?) |
| Mathilde Sénéchal (1850–1907) | Marie-Thérèse Johanny (1857–?) |
| **Parents** | |
| Robert Casadesus (1878–1940) | Louise Marie Varnet [Varnay] (1879–1963) |

**Uncles and Aunts:**

Francis (1870–1954)

Rose (1873–1944)

Henri (1884–1947); daughter of Henri: Gisèle (1914–2017), Robert's first cousin, and her son Jean-Claude Casadesus (1935–).

Cécile (1884–1962)

Marius (1892–1981); son of Marius: Gréco (1950–), Robert's first cousin

*Created by* Thérèse Casadesus Rawson.

# Chronology of Performances

## MAJOR TOURS INCLUDING GABY

| | |
|---|---|
| 1923 | Trip to England with Maurice Ravel |
| 1926–1938 | Almost yearly trips to Poland |
| 1927 | First trip to Switzerland then yearly until late 1960s |
| 1929 | First trip to Italy then almost yearly in 1950s and 1960s |
| 1929 | First Tour of Russia |
| 1931 | Trip to Algeria |
| 1931 | Major Tour of South America |
| 1931 | Romania, Turkey, and Greece |
| 1932 | Second Tour of Russia, including Ukraine |
| 1932 | Trip to Mallorca |
| 1933 | Middle-Eastern Tour: Lebanon, Israël, and Egypt |
| 1934 | Switzerland and Austria |
| 1934 | Second trip to Egypt and Israël |
| 1935 | First United States and Canadian Tour: New York debut |
| 1935–1971 | Yearly United States and Canadian Tours, particularly extensive in the 1940s |
| 1936 | Last Russian Tour; Trip to Germany |
| 1938 | Budapest, Poland, and Latvia |
| 1939 | United States and Cuba, also again in 1951 |
| 1941 | Tour of Mexico |
| 1953 | Tour in Greece |
| 1955 | Trip to Spain |
| 1958 | Behind the Iron Curtain: Prague and Budapest |
| 1961 | Tour of Israël with Jean |
| 1963 | Tour of Japan |
| 1965 | Lebanon |
| 1965 | Tour of Yugoslavia |
| 1968 | Osaka Festival Japan |

1967/1970        Portugal
Robert performed mostly alone, but yearly in Belgium, Holland, Germany, and Scandinavia, before and after World War II.

# Discography

GABY CASADESUS
MOZART DEBUSSY RAVEL FAURE
Rameau Couperin Chabrier Satie Milhaud Chopin Mendelssohn, 1942–1948
1999 *Dante* Productions, HPC 155–157, 3 compact disc (CD) Box Set, Historical Piano Collection
https://www.amazon.co.uk/Casadesus-Plays-Debussy-Fauré-Mozart/dp/B000026BX4 (accessed February 22, 2024).
—CD 1
Mozart Concerto # 9 in E flat major K. 271
 Paul Paray and Orchestre Lamoureux
 (Paris, 1947)
Mozart Six Variations in F major K. 500
 (Paris, 1947)
Mozart Concerto # 25 in C major K.503
 Eugene Bigot and Orchestre Lamoureux
 (Paris, 1948)
—CD 2
Gaby Casadesus and French Music recorded in the US between 1942 and 1945
 Jean-Philippe Rameau (1683–1764)
 *Le Rappel* des *Oiseaux* (1724)
 *Musette en Rondeau* (1724)
 François Couperin (1668–1733)
 *Le Carillon de Cythère* (1722)
 *Les barricades mystérieuses* (1717)
 Emmanuel Chabrier (1841–1894)
 *Idylle* (1881)

Gabriel Fauré (1845–1924) I
    *Impromptu #2 in F minor op. 31 (1883)*
    Erik Satie (1866–1925)
    *Gnossienne # 3 (1890)*

Claude Debussy (1862–1918)
    *Deux Arabesques* (1888–1891)
    Arabesque No. 1
    Arabesque No. 2

*Danse (Tarentelle Syrienne)* (1890)
    *Pour le Piano* (1894–1901)
    I Prélude
    II Sarabande
    III Toccata
    *Children's Corner* (1906–1908)
    III Serenade for the doll
    VI Golliwogg's cake-walk
    *Preludes* (1er livre) (1909–1910)
    II Voiles
    IX Sérénade Interrompue
    VIII La fille aux cheveux de lin
    XII Minstrels
    Maurice Ravel (1875–1937)
    *Pavane pour une infante défunte* (1899)
    *Jeux d'eau (*1901)
    *Miroirs* (1904–1908)
    II Oiseaux Tristes
    *Prélude* (1913)
    *Menuet sur le nom de Haydn* (1909)
    *Le Tombeau de Couperin* (1914)
    I Prélude
–CD 3
    Frédéric Chopin (1810–1849)
    *Four Impromptus*
    Recorded in Paris 1948

    Felix Mendelssohn-Bartholdy (1809–1847)
    *12 Songs without words* (*Lieder ohne Worte)*
    Recorded in Paris, 1947

    Gabriel Fauré (1845–1924)

*Ballade pour piano et orchestre* op. 19 (1877, orchestrated 1881)
Manuel Rosenthal and Orchestre Lamoureux (Paris, 1948)
Darius Milhaud (1892–1974)
*Le Bal Martiniquais* op. 249 (Dec. 1944) For Two Pianos
Recorded with Robert, USA, 1945

GABY CASADESUS PLAYS ROBERT CASADESUS
Eight Etudes, op. 28,
Piano Sonata No. 4, op. 56
Recorded in New York, *CBS* 1975; 2019, Sony Music Entertainment
https://music.apple.com/us/album/gaby-casadesus-plays robertcasade-
sus remastered/1452258414

**Collaborations**
Camille Saint-Saëns
*Carnival of the Animals*, R.125
Philippe Entremont, Gaby Casadesus, Yo-Yo Ma
*Variations on a Theme by Beethoven*, op. 35 and *Polonaise* op. 77 for
Two Pianos
Gaby Casadesus, Philippe Entremont, 1978, Sony Classical.

*Duo Piano with Her Husband Robert and Three Piano with Son Jean*
Robert Casadesus—The Complete Columbia Sony Classical Album
Collection 19075853652,
65 CD Box Set, March 2019. Box set contains recordings by ROBERT,
ROBERT and GABY, ROBERT, GABY and JEAN, as well as a few by
GABY and JEAN as soloists. Selected recordings featuring Gaby from
box set listed below (composers in alphabetical order).

BACH
Concerto No 1 in C minor for two harpsichords (pianos), BWV 1060
Concerto No. 2 in C major for two harpsichords (pianos), BWV 1061
Zurich Chamber Orchestra, Edmond de Stoutz Switzerland, June 1967,
CD 55
Concerto No 1 in D minor for three harpsichords (pianos), BWV1063
Dimitri Mitropoulos, New York Philharmonic New York 1950 CD 10
Eugene Ormandy, The Philadelphia Orchestra, 1962, CD 47
Concerto No 2 in C major for three harpsichords, BWV 1064
Pierre Dervaux, Orchestre des Concerts Colonne, Paris 1966, CD 53

BARTÒK

Sonata for two pianos and percussion—Jean-Claude Casadesus/Jean-Pierre Drouet, Paris, 1963, CD 48

CASADESUS
Concerto for three pianos, op. 65
Pierre Dervaux, Orchestre des Concerts Colonne, Paris, 1966, CD 53
*Trois Danses méditerranéenes* for two pianos, op. 36 (1944), 1950/1951, CD 7

CHABRIER
*Trois Valses Romantiques* pour deux pianos, 1950/51 CD 7

DEBUSSY
*En blanc et noir* (For Two Pianos)
*Six Epigraphes Antiques* (For Piano Four Hands), 1955, CD 22
*Petite Suite* (For Piano Four Hands), 1959, CD 43

FAURÉ
*Dolly* (For Piano Four Hands), 1959, CD 43

MILHAUD
*Le Bal Martiniquais* (For Two Pianos), 1945

MOZART
Concerto No. 10 in E-Flat Major for Two Pianos and Orchestra, K. 365
George Szell conducting the Columbia Symphony Orchestra, 1955
Mozart Bicentennial Commemorative Issue, CD 31
Concerto No. 10 in E-Flat Major for Two Pianos and Orchestra, K. 365
Eugene Ormandy and the Philadelphia Orchestra, 1960, CD 42
Sonata for in D major Two Pianos K. 448, 1953, CD 26
Variarions in G major for Piano Four Hands, K. 501, 1954

RAVEL
*Habañera* Piano Four Hands, 1951, CD 13
*Ma Mère l'Oye* Piano Four Hands, 1951

SATIE
*Trois Morceaux en forme de poire* Piano Four Hands, 1946, CD 5

SCHMITT

*Une semaine du petit elfe ferme-l'œil* for Two Pianos, op. 58, 1956, CD 33

*Trois Rapsodies* for Two Pianos, op. 53, 1956

SCHUBERT

*Andantino varié* for Piano Four Hands, op. 81 No. 1, 1954, CD 26

*Fantaisie* in F minor for Piano Four Hands, op. 103, 1954

# Index

Photo insert images are indicated by *p1, p2, p3,* etc.

as conductor, 154; family of, 91;
as orchestra leader, 94; Walter and,
93–94
Toscanini, Madame, 95
Toulon, 55
Toulouse-Lautrec, Henri de, 172
Truc, Georges, 101
Truman, Harry S., 150–51
Truman, Margaret, 150–51
Tully Hall, 180
Tuttle, Mrs., 32

United States, 33, 105; religion in,
102–3
Uruguay, 66

Valabrègue-Wurzburger, Odette, 182–83
Valdemossa, 74
Valéry, François, 36
Vallin, Ninon, 28, 63, 65
Valmalète, Madeleine de, 32
Vanderbilt, Cornelia, 132
Van Gogh, Vincent, 106
Varengeville-sur-Mer, 40
Varèse, Edgar, 132
Varnet, Miss, 17
Vaurabourg, Andrée, 144
Vaux-le-Pénil, 54
Verdi, 92–93
Verdi, Giuseppe: works, 103
Vidal, Paul, 32
Vienna Philharmonic, 158

Viñes, Ricardo, 65, 82
Vladivostok, 97
Voisin, 44–45
Vronsky, Vitya, 182

Wagner, Richard, 7, 65, 99; works, 46
Wagner, Wieland, 158
Wailing Wall, 76
Waldmann, Frédéric, 180
Wallace Collection, 152
Walter, Bruno, 91, 92; Toscanini and,
93–94
Webern, Anton, 125
Wesendonck, Mathilde, 42
*West Side Story*, 167
Widor, Charles-Marie, 31, 32
Wiener, Jean, 6
Wilhelmina (Queen), 165
*Wisconsin, S.S.* (ship), 147
World Federation of International Music
Competitions, 183
World War I, 4–6, 49
World War II, 100–101; Fontainebleau
Conservatory during, 33–35
WQXR, 126

Young People's Concerts, 138
Ysaÿe, Eugène, 65
Yucatán, 168

Zurich, 42

For more information concerning Robert Casadesus: www.robertcasadesus.com

# About the Collaborators

**Thérèse Casadesus Rawson**, PhD, is the daughter of the late French pianists Robert and Gaby Casadesus and was educated both in France and in the United States. She earned a master's in English literature from the Sorbonne in Paris and received a PhD in French language and literature from the University of Pennsylvania in 1977. She taught French, humanities, French diction, and French vocal repertoire to singers at the Curtis Institute of Music in Philadelphia for nearly thirty years.

In addition to teaching, Thérèse Casadesus Rawson performs as a soprano focusing on Bach and French repertoire. She is also active as a lecturer in a variety of topics pertaining to French culture and the arts. She continues to be involved with French or Franco-American cultural institutions. She was President of the Alliance Française de Philadelphie for nearly ten years and has been President of the Fontainebleau Associations for twenty-five years: the stateside support group which helps organize and finance the summer Music and Fine Arts program at the Château de Fontainebleau, France.

The French Government awarded Thérèse Casadesus Rawson the Palmes Académiques in recognition of her teaching activities and, in 2001, she was named to the rank of Chevalier des Arts et Lettres, an acknowledgement of her efforts on behalf of Franco-American cultural affairs.

**Lawrence (Larry) Lockwood** earned a Bachelor of Arts degree from Dartmouth College, Hanover, New Hampshire. He became a versatile multi-linguist with experience that also encompasses translation in other fields such as law, finance, medicine, and archeology, and considers it a distinct honor to have participated in giving English-speaking readers access to the extraordinary life of pianist Gaby Casadesus and her husband Robert, with whom she partnered through their career. One of Larry Lockwood's first book-length translations was *New Discoveries in China* (1983) by the prominent art historians Danielle and Vadime Elisseeff. He lives in North Andover, Massachusetts, and, when he is not actively translating and interpreting, he eagerly pursues interests in trail running, genealogy, nutrition, and art history.